Annett Zinsmeister (Hg./Ed.)

Kunst
und/oder
Design?

Ein Grenzgang

Art
and/or
Design?

Crossing Borders

edition weissenhof

Content

Inhalt

Annett Zinsmeister

Kunst und/oder Design? Ein Grenzgang
—
Art and/or Design? Crossing Borders

Where is the boundary between art and design?[1] What differences exist between fine and applied art? Artists design rooms and buildings, furniture and lamps, and even offer furnishing advice, while designers create non-functional objects as unique works or in very small editions. In an age when artists are poaching audaciously from other disciplines, the markets for fine and applied art are converging, and controversy is sparking over different taxation rates for the creative industries, the question is raised — what is the current position regarding disciplinary distinctions and dividing lines?

The interrelations of free and applied arts are by no means easy to determine. Today, the distinction between *free* = independent, wild, untrammeled and *applied* = servicable, conforming, purposeful, no longer stands up to real scrutiny. Is so-called *free art* really so free and untrammeled, and is design, as *applied art,* really as tied down and purpose-oriented as these equations might suggest? Or do these terms turn out to be a myth when examined more closely? The work of many contemporary artists is also tied to a purpose: on the one hand, there are external obligations in the case of commissoned works for private, municipal and institutional clients that frequently need to fulfil their users' demands; the announcement of an Art with Architecture competition often calls for practical functions from especially the art as well, like specific colour and light design in order to generate the desired spatial effects, etc. On the other hand, many art projects can be scarcely distinguished from design projects, as they are set out specifcally to fulfil functions, like the *comfort* and *living units* and *escape vehicles* by American artist Andrea Zittel or the *west wagon station encampment.* And Christine Hill, an american artist based in Berlin explicitly defines her artwork as providing a service, illustrating this with the example of her installation *Do-It-Yourself Bauhaus* in the present volume.[2] Wolfgang Ulrich, who has already written many outstanding publications on the subject, discusses here more and new forms of applied art.[3] And so art is not necessarily measured in terms of non-conformism and occasionally it is far from existence merely to please itself. Vice versa, many designers operate free of such constrictions; they turn away from the functional fulfilment of purpose attributed to design and are sounding out new levels of meaning in their field, as well as new forms of representation and, necessarily, new approaches to distribution as well. The Spanish designer duo Rosario Hurtado and Roberto Feo, who operate under the name El Ultimo Grito give in this volume an insight in their post-disciplinary understanding of design.[4] Dutch design theorist Louise Schouwenberg presents works by young dutch designers[5], which do not fit in common

Wo verläuft die Grenze zwischen Kunst und Design?[1] Worin unterscheiden sich freie von angewandten Künsten? Künstler entwerfen Räume und Gebäude, Mobiliar und Lampen und bieten Einrichtungsberatungen an, Designer gestalten zweckfreie Objekte als Unikate und in Kleinstauflagen. In einer Zeit, in der sich Künstler als Wilderer in fremden Disziplinen behaupten, sich die Märkte für freie und angewandte Künste angleichen und ein Streit um unterschiedliche Besteuerungen von Kreativleistungen entbrennt, stellt sich die Frage, wie es aktuell um fachspezifische Differenzierungen und Grenzziehungen bestellt ist.

Das Verhältnis von freien zu angewandten Künsten ist kein einfach zu bestimmendes. Die Unterscheidung in *frei* = unabhängig, wild, ungebunden und *angewandt* = dienlich, angepasst, zweckgebunden kann bei genauer Betrachtung heute nicht mehr standhalten. Ist die *bildende Kunst* wirklich so frei und ungebunden und ist das Design als *angewandte Kunst* wirklich so angepasst und zweckorientiert, wie es diese Gleichsetzungen suggerieren? Oder entpuppen sich diese Begriffe nicht bei genauer Betrachtung als Mythos? Viele Künstler arbeiten seit jeher zweckgebunden: Auftragsarbeiten für private, kommunale und institutionelle Kunden haben oftmals Anforderungen der Nutzer zu erfüllen; auch Ausschreibungen für Kunst am Bau fordern bisweilen gerade von der Kunst dienende Funktionen ein, etwa spezifische Farb- und Lichtgestaltungen, um gewünschte Raumwirkungen zu erzeugen. Es gibt zahlreiche Kunstprojekte, die von Designprojekten kaum zu unterscheiden sind, sie sollen und wollen Funktionen erfüllen wie beispielsweise die *comfort* und *living units* und die *escape vehicles* der amerikanischen Künstlerin Andrea Zittel. Und die in Berlin lebende Amerikanerin Christine Hill versteht ihre Kunst sogar explizit als Dienstleistung. Mit der Vorstellung der Installation *Do-It-Yourself Bauhaus* gibt sie in diesem Band Einblick in ihre künstlerische Arbeit.[2] Wolfgang Ullrich, der sich bereits durch zahlreiche Publikationen zum Thema hervorgetan hat, erörtert aus theoretischer Sicht weitere und neue Formen einer angewandten Kunst.[3] Kunst misst sich also nicht zwingend am Nonkonformismus und ist bisweilen weit davon entfernt, sich selbst zu genügen. Im Gegenzug spielen sich viele Designer frei von derlei Zwängen, sie verabschieden sich von der dem Design zugeschriebenen funktionalen Zweckerfüllung und loten neue Bedeutungsebenen in ihrem Tätigkeitsfeld aus sowie neue Repräsentationsformen und notwendigerweise auch neue Distributionswege. Das spanische Designerduo Rosario Hurtado und Roberto Feo, die unter dem Namen El Ultimo Grito agieren, geben in diesem Band Einblick in ihr post-disziplinäres Selbstverständnis als Designer.[4] Die niederländische Designtheoretikerin Louise Schouwenberg stellt die Werke junger

categories and Katia Baudin provides a curatorial perspective of current boundary-crossing art and design projects.[6] Where did these common and perhaps now questionable concepts originate, and can the relations between art and design, between free and applied arts, be defined more accurately from a historical vantage point? Is there, or has there ever been a boundary that can be clearly delineated, and if so, when did it become so indistinct?

From antiquity into the modern age, the term *free art* (*artes liberales*) 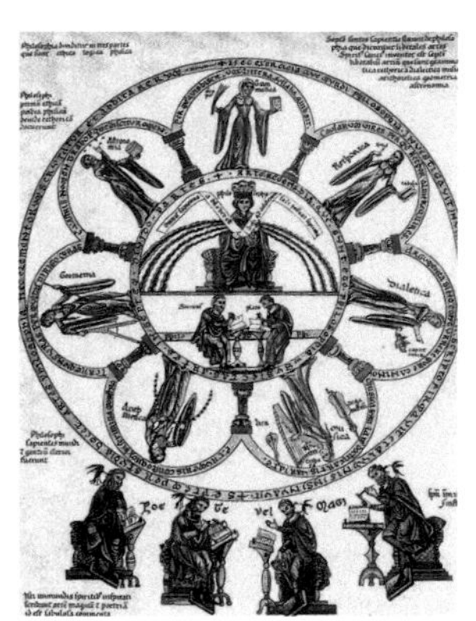 referred to the capacity of a free man (*homo liber*) to work creatively. Intellectual and linguistic skills as well as scientific activities like grammar, dialectics and rhetoric, geometry and arithmetics, astronomy and music were considered as so-called *free* art. Painting and sculpture, as well as a large number of manual skills in the fields of textiles, metal-working, agriculture, building etc. were categorised as *mechanical* or *practical arts* (*artes mechanicae*), based on technical, artisanal knowledge (*techne*[7]) and not serving science but the more profane need to earn a living. Slaves — that is, those who were *not free* — could practice these manual activities, and comparatively less recognition was granted to the *practical arts* as a consequence. Painters and sculptors cannot enter Plato's ideal state, as they are not active creatively but merely copy and reproduce nature, i.e. something that already exists, and so do not create anything new — quite by contrast to philosophers, poets and musicians.[8]

Until the modern era, therefore, *free art* had little in common with what we understand by it today. An evaluating line had already been drawn between high art and low art, but intellectual abilities were placed above artisanal skills and not fine art above applied art. The distinction was made between intellectual knowledge and artisanal skill. The fine artist was regarded as a "banauson", as an uneducated tradesman.

As from the mediaeval period, crafts and guilds regulated procedures for artistic training, trade and competition, as well as setting qualitative standards. The nature of artistic realisation was agreed in a contract with the client: "The prices of the artworks were determined according to format, number, the figures represented, the value of the paints and other materials used, etc."[9] The value of an artwork was measured according to work defined by its nature and dimensions. The artist as a person did not play any part in the matter at that stage. It was only with the combination of scientific research and artistic practice in the modern age that the fine artist's self-image and reputa-

holländischer Designer vor[5], die sich tradierter Kategorien entziehen und Katia Baudin bietet aus kuratorischer Sicht Einblick in aktuelle grenzüberschreitende Kunst - und Designprojekte.[6] Welchen Ursprung haben diese gängigen und vielleicht mittlerweile fragwürdigen Begrifflichkeiten und lässt sich das Verhältnis von Kunst und Design, von freien zu angewandten Künsten aus historischer Sicht näher bestimmen? Gibt oder gab es je eine klar zu bestimmende Grenze und wenn ja, wann ist diese unscharf geworden?

Der Begriff der *freien Künste (artes liberales)* bezeichnete von der Antike bis in die Neuzeit das Vermögen des freien Mannes *(homo liber),* schöpferisch tätig zu sein. Als sogenannte *freie Kunst* galten intellektuelle und sprachliche Fertigkeiten sowie wissenschaftliche Tätigkeiten wie die Grammatik, Dialektik und Rhetorik, Geometrie und Arithmetik, Astronomie und Musik. Die Malerei und Bildhauerei sowie eine Vielzahl handwerklicher Tätigkeiten in den Bereichen Textil, Metall, Landwirtschaft, Bauen usw. waren den *mechanischen* oder *praktischen Künsten (artes mechanicae)* zugeordnet, die auf einem technischen, handwerklichen Wissen *(techne[7])* beruhten und nicht der Wissenschaft, sondern dem profanen Broterwerb dienten. Auch Sklaven – also Unfreie – konnten diese manuellen Tätigkeiten ausführen, entsprechend wurde den praktischen Künsten wenig Ansehen zuteil. In Platons idealem Staat haben Maler und Bildhauer keinen Zugang, da sie nicht schöpferisch tätig sind und lediglich die Natur, also bereits Bestehendes, ab- und nachbilden, anstatt Neues zu erschaffen - ganz im Gegensatz zu Philosophen, Dichtern und Musikern.[8]

Bis in die Neuzeit hatte die *freie Kunst* also wenig gemein mit dem, was wir heute darunter verstehen. Die wertende Grenze zwischen höherer Kunst und niederer Kunst wurde bereits gezogen, doch wurden intellektuelle Fertigkeiten über handwerkliche gestellt und nicht die bildnerische Kunst über die angewandte. Die Grenze verlief zwischen geistigem Wissen und handwerklichem Können. Der bildende Künstler galt schlicht als „banauson", als ungebildeter Handwerker.

Seit dem Mittelalter regelten Zünfte und Gilden die Abläufe in der künstlerischen Ausbildung, in Handel und Wettbewerb sowie qualitative Standards. Die Art der künstlerischen Ausführung war mit dem Auftraggeber vertraglich vereinbart:„Die Preise der Kunstwerke waren festgelegt nach Format, Anzahl der dargestellten Figuren, Wert der verwendeten Farben und anderer Materialien etc."[9] Der Wert des Kunstwerkes bemaß sich an einer nach Art und Umfang definierten Arbeit; Der Künstler als Person, spielte hingegen keine Rolle. Erst mit der Verbindung von wissenschaftlicher Forschung und künstlerischer Praxis in der Neuzeit wandelten sich das Selbstverständnis und das Ansehen

tion changed: they appeared increasingly by name and as an individual. The first self-portraits, whose purpose was to document artistic authorship, are known in architecture as from the 13th century; it was not until the mid-15th century that self-portraits of artists began to emerge, as well as the first autobiographies, e.g. by Lorenzo Ghiberti.[10] The register of numerous artists' lives and works written by Giorgio Vasari and published in 1550, *Le vite de´ più eccellenti pittori scultori e architettori*, is regarded as the first recording of art history.[11]

Vasari also founded the first academy of drawing in Florence in 1563. The *Accademia del Disegno* meant that fine art was no longer taught on a purely artisanal level in workshops but was granted its first social recognition through the teaching of scientific insights. Alongside theoretical lectures in geometry, anatomy, perspective and analytical drawing (drawing based on plastic models, nude and landscape drawings), the copying of important works was a central component of artistic training from then onwards. Reproduction of nature had been the key assignment of artistic activity since antiquity, and remained the fundamental concept of training until into the 20th century: the aim was *mimesis*, reproduction true to nature, which was to be achieved through *imitatio*, the art of copying. Also Architecture was a subject at the Academy, it is based is based on the combination of creative design practice and scientific knowledge, but it was mainly attributed to the mechanical arts; only since the writings of architect Vitruvius has it occasionally been seen as a free art. Accordingly, the *Accademia del Disegno* was not only the first institution for the teaching of the fine arts but also the first school of architecture with regulated instruction.[12]

Brunelleschi's discovery of central perspective had introduced scientific methods into art. The process of perspective construction enabled not only the correct representation of space but also linked the scientific activity of *artes liberales* to the artisanal work of *artes mechanicae*. Here, for the first time, *techne* became an instrument of science and social recognition was therefore given to fine art. Alberti's tract *Della Pittura* in 1435 was the first treatise of art theory, at the same time standardising the knowledge spectrum of artistic practice.

"What do we teach those who want to become artists in order to assure profiency? If all the rules and standards are down, what happens to drawing, composition, the material of the artist and the like? And finally, of course, it is a crisis for art criticism itself: how does one judge, what are the appropriate responses, where are the standards, how can one evaluate?"[13] From a historical point of view, the much discussed and controversial statement: "Kunst kommt von Können" (art comes from ability) is quite justified. In German the word *Kunst* is

der bildenden Künstler: Sie traten zunehmend namentlich und als Individuen in Erscheinung. Die ersten Selbstporträts, die den Zweck halten, die künstlerische Urheberschaft zu dokumentieren, sind seit dem 13. Jahrhundert zunächst in der Architektur bekannt und erst ab Mitte des 15. Jahrhunderts entstehen Selbstbildnisse von Künstlern sowie die ersten Autobiografien wie zum Beispiel von Lorenzo Ghiberti.[10] 1550 erschien erstmals eine Aufzeichnung zahlreicher Künstlerleben und Kunstwerke von Giorgio Vasari: *Künstler der Renaissance: Lebensbeschreibungen der ausgezeichnetsten Maler Bildhauer und Architekten der Renaissance*, die als Anfang der Kunstgeschichtsschreibung gilt.[11]

Jener Vasari gründete zudem die erste Zeichenakademie 1563 in Florenz. Mit der *Accademia del Disegno* wurde die Ausbildung zur Malerei und Bildhauerei um die Vermittlung wissenschaftlicher Kenntnisse erweitert und erhielt so erstmals gesellschaftliche Anerkennung. Neben theoretischen Vorlesungen in Geometrie, Anatomie, Perspektive und dem analytischen Zeichnen (Zeichnen nach plastischen Modellen, Akt- und Landschaftszeichnen) war von nun an das Kopieren bedeutender Werke zentraler Bestandteil der künstlerischen Ausbildung. Die Nachbildung der Natur war seit der Antike die Kernaufgabe bildnerischer Tätigkeit und grundlegendes Ausbildungskonzept bis ins 20. Jahrhundert: *Mimesis,* die naturgetreue Nachbildung war das Ziel, das durch *imitatio,* die Kunst des Kopierens erreicht werden sollte. Auch die Architektur war ein Lehrfach an der Akademie. Zumal sie wesentlich auf der Verbindung von gestalterischer Praxis und wissenschaftlicher Kenntnis basiert, doch wurde sie meist den mechanischen Künsten und erst seit den Schriften des Architekten Vitruv gelegentlich auch den freien zugeordnet. Die *Accademia del Disegno* war nicht nur die erste Lehranstalt für die Vermittlung bildender Künste, sondern auch die erste Architekturschule mit einem geregelten Unterrichtsbetrieb.[12]

Brunelleschis Entdeckung der Zentralperspektive hatte wissenschaftliche Methoden in die Kunst eingeführt. Das Verfahren der Perspektivkonstruktion ermöglichte nicht nur eine korrekte Raumdarstellung, sondern verband die wissenschaftliche Tätigkeit der *artes liberales* mit den handwerklichen *artes mechanicae*. Hier wurde die *techne* erstmals zu einem wissenschaftlichen Instrumentarium und damit der bildnerischen Kunst gesellschaftliches Ansehen zuteil. Mit Albertis Traktat *Della Pittura* entstand 1435 die erste kunsttheoretische Darlegung zur Malerei, die zugleich den Wissensumfang der künstlerischen Praxis normierte.

„Was lehren wir jene, die Künstler werden wollen, um Fertigkeit und Können zu gewährleisten? Wenn keine der Regeln und Normen mehr gelten, was bedeutet das für das Zeichnen, die Komposition, die Mate-

derived etymologically from the Old High German *kunnan* and so it is directly connected linguistically to knowledge, skill or mastery. Johann Gottfried Herder's aphorism could be seen as a timeless attempt to make value judgements applicable to fine art as well: "Art comes from ability or knowing (nosse aut posse), perhaps from both; at least it must combine the two to a considerable degree. He who knows but lacks ability is a theorist, who one would scarcely trust in matters of ability; he who can do but knows nothing is a mere practitioner or craftsman; the true artist combines the two."[14]

The scientification of art as from the mid-15th century led to a de-limitation of artistic disciplines: Leonardo da Vinci was character-ised not only by his artisanal abilities in painting and sculpture but

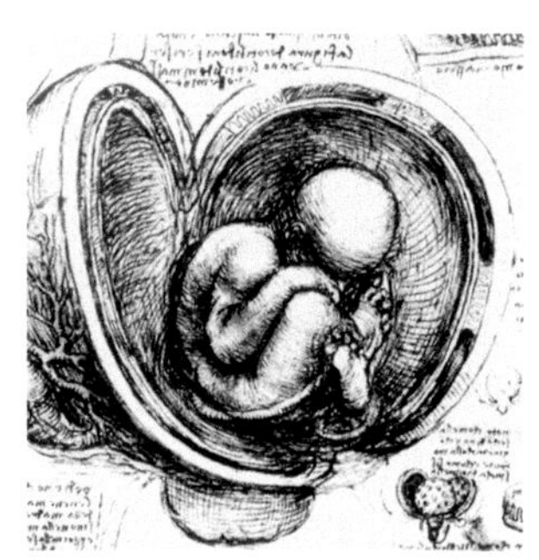

also by his experimental studies in various disciplines of medicine, mechanics, architectural construction etc., which he was able to document and illustrate in such an outstanding way. A wide spectrum of knowledge like this elevated da Vinci to the status of *uomo universalis*, a lead-ing image of courtly society that was also transferred to the fine artist[15] from that point onwards, and consequently called for new standards in art instruction.

It is remarkable that the basic idea, the starting point of the first art academy's foundation was the teaching of interdisciplinary knowledge to facilitate instruction as a universally educated artist. Numerous academies were founded until into the 18th century, becoming the new regulating institutions of artistic training. This meant that a new dividing line developed within the arts: painters and sculptors gained access to a more diversified system of instruction. They left the traditional professional organisations in order to become members of the academies. This change marked the beginning of the division into *fine* and *applied arts*.

As from the early modern era, different crafts of the artes *mechani-cae* had already united under one roof to form so-called manufactories. These were economically oriented organisational systems to increase productivity by optimising manual production processes, e.g. by sepa-rating work procedures. After industrialisation, in the 19th century the manufactories finally lost the economic competition that they had once co-established: industrial operations became increasingly mechanically organised. Along with unstoppable rationalisation, addi-tional delimitation came to the once unified spectrum of applied arts: the distinction between *handicraft* and *applied art*. Handicraft referred to the manual production of unique works and products in small series, as opposed to applied art that made it its task — in a combination of

rialien des Künstlers und ähnliches? Und schließlich ist es natürlich eine Frage für die Kunstkritik selbst: Wie wird beurteilt, wie sehen angemessene Reaktionen aus, wo finden sich Normen, wie lässt sich bewerten?"[13] Die vielfach diskutierte und streitbare Aussage: „Kunst kommt von Können" ist historisch betrachtet durchaus berechtigt. Etymologisch leitet sich der Begriff *Kunst* vom altdeutschen *kunnan* ab und steht damit in direktem sprachlichen Zusammenhang mit der (Er-)Kenntnis, dem Wissen, der Meisterschaft. Johann Gottfried Herders Aphorismus könnte als ein zeitloser Versuch gesehen werden, Bewertungsmaßstäbe auch für die bildende Kunst geltend zu machen: „Kunst kommt von Können oder Kennen her (nosse aut posse), vielleicht von beiden, wenigstens muß sie beides in gehörigem Grad verbinden. Wer kennt, ohne zu können, ist ein Theorist, dem man in Sachen des Könnens kaum trauet; wer kann ohne zu kennen, ist ein bloßer Praktiker oder Handwerker; der echte Künstler verbindet beides."[14]

Die Verwissenschaftlichung der Kunst führte ab Mitte des 15. Jahrhunderts zu einer Entgrenzung der künstlerischen Disziplinen: Leonardo da Vinci zeichnete sich nicht nur durch seine handwerklichen Fertigkeiten in der Malerei und Bildhauerei aus, sondern auch durch seine experimentellen Studien in unterschiedlichsten Fachgebieten in der Medizin, der Mechanik, Baukonstruktion usw., die er in herausragender Weise zu dokumentieren und illustrieren wusste. Mit einem derart breiten Wissensspektrum stieg da Vinci in den Rang eines *uomo universalis* auf, ein Leitbild der höfischen Gesellschaft, das von nun an auch auf den bildenden Künstler übertragen wurde[15] und neue Anforderungen an dessen Ausbildung stellte.

Es ist bemerkenswert, dass die Vermittlung von fächerübergreifenden Kenntnissen die Grundidee und der Ausgangspunkt für die Gründung der ersten Kunstakademie war, um die Ausbildung zu einem universal gebildeten Künstler überhaupt erst möglich zu machen. Bis ins 18. Jahrhundert wurden zahlreiche Akademien gegründet und etablieren sich als neue regulative Institutionen in der künstlerischen Ausbildung. Damit vollzog sich eine neue Trennlinie innerhalb der Künste: Maler und Bildhauer erhielten Zugang zu einem breiter gefächerten Ausbildungssystem. Sie verließen die traditionellen berufsständischen Organisationen, um als Mitglieder in die Akademien einzutreten. Dieser Wechsel markiert den Beginn der Unterscheidung in *bildende* und *angewandte* Künste.

Seit der frühen Neuzeit vereinigten sich bereits verschiedene Gewerke der *artes mechanicae* unter einem Dach zu sogenannten Manufakturen. Sie waren wirtschaftlich ausgerichtete Organisationssysteme

art and serial production — to design our entire world of goods. Quite simply, this was the foundation of what we now call *design*. New technologies and the ever more comprehensive design of the environment was celebrated, as from the mid-19th century, at extremely successful World Exhibitions that propagated new materials and production techniques by means of ambitiously designed products. Technical innovations stood for economic and social upswing, and new specialist skills were demanded in a blossoming applied arts industry; all this led to the foundation of numerous colleges and museums of applied art.

At the end of the 19th century a movement of art educators emerged, critical of existent training methods and their division between the rational and emotional. Alfred Lichtwark, founder of the Hamburg Museum für Kunst und Gewerbe (Museum of Arts and Crafts), was the main representative of this movement: "We do not wish to regard" art teaching "as it has frequently been understood, as a means of acclimatisation to order, cleanliness and mechanical persistancy, but as the development of a joy in assimilation and expression."[16] A number of associations were formed in the context of the diverse reform movements (Arbeitsrat der Kunst / Working Art Council, Werkbund, etc.) as well as artists' groups, small private schools and artists' colonies, which all experimented with new forms in art, applied arts and the teaching of art beyond traditional instruction methods and established boundaries.[17] Changes in art education were demanded in different ways, as indicated by Adolf Behne and Bruno Taut, for example, who even suggested in the *Arbeitsrat der Kunst* in 1918 that artistic instruction be abandoned altogether — without success, for only a year later surely the most historically important college of design ever opened its doors: the State Bauhaus in Weimar. Bringing together art academy and college of applied art, the Bauhaus stands for the reuniting of all work-oriented artistic disciplines, to be taught through a synthesis of artistic instruction and workshop training. In his *Bauhaus Manifesto* in 1919, founding director Walter Gropius proclaimed the abolition of the distinction between free and applied arts: "There is no essential difference between the artist and the craftsman. The artist represents a progression from the craftsman."[18] Art and the will to create were one: "art and technology a new unity" was the hypothesis; design and reproducibility the actuality that prepared the way for industrial design.

Two years before this, Marcel Duchamp had staged the perhaps most spectacular violation of boundaries ever by signing an industrially manufactured functional object with a pseudonym and attempting to submit it to the annual exhibition of the newly founded Society of *Independent Artists* in New York. This urinal entitled *Fountain* triggered

zur Steigerung der Produktivität, indem sie manuelle Herstellungsprozesse unter anderem durch eine Zergliederung von Arbeitsläufen wirtschaftlich optimierten. Mit der Industrialisierung verloren die Manufakturen im 19. Jahrhundert gegen die zunehmend maschinell organisierten Industriebetriebe den ökonomischen Wettlauf, den sie einst mitbegründet hatten. Mit der unaufhaltsamen Rationalisierung entstand eine weitere Abgrenzung in dem einst geeinten Spektrum der praktischen Künste: Die Unterscheidung in *Kunsthandwerk* und *Kunstgewerbe*. Das Kunsthandwerk berief sich auf die manuelle Fertigung von Unikaten und Produkten in Kleinserien im Gegensatz zum Kunstgewerbe, das sich in der Verbindung von Kunst und serieller Produktion die Gestaltung unserer gesamten Warenwelt zur Aufgabe machte und schlicht das begründete, was wir heute *Design* nennen. Die nun um sich greifende Gestaltung von Lebenswelt wurde ab Mitte des 19. Jahrhunderts mit überaus erfolgreichen Weltausstellungen gefeiert, die neue Materialien und Fertigungstechniken mittels anspruchsvoll gestalteter Produkte propagierten. Technische Innovationen standen für wirtschaftlichen und gesellschaftlichen Aufschwung, neue Fachkompetenzen waren in einer aufblühenden Kunstgewerbeindustrie gefragt, die zur Gründung zahlreicher Kunstgewerbeschulen und -museen führte.

Ende des 19. Jahrhunderts formierte sich eine Kunsterziehungsbewegung, die die einseitigen Ausbildungsmethoden und die Trennung von Ratio und Gefühl kritisierte. Alfred Lichtwark war der Gründer des hamburgischen Museums für Kunst und Gewerbe und der Hauptvertreter der Bewegung: „Wir wollen" den Kunstunterricht „nicht, wie er vielfach aufgefasst worden ist als ein Mittel der Gewöhnung an Ordnung, Sauberkeit und mechanische Beharrlichkeit, sondern als die Entwicklung der Auffassungs- und Ausdrucksfreudigkeit betrachten."[16] Im Kontext der vielgestaltigen Reformbewegungen entstanden zahlreiche Verbände (Arbeitsrat der Kunst, Werkbund etc.) und Künstlergruppen sowie kleine Privatschulen und Künstlerkolonien, die mit neuen Formen in der Kunst, dem Kunstgewerbe und der Kunstvermittlung jenseits tradierter Lehrformen und Grenzziehungen experimentierten.[17] Auf welch unterschiedliche Weise Veränderungen in der künstlerischen Ausbildung eingefordert wurden, zeigen unter anderem Adolf Behne und Bruno Taut, die sich im Arbeitsrat der Kunst 1918 für die Abschaffung der künstlerischen Ausbildung aussprachen – ohne Erfolg, denn nur ein Jahr später wurde die wohl historisch bedeutsamste Hochschule für Gestaltung eröffnet: das Staatliche Bauhaus in Weimar. Mit der Zusammenlegung von Kunstakademie und Kunstgewerbeschule steht das Bauhaus für die Wiedervereinigung

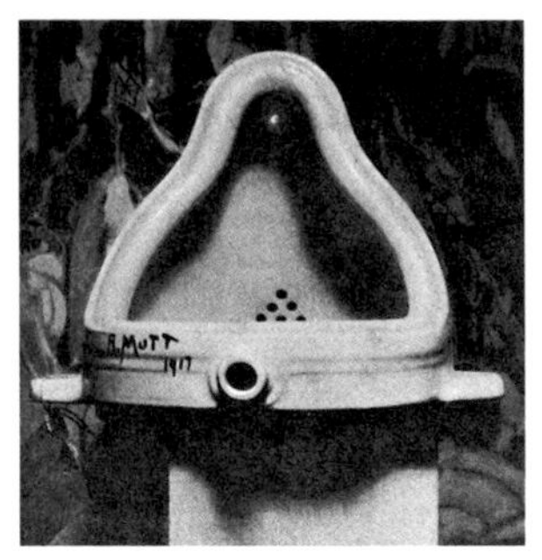

hefty discussions, being refused as an object that could not be categorised as art. Only a week after the exhibition opening, however, it did find a way into the art world: Alfred Stieglitz showed it in his Galerie 291, placed on a white pedestal immediately in front of the painting *The Warriors* by Marsden Hartley.

The 20th century stands for a struggle for disciplinary boundaries and spectacular boundary crossings. It was a multicoloured kaleidoscope of events, manifestos, rebellions, demontage and innovations, from which only very fragmentary, diverse elements can be selected and returned to the reader's attention in this context: in his famous work *Das Kunstwerk im Zeitalter der technischen Reproduzierbarkeit* (The Work of Art in the Age of Mechanical Reproducibility), Walter Benjamin attributed the "demolition of the aura" to art in reproduction and granted only a difficult position to photography as an artistic discipline. Meanwhile, with Andy Warhol and Pop Art, a new chapter began: Warhol, who had made a name for himself in the 50s as a well-paid commercial graphic designer, became an artist at the very moment when he abandoned the will to design: his first exhibition in the Ferus Galerie, Los Angelos in 1962 showed a series of reproductions of *Campbell's Soup* cans, which differed only because of their written labels indicating 32 flavours. "It was like being in an advertising agency," Californian artist Ed Moses commented.[19]

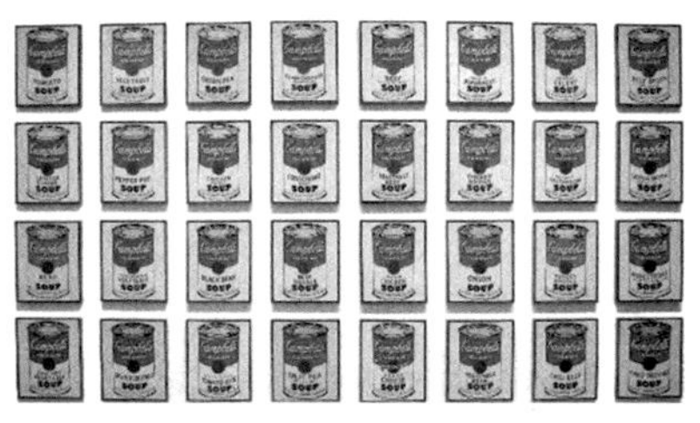

"When I think about it, it is obvious to me that it is a mistake to paint. It means lending dimension to thought and then painting it as well. My painterly instinct tells me: 'If you don't think, you're doing the right thing.'" And so Andy Warhol did what he could do anyway, and he painted what was already there; and so serial production and business came to the fore and stayed there: "After art the next logical step is commercial art. I began as a commercial artist and I want to finish as a commercial artist. [...] Being good in business is the most fascinating art."[20]

In 1966, only a few years after Andy Warhol's breakthrough as an artist, Italian designer Bruno Munari declared: *Design as Art*.[21] He maintained that the elitist myth of art should be destroyed, art should break out of its closed circle and re-establish its connections to life: "Today it has become necessary to demolish the myth of the 'star artist' who only produces masterpieces for a small group of ultra-intelligent people."[22] The way to achieve this was serial production, which could reach a wide audience at a small price — for that reason, Munari saw

aller werkkünstlerischen Disziplinen, die in einer Synthese von künstlerischem Unterricht und Werkstattausbildung vermittelt werden sollten. Bereits in seinem *Bauhaus Manifest* von 1919 proklamierte der Gründungsdirektor Walter Gropius die Aufhebung der Trennung von freien und angewandten Künsten: „Es gibt keinen Wesensunterschied zwischen dem Künstler und dem Handwerker. Der Künstler ist eine Steigerung des Handwerkers."[18] Kunst und Gestaltungswille waren eins: „Kunst und Technik eine Einheit", hieß das Postulat, Gestaltung und Reproduzierbarkeit das Faktum, das im 20. Jahrhundert dem industriellen Design den Weg bereitete.

Zwei Jahre zuvor hatte Marcel Duchamp die wohl spektakulärste Grenzverletzung inszeniert, als er ein industriell gefertigtes Gebrauchsobjekt mit einem Pseudonym signierte und in die Jahresausstellung der neu gegründeten *Society of Independent Artists* in New York einzubringen versuchte. Das Urinal mit den Titel *Fountain* löste heftige Diskussionen aus und wurde als nicht der Kunst zuzuordnendes Objekt zurückgewiesen. Nur eine Woche nach der Eröffnung der Ausstellung fand es dennoch Eingang in die Kunstwelt: Alfred Stieglitz zeigte es in seiner Galerie 291 auf einem weißen Sockel platziert, direkt vor dem Gemälde *The Warriors* von Marsden Hartley.

Das 20. Jahrhundert steht für ein Ringen um disziplinäre Grenzen und spektakuläre Grenzüberschreitungen, und bietet ein vielfarbiges Kaleidoskop an Ereignissen, Manifesten, Rebellionen, Demontagen und Innovationen, aus denen hier nur sehr fragmentarisch bunte Splitter aufgegriffen und in Erinnerung gerufen werden können. In seinem berühmten Werk *Das Kunstwerk im Zeitalter der technischen Reproduzierbarkeit* bescheinigte Walter Benjamin der Kunst die „Zertrümmerung der Aura" im Falle der Vervielfältigung und bescherte der Fotografie als künstlerischer Disziplin einen schweren Stand. Mit Andy Warhol und der Pop Art wurde indes ein neues Kapitel aufgemacht: Warhol, der sich in den 50er Jahren als gut bezahlter Gebrauchsgrafiker einen Namen gemacht hatte, wurde bezeichnenderweise in dem Moment zu einem Künstler, als er seinen Gestaltungswillen aufgab: Seine erste Ausstellung 1962 in der Ferus Galerie in Los Angeles zeigte eine Serie von Abbildungen der *Campbells-Soup*-Dosen, die sich nur aufgrund der Aufschrift von 32 Geschmacksrichtungen unterschieden. „Es sah aus wie in einer Werbeagentur", kommentierte der kalifornische Künstler Ed Moses.[19] „Wenn ich darüber nachdenke, wird mir klar, dass es ein Fehler ist zu malen. Es bedeutet einem Gedanken Dimension zu verleihen und ihn dann auch noch anzumalen. Mein malerischer Instinkt sagt mir: ‚Wenn du nicht denkst, tust du das Richtige.'" Andy Warhol tat demnach das, was er handwerklich beherrschte und malte,

design as the art of the future, as only design provides answers or rather solutions to aesthetic problems in response to socially relevant questions. Production and distribution were foremost on both sides: art was to discover fresh contact with life and the masses via trivi-

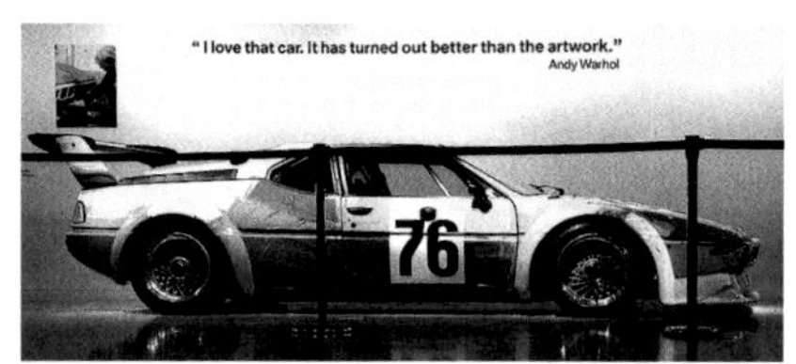

alisation, usefulness and multiplication. A few years later, the publication *Design for the Real World*[23], appeared first in Sweden and then in America. This work by American industrial designer Victor Papanek, a lecturer at California Institute of the Arts, provided a social agenda for industrial design, a call to designers to question and re-orient their role and the task of industrial design as such in order to find new, relevant social starting points for the design and development of products that were directed promarily towards market interests.

In Germany, after a fatal political and cultural break, war and postwar reconstruction there was a need to reconnect within the international context. Colleges here attempted to revert to the end of avant-garde modernism imposed by the National Socialists, a modernism that had developed further into the so-called International Style in America.

The years of the economic miracle and suppression of the past were followed by rebellions, discourse and concept took the place of form. The wild 60s and 70s redeemed the demand for art = life, albeit in a socially critical way, in fact turning away from the world of commerce and consumer goods: Fluxus and Happenings questioned the tradi-tional boundaries more than ever, art was celebrated as a temporary event or, as Concept Art, it bade farewell to formal issues and claims to materialisation. In place of serial productivity came consumer criticism and individual perception. Urban space emerged as a social playground where the boundaries between art, design and architec-ture gained in fluidity. The trio of architects and artists Haus Rucker Co drew public attention when they paraded through the streets of Vienna in the sixties and seventies with so-called *Mind Expanders*. Their aim was to see urban space literally with fresh eyes and bring art into public space and closer to an audience across all social classes by means of installations and playful Happenings. However, this was not only a matter of playfulness and fun but also involved debate with our environment, with the development of new technologies, ways of life, and questions regarding the future of our society. They developed a critical stance and visionary approaches to elementary problems, lacking in many actions and projects which have been reviving such urban interventions for several years now.

was ohnehin schon da war; von nun an traten die serielle Produktion sowie das Geschäft in den Vordergrund: „Nach der Kunst folgt als nächster Schritt die kommerzielle Kunst. Ich habe als kommerzieller Künstler begonnen und möchte als Künstler-Geschäftsmann aufhören. (…) Die faszinierendste Kunst ist, gute Geschäfte zu machen."[20]

1966, nur wenige Jahre nach Andy Warhols Durchbruch als Künstler, erklärte der italienische Designer Bruno Munari: *Design as Art*.[21] Der elitäre Mythos der Kunst solle zerstört werden, die Kunst sollte ausbrechen aus ihrem geschlossenen Kunstzirkel und wieder Anschluss an das Leben finden: „Today it has become necessary to demolish the myth of the star artist who only produces masterpieces for a small group of ultra-intelligent people."[22] Der Weg, dies zu erreichen, ist die serielle Produktion, die bei kleinem Preis ein großes Publikum erreichen kann – daher ist für Munari das Design die Kunst der Zukunft, denn nur das Design liefert Antworten bzw. ästhetische Problemlösungen auf gesellschaftsrelevante Fragen. Die Produktion und Distribution standen auf beiden Seiten im Vordergrund: Kunst soll über Trivialisierung, Nutzbarmachung und Vervielfachung Anschluss an das Leben und an die Masse finden. Wenige Jahre später erschien zunächst in Schweden, dann in Amerika das Buch *Design for the Real World*.[23] Die Schrift des amerikanischen Industriedesigners Victor Papanek, der zudem am California Institute of the Arts lehrte, war eine soziale Agenda, ein Aufruf an Designer, ihre Rolle und die Aufgabe des Industrial Design zu hinterfragen und neu auszurichten, um für die Gestaltung und Entwicklung von Produkten, die sich primär an Marktinteressen ausrichteten, neue und gesellschaftsrelevante Ansätze zu finden.

In Deutschland galt es indes nach einer fatalen politischen und kulturellen Zäsur, Krieg und Wiederaufbau den Anschluss zu suchen. Die Hochschulen versuchten an das von den Nationalsozialisten erzwungene Ende einer avantgardistischen Moderne, die sich in Amerika zum sogenannten Internationalen Stil weiterentwickelt hatte, anzuknüpfen.

Den Jahren des Wirtschaftswunders und der Verdrängung folgte die Revolte, an die Stelle der Form traten Diskurs und Konzept. Die wilden 60er und 70er lösten die Forderung Kunst = Leben ein, jedoch gesellschaftskritisch und in Abkehr von Kommerz und Warenwelt: Fluxus und Happenings stellten mehr denn je tradierte Grenzen infrage, Kunst wurde als temporäres Ereignis gefeiert oder verabschiedete sich als Konzeptkunst von Formfragen und Materialisierungsansprüchen. An die Stelle serieller Produktivität traten Konsumkritik und die individuelle Wahrnehmung. Der urbane Raum wurde zur gesellschaftlichen Spielwiese, die Grenzen zwischen Kunst, Design und Architektur begannen zu fließen. Das Architekten- und Künstlertrio Haus Rucker Co

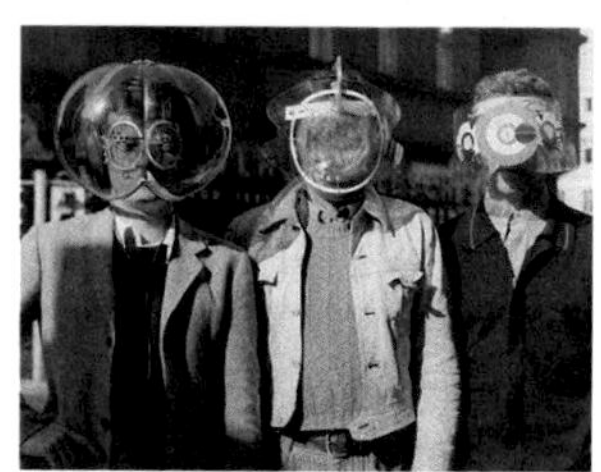

This experimental, physical elation was followed by a politicising and de-sensitising, and by an apparently limitless expansion of the art concept, which inevitably led to the dissolution of boundaries within the arts. New technologies facilitated new forms of representation and expression and consolidated this process. No limits were set to artistic expression. One perhaps symptomatic example is the career of American artist, designer and architect Vito Acconci: originally a literary figure, in 1972 he suddenly drew discussion as a "fine" artist following his provocative performance *Seedbed*, at which he publicly masturbated during an exhibition opening in the Sonnabend Galerie in NYC. Then, in the eighties and nineties, he began to design furniture and rooms; And in the context of the Cultural Capital Programme in Graz in 2003 the architecture of so called Murinsel was realised for an event venue — a floating platform in the river Mur.

In the eighties and nineties remembrance developed fresh ascendancy over forgetfulness — postmodernism over deconstructivism. Works oriented on the avant-garde of modernism were developed by architects who investigated space and the self-understanding of architecture in an artistic way and so received only limited recognition in their own specialist fields, like John Hejduk, Zaha Hadid and Daniel Libeskind, to name but a few. The nineties disclosed this field of conflict in face of an extremely critical attitude towards artistic positions in architecture — and today the fronts in self-understanding have hardened, although in practice the borders are fluid.

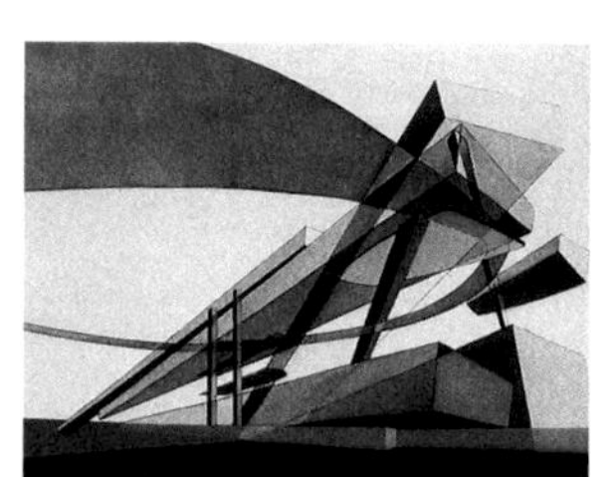

The duo of architects Elizabeth Diller and Ricardo Scofidio made their name at the beginning of the nineties with multimedia installations that approached the topic of space from a critical perspective. It was only in 2002, with the realisation of the *Blur Buildung* in the context of the Swiss Expo, that they were acknowledged seriously or indeed at all within their own professional field. The *Blur Building* has drawn considerable attention: the so-called building systematically evades spatial categories, functions and materialisation as a technically produced, real cloud. It is an architecture of the event, which abandons the fundamental claim to exist as designed casing and form, being satisfied with an ephemeral, constantly transforming manifestation. It cannot be sorted into any category as a result: is it art, design, architecture?

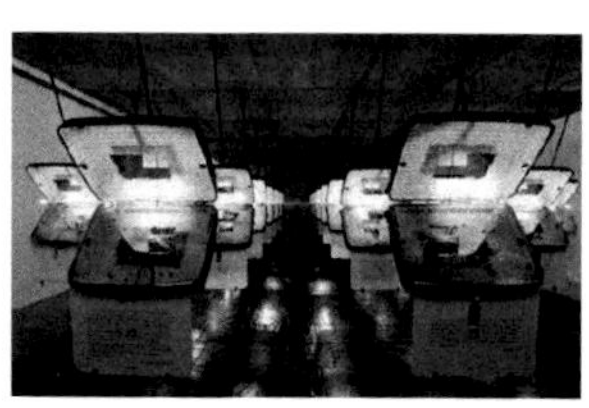

errang in den 60er und 70er Jahren Aufmerksamkeit, als sie mit sogenannten *Mind Expandern* durch die Straßen Wiens zogen, um den städtischen Raum buchstäblich mit anderen Augen zu sehen, und mittels Installationen und spielerischer Happenings die Kunst in den öffentlichen Raum und einem Publikum quer durch alle Gesellschaftsschichten näherbrachten. Doch ging es dabei nicht nur um Spiel und Spaß, sondern auch um eine Auseinandersetzung mit unserer Umwelt, mit der Entwicklung neuer Technologien, um Lebensformen und um Fragen an die Zukunft unserer Gesellschaft. Sie entwickelten eine kritische Haltung und visionäre Lösungsansätze zu elementaren Problemen, welche viele Aktionen und Projekte, die seit einigen Jahren diese urbanen Interventionen re-aktualisieren, vermissen lassen.

Dem experimentellen Sinnesrausch folgte die Politisierung und Entsinnlichung und eine scheinbar grenzenlose Erweiterung des Kunstbegriffs, die zwangsläufig zu einer Auflösung von Grenzziehungen innerhalb der Künste führen musste. Neue Technologien ermöglichten neue Darstellungs- und Ausdrucksformen und unterstützten diesen Prozess. Dem künstlerischen Ausdruck waren keine Grenzen gesetzt. Ein vielleicht symptomatisches Beispiel ist der Werdegang des amerikanischen Künstlers, Designers und Architekten Vito Acconci: Ursprünglich Literat, brachte er sich 1972 mit seiner provokanten Performance *Seedbed* als „bildender" Künstler ins Gespräch, indem er zur Ausstellungseröffnung in der Sonnabend Galerie in NYC öffentlich onanierte. In den 80er und 90er Jahren begann er, Möbel und Räume zu entwerfen. Und 2003 wurde im Rahmen des Kulturhauptstadtprogramms in Graz der architektonische Entwurf für die sogenannte Murinsel als schwimmende Plattform in der Mur realisiert.

In den 80er und 90er Jahren stellte sich das Erinnern gegen das Vergessen – Postmoderne versus Dekonstruktivismus. In Anlehnung an die Avantgarde der Moderne entstanden Arbeiten von Architekten, die sich auf künstlerische Art und Weise mit Raum und dem Selbstverständnis von Architektur auseinandersetzten und nur bedingt Anerkennung in den eigenen Fachkreisen erhielten, wie zum Beispiel John Hejduk, Zaha Hadid, Daniel Libeskind, um nur einige wenige zu nennen. Die 90er Jahre machten dieses Spannungsfeld deutlich angesichts der überaus kritischen Haltung gegenüber künstlerischen Positionen in der Architektur – und noch heute sind die Fronten im Selbstverständnis bisweilen verhärtet, auch wenn die Grenzen in der Praxis fließend sind.

Das Architektenduo Elizabeth Diller und Ricardo Scofidio machten sich Anfang der 90er Jahre einen Namen mit multimedialen Installationen, die sich dem Thema Raum aus einer kritischen Perspektive näherten. Erst 2002 wurden sie mit der Realisierung des *Blur*

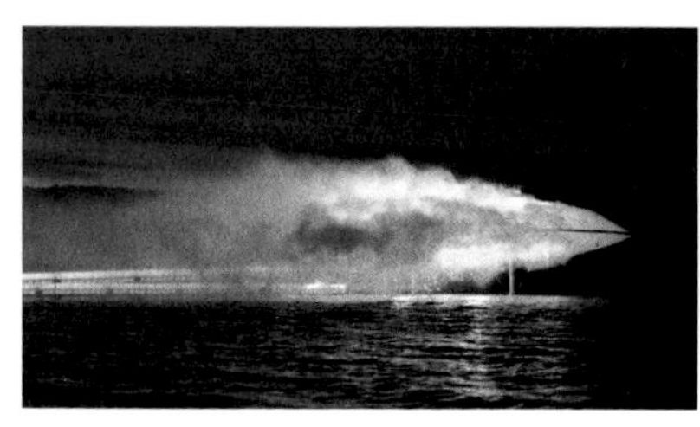

In the field of product design, designers in the nineties also embarked upon new paths: they questioned the content and significance of functional objects, as well as the processes of design, production and distribution, and in general terms their own assignment as the designers of our living environment. The outcome of the conceptually influenced design process was no longer industrially manufactured everyday products but objects that ocassionally thematised uncomfortable aspects rather than offering reassuring solutions. In this context, designer duo Anthony Dunne and Fiona Raby coined the term *critical design*. *Critical design* locates the task of design in a cultural-political context and sees itself as debate with the present and future of our living environment; it takes up the aforementioned tendencies within the design scene of the 70s. *Critical Design* formulates an attitude, a position, and re-investigates the setting of assignments in design. What are people's current needs, beyond well-designed everyday products?

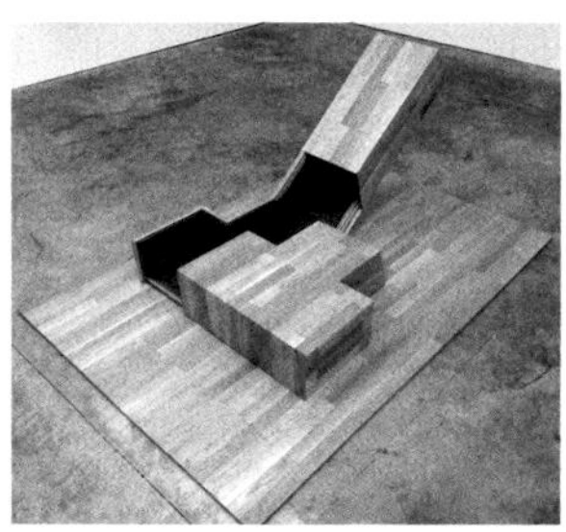

Anthony Dumme and Fiona Raby both teach at the Royal College of Art in London, a college where many young, lateral-thinking and meanwhile successful designers studied — like Pieke Bergmanns from the Netherlands. She uses the term *design virus* to describe her objects as viral, since they emerge from the manipulation of standardised production processes. At this point I should also mention the Design Academy Eindhoven and the Haute école d'art et de design in Geneva, which are both characterised by their innovative study programmes in the field of design; a fertile basis upon which design is taught, learnt, researched and developed from novel standpoints.[24]

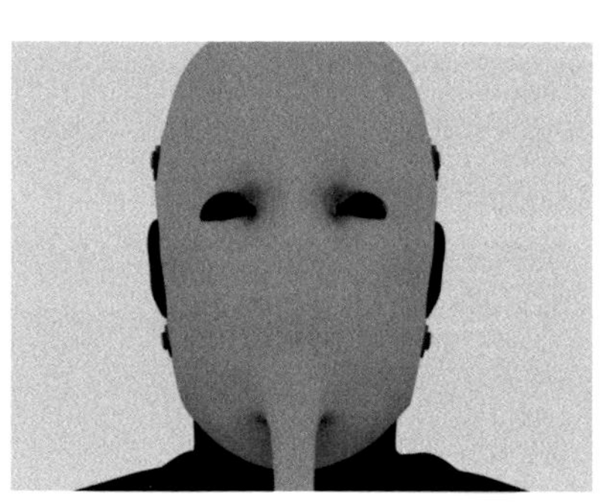

Concepts and products of *critical* and *social design* do not necessarily conform to the market, they do not primarily fulfil the requirements of formally attractive functional everyday objects that can be manufactured industrially; instead they embody attitudes, individual responses to socially relevant questions. These experimentally developed prototypes are not designed for serial production and cannot be subordinated to the dictates of usefulness; rather, they aim to raise questions in a socially critical but also humorous manner, and present innovative offers to meet the changing needs of individuals in a post-industrial society. The marketing of these products, mainly unique works

Building im Rahmen der Schweizer Expo von der eigenen Berufssparte ernst oder überhaupt zur Kenntnis genommen. Das *Blur Building* hat für viel Aufmerksamkeit gesorgt, denn als technisch inszenierte reale Wolke entzieht sich das sogenannte Gebäude gezielt räumlichen Kategorien, Funktionen und einer Materialisierung. Es ist eine Architektur des Ereignisses, die sich von dem grundlegenden Anspruch, gestaltete Hülle und Form zu sein, verabschiedet. Sie begnügt sich damit, ephemere, sich ständig wandelnde Erscheinung zu sein und lässt sich demnach in keine Schublade einsortieren: Ist das Kunst, Design, Architektur?

Auch im Bereich des Produktdesign schlugen in den 90er Jahren Designer neue Wege ein: Sie stellten den Inhalt und die Bedeutung von Gebrauchsobjekten infrage, den Prozess der Gestaltung, der Produktion und Distribution sowie generell ihre Aufgabe als Gestalter von Lebenswelt. Aus dem konzeptuell geprägten Designprozess gingen keine industriell gefertigten Alltagsprodukte hervor, sondern Objekte, die bisweilen unbequeme Aspekte thematisierten, anstatt Komfortlösungen zu bieten. Das Designerduo Anthony Dunne und Fiona Raby haben den Begriff *critical design* geprägt. *Critical design* verortet die Aufgabe des Designs in einem kulturpolitischen Kontext; es versteht sich als eine Auseinandersetzung mit der Gegenwart und Zukunft unserer Lebenswelt und knüpft an bereits oben genannte Tendenzen innerhalb der Designszenen in den 70er Jahren an. *Critical Design* formuliert eine Haltung, eine Position und lotet die Aufgabenstellung des Designs neu aus. Was sind die aktuellen Bedürfnisse der Menschen jenseits wohlgestalteter Alltagsprodukte?

Anthony Dunne und Fiona Raby unterrichten beide am Royal College of Art in London, eine Hochschule an der viele der jungen querdenkenden und mittlerweile auch erfolgreichen Designer studiert haben, wie beispielweise die Niederländerin Pieke Bergmanns. Mit dem Begriff *design virus* beschreibt sie ihre Objekte als viral, da sie aus der Manipulation standardisierter Produktionsprozesse emergieren. Auch die Design Academy Eindhoven und die Haute école d'art et de design in Genf sind in diesem Zuge zu nennen, da sie sich durch innovativen Studienprogramme auszeichnen und einen Nährboden schaffen, auf dem Design unter neuen Gesichtspunkten gelehrt, gelernt, erforscht und entwickelt wird.[24]

Konzepte und Produkte des *critical* und *social design* sind nicht unbedingt marktkonform, sie erfüllen nicht primär Ansprüche an einen industriell zu fertigenden funktionalen und formschönen Alltagsgegenstand, sondern verkörpern Haltungen: individuelle Antworten auf gesellschaftsrelevante Fragen. Die experimentell entwickelten Prototypen werden nicht für die Serienproduktion entworfen und ordnen

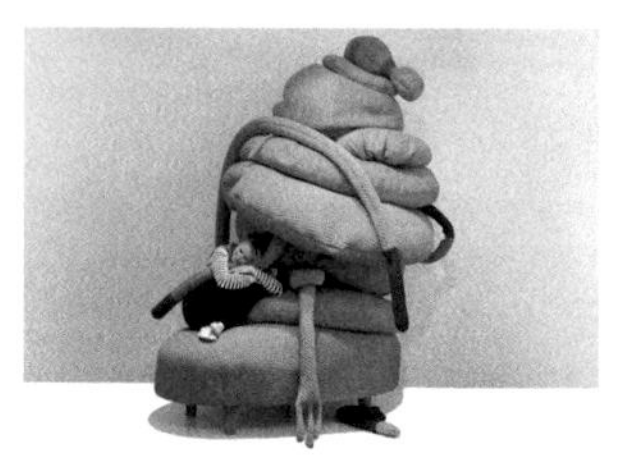

and small editions involving complicated production processes, therefore calls for new strategies and distribution systems and presents difficulties to many young designers wishing to secure their economic survival.

Is there still a boundary between art and design? Who defines the category into which artistic objects and projects are sorted? Is it a matter of functionality, specific purpose, the authors, or rather the strategy of marketing or even customs officials?

In 2007 a design fair of the same name was opened alongside *Art Basel/Miami.* Both fairs see themselves as a global forum for art and design, presenting twice yearly in direct proximity and lucrative co-existence, first in Basel and later in Miami. But the clear spatial boundary drawn between the fairs does not necessarily permit any conclusions about clear differentiation between the exhibits shown. Here, it is interesting to observe that *Design Basel/Miami* offers contemporary design and art to equal degrees alongside the customary share of design classics from the world of furniture - whereby it is often not really possible to distinguish one from the other. Far more, the boundaries

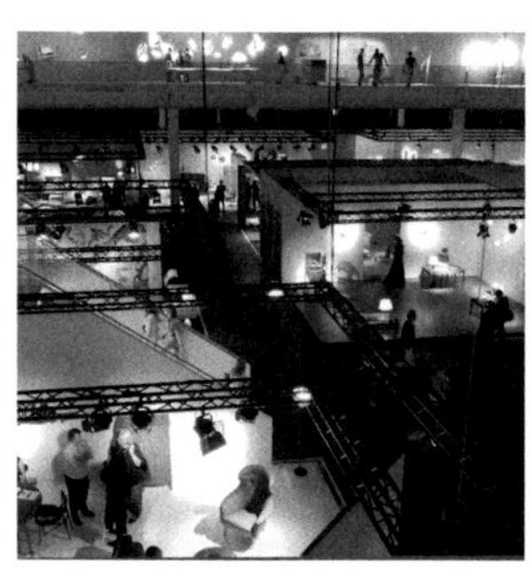

on the world market are becoming indistinct and there is an obvious trend in that direction. An exclusive world market for unique works of design and small editions is being established. These are objects that are no longer designed and produced for their functional value but as exhibition pieces for collections, thus deliberately apart from the customary distribution networks in the field of design. The new marketing strategy is not multiplication but scarcity, which — in the nineties — had already granted unprecedented commercial success to contemporary photography, which had needed to struggle a long time for artistic recognition — as a serial product. In design as well, the price segment for unique works knows no upward limit, not necessarily addressing the audience in search of a functional object first and fore-

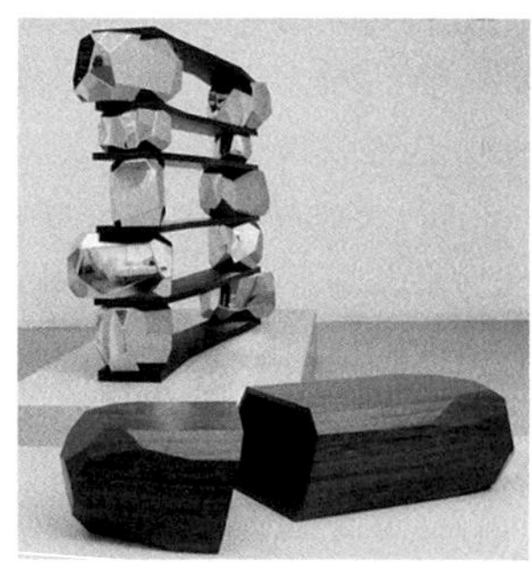

most. In 2011, a shelf by designer Arik Levy, for example, was put up for sale in a small edition of 5 at a price of 100,000 EUR per piece: a price that can scarcely tolerate any trace of usage. A new market is developing for designers and architects here, providing new distribution paths and networks appealing to a new set of customers in the field of applied arts. As a rule, it concerns a luxury segment, which justifies the exquisite price level by means of scarcity, high-quality materials and a return to artisanal realisation.[25]

sich nicht einem Diktat der Nutzbarkeit unter, sie wollen vielmehr Fragen aufwerfen, gesellschaftskritisch, aber auch humorvoll, und den sich wandelnden Bedürfnissen von Individuen in einer postindustriellen Gesellschaft innovative Angebote unterbreiten. Die Vermarktung dieser Produkte, meist aufwendig hergestellte Unikate und kleine Editionen, erfordert demnach neue Strategien und Vertriebssysteme und stellt viele junge Designer vor die Herausforderung, ihre existenzielle Grundlage zu sichern.

Gibt es noch eine Grenze zwischen Kunst und Design? Wer definiert, in welche Kategorie künstlerische Objekte und Projekte einsortiert werden? Sind es Funktionalität, Zweckbestimmung, die Autoren, die Strategie der Vermarktung oder gar der Zoll?

2007 wurde begleitend zur *Art Basel/Miami* die Designmesse *Design Basel/Miami* eröffnet. Beide Messen verstehen sich als globales Forum für Kunst und Design, und präsentieren sich zweimal im Jahr in direkter Nachbarschaft und lukrativer Koexistenz, zuerst in Basel, dann in Miami. Doch die zwischen den Messen eindeutig gezogene räumliche Grenze lässt nicht unbedingt Rückschlüsse zu auf eine klare Ausdifferenzierung der gezeigten Exponate. Dabei ist interessant zu beobachten, dass die *Design Basel/Miami* neben dem üblichen Anteil an Designklassikern aus dem Möbelbereich, zeitgenössisches Design und Kunst gleichermaßen anbietet – wobei häufig das eine vom anderen nicht recht zu unterscheiden ist. Vielmehr werden die Grenzen auf dem Weltmarkt unscharf und dies mit eindeutiger Tendenz. Es etabliert sich ein exklusiver Markt für Designunikate und Kleinstauflagen, die nicht mehr wegen ihres Gebrauchswerts entworfen und hergestellt werden, sondern als Ausstellungsobjekte für Sammlungen und sich somit gezielt von den im Designbereich gängigen Distributionsnetzen lösen. Nicht Vervielfältigung, sondern Verknappung heißt die neue Vermarktungsstrategie, die in den 90er Jahren bereits der zeitgenössischen Fotografie, die als serielles Produkt lange um künstlerische Anerkennung ringen musste, einen nie dagewesenen kommerziellen Erfolg bescherte. Das Preissegment für Unikate kennt auch im Designbereich nach oben keine Grenzen und spricht nicht unbedingt jenes Publikum an, das in erster Linie ein funktionales Objekt erwerben möchte. Ein Regal des Designers Arik Levy wurde beispielsweise 2011 in einer Kleinstauflage von fünf Exemplaren für ca. 100.000 Euro pro Stück angeboten: ein Preis, der kaum Gebrauchsspuren duldet. Es entwickelt sich hier ein neuer Markt für Designer und Architekten, der im Bereich der angewandten Künste neue Vertriebswege und -netze für eine neue Kundschaft anbietet. Dabei handelt es sich in der Regel um ein Luxussegment, das durch Verknappung, hochwertige Materialität und die Rückkehr zum Kunsthandwerk eine exquisite Preislage rechtfertigt.[25]

Owing to a special European regulation, art objects in Germany are subject to a reduced rate of value-added tax of seven per cent. Since the EU-commission called upon Germany to abolish this reduced taxation rate, numerous protests have been made in the field of artistic production. Quite correctly, as the absurdity of the existing taxation chaos in the art world is made clear by the following example: artists or gallery-owners who develop or sell artworks using light face a requirement to levy tax of 19% on these objects. This is due to the simple fact that such works contain lighting materials that could also be used commercially in other contexts. The mere possibility of different use alters the classification of an object, so that it loses its status as art and is treated as a functional object. A prominent example of this strange evaluation of art by the German tax authorities is the work of artist Gunter Demnig, who successfully defended himself against back

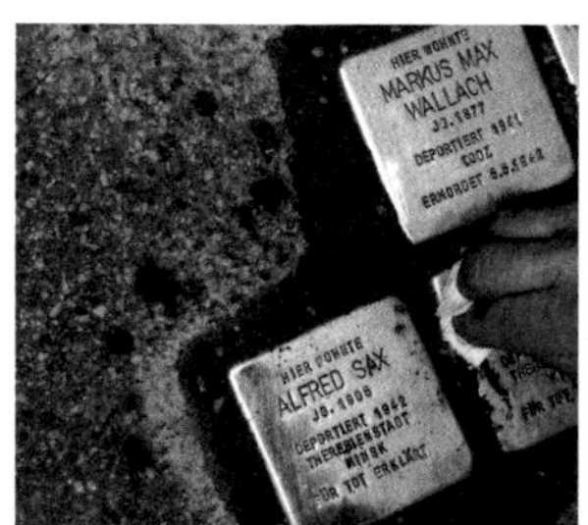

taxation of his internationally known project *Stumbling Blocks* in 2011: after the *Stumbling Blocks* had been classified according to expert assessment by the relevant tax authority as 'brass-plate information signs', Demnig was called upon to pay back tax of circa 150,000 euros. He made the matter public and the demands from the tax office were dropped. Israeli designer Eyal Burstein, who launched a conceptual design label in Berlin going by the name Beta Tank, published a book on this subject in the same year: *Taxing art — when objects travel*. Burstein, who studied design — at the Royal College of Art in London, significantly — not only faced the absurdity of his objects' constantly changing classification in the context of German taxation law, but also following various customs procedures endured by his works when travelling to exhibitions. Deflated, he noted: "Today it is not the object itself but rather its ecomomic functionality that determines its categorization. Astonishingly, it is often customs officials who subjectively decide what constitutes art and design based on their personal views and erratic local tax laws."[26]

In the course of the 20th century art left behind elementary forms, principles and styles in both the artisanal and the formal field. Today, many an artist succeeds less as a designer than as a cook, model, theorist or furnishing adviser etc.[27] One aim of art — so it seems — was a provocative crossing of supposed boundaries, as illustrated by Duchamp as early as 1917 with the consequence that such boundaries scarcely exist at all in contemporary fine art: artists are trying to break down open doors, at least to some extent. "Obviously, art values have become a form of life. (...) no doubt for that reason, too, many artworks

Aufgrund einer Sonderregelung innerhalb Europas sind Kunstgegenstände in Deutschland mit einem ermäßigten Mehrwertsteuersatz von sieben Prozent belegt. Seit die EU-Kommission Deutschland dazu aufgefordert hat, diesen verminderten Steuersatz abzuschaffen, regten sich im Bereich der Kulturschaffenden zahlreiche Proteste. Zu Recht, denn welch absurdes Besteuerungschaos im Kunstbereich bereits wirksam ist, verdeutlicht folgendes Beispiel: Künstler oder Galeristen, die Kunstwerke mit Licht entwickeln oder verkaufen, sehen sich mit der Auflage konfrontiert, diese Arbeiten mit 19 Prozent zu versteuern. Dies ist dem einfachen Umstand geschuldet, dass diese Werke Leuchtmittel beinhalten, die auch anderweitig kommerziell verwendet werden könnten. Allein diese Möglichkeit einer anderen Nutzung verändert die Klassifikation eines Objektes, sodass es den Kunststatus verliert und als Gebrauchsgegenstand gehandelt wird. Ein prominentes Beispiel für diese befremdliche Kunsteinschätzung der deutschen Steuerbehörden ist die Arbeit des Künstlers Gunter Demnig, der sich 2011 gegen eine Nachbesteuerung seines international bekannten Projektes *Stolpersteine* erfolgreich zur Wehr gesetzt hat: Nachdem laut Gutachten einer zuständigen Zollbehörde die Stolpersteine als „Hinweisschilder aus Messingblech" klassifiziert worden waren, wurde Demnig eine Steuernachzahlung von rund 150.000 Euro abverlangt. Er ging an die Öffentlichkeit woraufhin die Forderungen seitens des Finanzamtes fallengelassen wurden. Zu diesem Thema hat der israelische Designer Eyal Burstein, der unter dem Namen Beta Tank in Berlin ein konzeptuelles Designlabel gestartet hat, im selben Jahr ein Buch veröffentlicht: *Taxing art – when objects travel*. Burstein, der bezeichnenderweise am Royal College of Art in London Design studierte, hat die Absurdität der sich ständig ändernden Klassifikation seiner Objekte nicht nur im Rahmen der deutschen Steuergesetzgebung kennengelernt, sondern auch anhand der unterschiedlichen Zolldurchgänge, die seine Objekte auf ihren Reisen zu Ausstellungen durchliefen. Ernüchtert stellte er fest: „Today it is not the object itself but rather its economic functionality that determines its categorization. Astonishingly, it is often customs officials who subjectively decide what constitutes art and design based on their personal views and erratic local tax laws."[26]

Die Kunst verabschiedete sich im Laufe des 20. Jahrhunderts von elementaren Formen, Grundlagen und Stilen sowohl im handwerklichen als auch im formalen Bereich. Viele Künstler heute behaupten sich weniger als Gestalter denn als Koch, als Model, als Theoretiker, Einrichtungsberater etc.[27] Ein Ziel der Kunst – so scheint es – war die

today seem like art clichés — they merely double the inevitable, they are not conceived with more invention, not made with any more care than things produced by everyday culture."[28] So is the designer perhaps the artist of the future after all, as Munari predicted 50 years ago? Despite current trends, the design of functional objects is still bound to their function: but the extent to which they have to comply with that function is another matter altogether. Even today, pleasure over a chair's beautiful form may fail to reduce our annoyance if it is uncomfortable, and a lemon squeezer that gives the user a pain in the arm rather than providing the optimum amount of lemon juice may embellish any kitchen as an object with beautiful form but it will always be replaced by an object that works better sooner or later. This simple yet complex standard makes the design of functional goods easy and difficult in the same breath. Easy, as the setting of clear parameters provides something like a guideline or safety rail for design, along which we can orient our work. Difficult, as such functions not only require — depending on their nature and complexity — wide-ranging competencies but also impose technical and formal limits on design. However, this clearly set out framework has become as permeable as the understanding of free art and its protagonists. There is a new focus on socially relevant and sociopolitical questions; fundamental debate with advancing social transformation that forces us to search for new answers.

New technologies and virtual networks are altering and accelerating our everyday lives to an unprecedented degree: they are changing our needs and patterns of behaviour, influencing our relationships to real people and places, and also our perceptions of space. The production, teaching and acquisition of knowledge cannot remain untouched by this. New questions demand new answers and concepts for responsible dealings with our fellow men and the environment, for sustainable, ecological design that conserves resources; design that is oriented on cultural values and human needs and not only on market interests; design that focuses on existential problems and opens the question of ethical responsibility for disposition in both free and applied art.[29]

This volume brings together different perspectives on the relations between free and applied art. Artists and designers are given the same opportunity to speak as theorists and curators — almost all of them are united by their active involvement in teaching within the disciplines of art, design and architecture. Their essay contributions offer insights into diverse fields of activity and working methods, and open up an exciting discursive field. In parallel, we are releasing the illustrated

provozierende Überschreitung vermeintlicher Grenzen, wie es Duchamp bereits 1917 vor Augen führte, mit der Konsequenz, dass es in der freien Kunst diese Grenzen kaum noch gibt. „Die Werte der Kunst sind offenbar zu einer Lebensform geworden. (...) Wohl auch deshalb wirken viele Kunstwerke heute wie Kunstklischees – sie verdoppeln nur das Selbstverständliche, sie sind nicht erfindungsreicher gedacht, nicht sorgfältiger gemacht als das, was die Alltagskultur hervorbringt."[28] Ist also doch der Designer der Künstler der Zukunft, wie Munari dies vor 50 Jahren prophezeite? Trotz aktueller Trends ist die Gestaltung funktionaler Objekte immer noch an ihre Funktion gebunden, inwieweit sie ihr Folge leisten muss, steht dabei auf einem anderen Blatt. Auch heute mag die Freude an der schönen Form eines Stuhles den Ärger wenig mindern, wenn er unbequem ist, eine Zitronenpresse, die dem Benutzer Muskelkater beschert anstelle der optimalen Menge an Zitronensaft wird als formschönes Objekt vielleicht die Küche zieren, aber in jedem Fall durch einen besser funktionierenden Gegenstand ersetzt werden. Diese schlichte und doch komplexe Maßgabe macht die Gestaltung von Gebrauchsgütern einfach und schwer zugleich. Einfach, da die Vorgabe klarer Parameter gleichsam eine Richtschnur oder Leitplanke für die Gestaltung bietet, an der man sich orientieren kann. Schwierig, da die Funktion je nach Art und Komplexität nicht nur breit gefächerte Kompetenzen voraussetzt, sondern der Gestaltung auch technische und formale Grenzen setzt. Doch dieser klar gesteckte Rahmen ist ebenso brüchig geworden wie das Selbstverständnis der freien Kunst und ihrer Protagonisten. Es treten gesellschaftsrelevante und soziopolitische Fragen in den Vordergrund und fordern die grundlegende Auseinandersetzung mit einem fortschreitenden gesellschaftlichen Wandel, der uns zwingt, nach neuen Antworten zu suchen.

Neue Technologien und virtuelle Netzwerke verändern und beschleunigen unser Alltagsleben in nie dagewesenem Ausmaß: Sie verändern unsere Bedürfnisse und Verhaltensweisen, nehmen Einfluss auf unseren Umgang mit realen Personen. Auch die Produktion, die Vermittlung und Aneignung von Wissen bleibt davon nicht unberührt. Neue Fragestellungen erfordern neue Antworten und Konzepte für einen verantwortungsvollen Umgang mit unseren Mitmenschen und unserer Umwelt, für ein nachhaltiges, ressourcenschonendes, ökologisches Design, für eine Gestaltung, die sich an kulturellen Werten und menschlichen Bedürfnissen orientiert und nicht nur an Marktinteressen ausrichtet, die existenzielle Probleme in den Fokus rückt und die Frage nach einer ethischen Verantwortung der freien und angewandten Künste stellt.[29]

volume *Art? Design? Transdisciplinary Studies*, which elucidates the topic of interdisciplinary teaching concepts and, as a visual experiment, directly asks its reader or viewer the central question of this double publication: Where is the boundary between art and design? Into what category should I place each object, image, graphic, installation, or space? What can I use to demonstrate differences or common characteristics? The question of borders and crossings within the artistic disciplines is not easy to answer and offers a diverse range of fields of discourse. This is a beginning - looking forward to a continuation of the discussion.[30]

Der vorliegende Band vereint unterschiedliche Perspektiven auf das Verhältnis von freien und angewandten Künsten. Künstler und Designer kommen dabei ebenso zu Wort wie Theoretiker und Kuratoren – fast alle eint, dass sie auch in der Lehre tätig sind: in den Fachgebieten Kunst, Design und Architektur. Die Beiträge bieten Einblicke in die unterschiedlichen Tätigkeitsfelder und Arbeitsansätze und eröffnen ein spannendes diskursives Feld. Begleitend erscheint der Bildband *Kunst? Design? Transdisziplinäre Studien,* der die Frage nach Lehrkonzeptionen zwischen den Disziplinen erörtert und als visuelles Experiment die zentrale Frage dieses Doppelbandes an den Leser stellt: Wo verläuft die Grenze zwischen Kunst und Design? In welche Kategorie ordne ich das jeweilige Objekt, das Bild, die Grafik, die Installation, den Raum ein? Woran mache ich Unterschiede oder Gemeinsamkeiten fest? Die Frage nach Grenzziehungen und Überschreitungen innerhalb der künstlerischen Disziplinen ist nicht einfach zu beantworten und bietet facettenreiches Spektrum an Diskursfeldern. Dies ist ein Anfang und die Fortsetzung der Diskussion wünschenswert.[30]

Figures

Notes

[1] Here, the term design refers to applied art disciplines and includes architecture.
[2] See the essay by Christine Hill in this publication, p.083
[3] See the essay by Wolfgang Ullrich in this publication, p.065 also: Wolfgang Ullrich: *Tiefer hängen. Über den Umgang mit der Kunst.* Berlin 2003, *Was war Kunst? Biographien eines Begriffs.* Frankfurt/Main 2005, *Alles nur Konsum. Kritik der warenästhetischen Erziehung.* Berlin 2013
[4] See the essay by El Ultimo Grito in this publication, p.157
[5] See the essay by Louise Schouwenberg, p.105

037

Abbildungen

Anmerkungen

[1] Der Begriff Design meint hier angewandte künstlerische Disziplin und schließt die
Architektur mit ein.

[2] Siehe den Beitrag von Christine Hill in diesem Band, S. 083

[3] Siehe den Beitrag von Wolfgang Ullrich in diesem Band, S. 065 sowie: Wolfgang Ullrich:
Tiefer hängen. Über den Umgang mit der Kunst. Berlin 2003, *Was war Kunst? Biographien eines Begriffs.* Frankfurt/Main 2005, *Alles nur Konsum. Kritik der warenästhetischen Erziehung.* Berlin 2013

[4] Siehe den Beitrag von El Ultimo Grito in diesem Band, S. 157

[6] Siehe den Beitrag von Katia Baudin, p.041

[7] Detail about the term techné: Rudolf Löbl: *Texnh-Techne: Untersuchungen zur Bedeutung dieses Worts in der Zeit von Homer bis Aristoteles*. Vols. 1 and 2: Von den Sophisten bis Aristoteles. Königshausen & Neumann, Würzburg 1997, 2003. "Up until Plato and still in many Aristotelian texts, *techné* is used in the same sense as episteme (knowledge), referring both to *theoretical sciences*, like geometry and astronomy, and also to *practical skills*, like the art of the smith or the sculptor. However, in the work of Aristotle one also finds a narrower definition of *techné*; it is then contrasted, as the art of producing an object, with *episteme* as theoretical knowledge", in: Lexikon der Alten Welt. Zurich: Artemis 1965.

[8] Ibid., p.260

[9] Verena Krieger: *Was ist ein Künstler*, Cologne 2007, p.13

[10] Ibid., p.14

[11] Giorgio Vasari: *The Lives of the Most Excellent Painters, Sculptors, and Architects*, New York 2006, Original edition: *Le Vite de' più eccellenti architetti, pittori, et scultori italiani, da Cimabue infino a'tempi nostri: descritte in lingua toscana da Giorgio Vasari, pittore arentino – Con una sua utile et necessaria introduzione a le arti loro*. L. Torrentino, Florence 1550, 2 Vol

[12] Petra Libel – Osborne: *Gestaltungslehren in der Architektenausbildung*, Frankfurt, Berlin 2001, p. 21

[13] Arthur C. Danto: *Encounters and Reflections. Art in the Historical Present*, Berkley/ Los Angeles/ London 1990, p. 7

[14] Johann Gottfried Herder: *Kalligone, Von Kunst und Kunstrichterei*. Leipzig 1800, Volume 2, p. 3

[15] Verena Krieger: *Was ist ein Künstler*, Cologne 2007, p. 17

[16] Wolf Mannhardt (ed.): *Alfred Lichtwark*, Berlin 1917, p.57 quoted from: Petra Libel – Osborne: *Gestaltungslehren in der Architektenausbildung*, Frankfurt, Berlin 2001, p.37

[17] In 1902 sculptor and theorist Hermann Obrist, and painter and interior designer Wilhelm von Debschitz founded a private college in Munich. Here, in their so-called "Lehr- und Versuchsateliers für Angewandte und Freie Kunst" (Teaching and Experimental Studios for Applied and Free Art) Obrist and Debschitz first taught, for example, the subject "Fundamentals of Design", which was to set a precedent as the so-called "Vorkurs" (preliminary course) at the Bauhaus ca. 15 years later.

[18] Here, Gropius also expressed the opinion that art could not be taught at all.

[19] Jörg Burger: „Andy Warhol - Blums Entdeckung" in: *ZEIT Magazin*, 22.11.12, No.48, also online: www.zeit.de/2012/48/Andy-Warhol-Galerist-Irving-Blum/ (last access: 11.09.2013)

[20] Andy Warhol: *The philosophy of Andy Warhol (from A to B and back again)*, New York 1975, p.92

[21] Bruno Munari: *Design as Art*. Translated by Patrick Creagh, 1st edition Italy 1966, 1st translated edition 1971

[22] Bruno Munari: *Design as Art*, 2008, p.25

[23] Victor Papanek: *Design for the Real World; Human Ecology and Social Change (first Swedish edition 1970) new revised edition 1985* with numerous additions. Chicago 1985. On the current understanding and programme of Social Design, see Victor + Sylvia Margolin: "A 'Social Model' of Design: Issues of Practice and Research", in: *MIT Design issues*, Vol. 18, No. 4, Fall 2002

[24] For an insight into the practice of, and basic attitudes to the topic Art and / or Design? see the contributions by teaching staff at these colleges: Louise Schouwenberg p. 105, and Rosario Hurtado and Roberto Feo (El Ultimo Grito), p. 157

[25] On this, see the contributions Katia Baudin, p.041 and Alex Coles, p.131

[26] Eyal Burstein: *Taxing art – when objects travel*, 2011

[27] On this, see the contribution by Christine Hill p.083

[28] Hanno Rauterberg: „Einsamkeit, Freiheit, tiefes Glück. Wanderungen im Nebelmeer: Was die zeitgenössische Kunst von Werbung, Mode und Design unterscheidet" in: *Die Zeit*, 16.08.2007, No. 34

[29] On the relations between ethics and aesthethics, see: Annett Zinsmeister (ed.): *Ethics in Aesthetics?* Berlin 2012

[30] For the continuation of the discourse we have set up a blog that aims to provide space for answers, articles and further leading interdisciplinary issues: http://www.art-and-or-design.blogspot.de. We look forward to a continuation of the discussion.

5 Siehe den Beitrag von Louise Schouwenberg, S. 105

6 Siehe den Beitrag von Katia Baudin, S. 041

7 Zum Begiff Techné ausfurhlich: Rudolf Löbl: *Texnh-Techne: Untersuchungen zur Bedeutung* dieses Worts in der Zeit von *Homer bis Aristoteles.* Bd. 1 und 2: Von den *Sophisten bis Aristoteles.* Königshausen & Neumann, Würzburg 1997, 2003. „Bis zu Platon und noch in vielen aristotelischen Texten wird *techné* als gleichbedeutend mit ep, steme (Wissen) angewendet, und zwar sowohl auf *theoretische Wissenschaften,* wie die Geometrie und die Astronomie, als auch auf *praktische Fertigkeiten,* wie die Kunst des Schmiedes oder des Bildhauers. Man findet jedoch bei Aristoteles auch eine engere Definition der *techné;* sie wird dann als die Kunst, etwas hervorzubringen, der *episteme* als dem theoretischen Wissen gegenüber gestellt", in: Lexikon der Alten Welt. Zürich: Artemis 1965

8 Ebda. S. 260

9 Verena Krieger: *Was ist ein Künstler? Genie - Heilsbringer - Antikünstler. Eine Ideen- und Kunstgeschichte des Schöpferischen* Köln 2007, S.13

10 Ebda., S. 14

11 Giorgio Vasari: *Künstler der Renaissance: Lebensbeschreibungen der ausgezeichnetsten Maler Bildhauer und Architekten der Renaissance,* Hamburg 2012, Originalausgabe: *Le Vite de' più eccellenti architetti, pittori, et scultori italiani, da Cimabue infino a' tempi nostri: descritte in lingua toscana da Giorgio Vasari, pittore arentino – Con una sua utile et necessaria introduzione a le arti loro.* L. Torrentino, Florenz 1550, 2 Bde

12 Petra Libel-Osborne: *Gestaltungslehren in der Architektenausbildung,* Frankfurt/Berlin 2001, S. 21

13 Arthur C. Danto: *Reiz und Reflexion,* München 1994, S. 16

14 Johann Gottfried Herder: *Kalligone, Von Kunst und Kunstrichterei.* Leipzig 1800, Band 2, S. 3

15 Verena Krieger: *Was ist ein Künstler,* Köln 2007, S. 17

16 Wolf Mannhardt (Hg): *Alfred Lichtwark,* Berlin 1917, S. 57, zitiert nach: Petra Libel-Osborne: *Gestaltungslehren in der Architektenausbildung,* Frankfurt/Berlin 2001, S. 37

17 1902 gründeten der Bildhauer und Theoretiker Hermann Obrist und der Maler und Innenarchitekt Wilhelm von Debschitz eine Privatschule in München. In den sogenannten „Lehr- und Versuchsateliers für Angewandte und Freie Kunst" unterrichteten Obrist und Debschitz zum Beispiel erstmals das Fach „Grundlagen der Gestaltung", das ca. 15 Jahre später als sogenannter Vorkurs im Bauhaus Schule machen wird.

18 Gropius vertrat darin auch die Auffassung, dass Kunst nicht lehrbar sei.

19 Jörg Burger: „Andy Warhol – Blums Entdeckung" in: *ZEIT Magazin,* 22.11.12, Nr.48, auch online: www.zeit.de/2012/48/Andy-Warhol-Galerist-Irving-Blum/ (letzter Zugriff am: 11.09.2013)

20 Andy Warhol: The *philosophy of Andy Warhol (from A to B and back again),* New York 1975, S. 92

21 Bruno Munari: *Design as Art.* Translated by Patrick Creagh, Italienische Originalausgabe 1966, übersetzte Ausgabe 1971

22 Bruno Munari: *Design as Art,* 2008, S.25

23 Victor Papanek: *Design for the Real World; Human Ecology and Social Change* (schwedische Erstausgabe 1970) neu aufgelegt 1985 mit zahlreichen Ergänzungen. Chicago 1985. Zum aktuellen Verständnis und der Programmatik von Social Design, siehe Victor + Sylvia Margolin: „A „Social Model" of Design: Issues of Practice and Research" in: *MIT Design issues,* Vol. 18, No 4, Herbst 2002

24 Für einen Einblick in die Praxis und Grundhaltung zum Thema Kunst und / oder Design? siehe die Beiträge von lehrenden Persönlichkeiten dieser Schulen: Louise Schouwenberg, S. 105 und Rosario Hurtado und Roberto Feo (El Ultimo Grito), S. 157

25 Siehe hierzu die Beiträge von Katia Baudin, S.041 und Alex Coles, S.131

26 Eyal Burstein: *Taxing art – when objects travel,* Berlin 2011

27 Siehe hierzu der Beitrag von Christine Hill S.083

28 Hanno Rauterberg: „Einsamkeit, Freiheit, tiefes Glück. Wanderungen im Nebelmeer: Was die zeitgenössische Kunst von Werbung, Mode und Design unterscheidet" in: *Die Zeit,* 16.08.2007, Nr. 34

29 Zur Frage nach dem Verhältnis von Ethik und Ästhetik siehe: Annett Zinsmeister (Hg.): *Ethics in Aesthetics?* Berlin 2012

30 Für die Fortführung des Diskurses wurde ein Blog eingerichtet, der Raum bieten soll für Antworten, Beiträge und weiter führende interdisziplinäre Fragestellungen: http://www.art-and-or-design. blogspot.de. Wir freuen uns auf eine Fortsetzung der Diskussion.

Katia Baudin

Identitätskrise? Zur Frage der Abgrenzung zwischen Kunst und Design
—
Identity Crisis? Border Issues between Art and Design

Is art design and design art? The very question at the heart of this publication has its roots just a few steps away, nearly one hundred years earlier. The celebrated Weißenhofsiedlung in Stuttgart was created in 1927 within the framework of the Werkbund exhibition *Die Wohnung* under Mies van der Rohe's general direction. He invited the leading

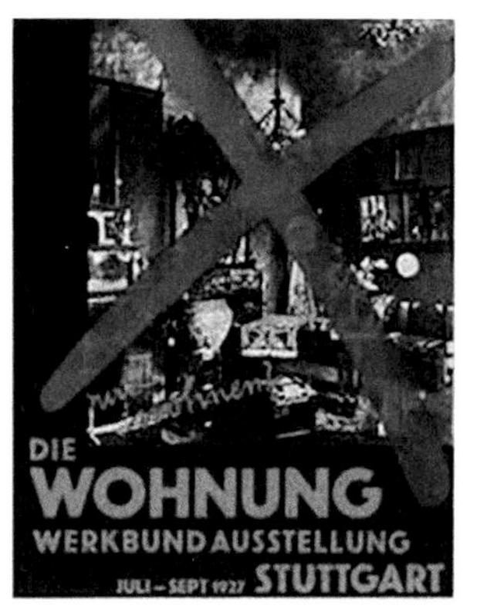

architects of the time, including J.J.P. Oud, Le Corbusier with Pierre Jeanneret, and Walter Gropius, to create a new typology for modern living.[2] The artist Willi Baumeister was also invited — albeit in a dual capacity. While — as could be expected — he painted murals in several of the model homes, his contribution was perhaps even more important in another, applied field. He created the exhibition's visual identity, designing everything from its letterhead to publications, posters, and advertisements. Baumeister was recognized in his time not only as an artist, but also — and perhaps even more so — as a graphic designer, landing in 1928 a professorship at the prestigious Frank-furter Städelschule not in the art department, but in the field of advertising, typography, and textile printing *(Gebrauchsgraphik, Typographie und Stoffdruck)*; and founding the same year, with like-minded artists including Kurt Schwitters and Lazlo Moholy-Nagy, a network for graphic designers, the *ring neue werbegestalter*.

Baumeister was one of many artists of his time to cross the borders between disciplines with ease, obliterating the traditional hierarchies between the "high" fine and the "low" applied arts. However, for crossing did not mean erasing the borders. While his work as a painter marked his approach towards graphic design and typography, he believed in a clear separation of the fields, stating in 1948: "I always had two activities, 1. typography, poster, stage, textile designs, and so on, 2. fine art with which I could consistently make modern art without compromises or concessions."[3] As the introductory quote to this essay, taken from his influential manifest *Neue Typographie* (1926) also illustrates, for Baumeister, the difference between art and (graphic)

Typographie beruht vor allem in der Aufteilung einer begrenzten Fläche. Der Typograph steht zu Beginn seiner werkbewußten Tätigkeit vor derselben Aufgabe wie der Maler. Die Grundsätze der Flächenaufteilung sind verschieden. Die Druckseite enthält Bildhaftes und Mitteilungen. Beim Plakat überwiegt das Bildhafte. Bei der Typographie ist die Mitteilung bildhaft zu gestalten. Die symmetrische Anordnung einer Druckseite, bei einem Inserat, Plakat usw. ist nichts anderes als das Dekorieren einer Fassade.[1] Willi Baumeister

Ist Kunst Design und Design Kunst? Ansätze für diese Frage finden sich bereits vor 100 Jahren zum Beispiel im Hinblick auf die vielgerühmte Weißenhofsiedlung in Stuttgart, die 1927 im Rahmen der Werkbund-Ausstellung „Die Wohnung" unter der Leitung von Mies van der Rohe entstand. Er lud führende Architekten der Zeit – darunter J.J.P. Oud, Le Corbusier mit Pierre Jeanneret und Walter Gropius – ein, eine neue Typologie für das moderne Wohnen zu schaffen.[2] Auch der Künstler Willi Baumeister war eingeladen, allerdings in einer Doppelfunktion. Neben seinen Wandgemälden für einige der Modellhäuser war sein Beitrag im Bereich der angewandten Kunst womöglich noch wichtiger. Er prägte das visuelle Erscheinungsbild der Ausstellung, indem er Briefkopf, Publikationen, Plakate und Anzeigen gestaltete. Baumeister war zu seiner Zeit als Künstler anerkannt und vielleicht noch bekannter als Grafikdesigner, zumal er 1928 an der renommierten Frankfurter Städelschule eine Professur nicht etwa in der Abteilung für freie Kunst, sondern im Bereich Gebrauchsgrafik, Typografie und Stoffdruck erhielt. Im selben Jahr gründete er mit gleichgesinnten Künstlern wie Kurt Schwitters und László Moholy-Nagy ein Netzwerk für Grafikdesigner: den *ring neue werbegestalter*.

Baumeister war einer der vielen Künstler seiner Zeit, die die Grenzen der Disziplinen leichtfüßig überschritten, indem sie die traditionelle Hierarchie von „hoher" freier Kunst und „niederer" angewandter Kunst auflösten. Für Baumeister bedeutete das Überschreiten der Grenzen jedoch nicht ihre Auslöschung. Auch wenn seine Arbeit als Maler seine Tätigkeit als Grafikdesigner und Typograf prägte, glaubte er doch an eine klare Trennung dieser Bereiche. 1948 sagte er: „ich hatte immer zwei tätigkeiten, 1. typografie, plakate, bühnenbilder, textil-entwürfe usw., 2. freie kunst, damit konnte ich ohne kompromisse und konzession konsequent moderne kunst machen."[3] Gemäß dem hier vorangestellten Zitat aus seinem richtungsweisenden Manifest *Neue Typographie* (1926) ist der Unterschied zwischen Kunst und (Grafik-)Design durch die Auffassung von Ziel und Zweck bestimmt: Während Kunst nutzlos sein kann, muss Design nützlich sein.

design resides in the notion of objective and purpose: while art can be useless, design needs to be useful.

This viewpoint is also shared, albeit with a certain irony, several decades later by the recently deceased American artist Richard Artschwager, who exclaimed, "Art is useless; furniture is useful."[4] A precursor of the current trend, Artschwager spent years of making furniture before switching over to art in the nineteen-sixties. He applied his carpentry skills to make sculptures that resemble furniture, seemingly blurring the boundaries and letting the viewer decide: "If you sit on it, it's a chair; if you walk around it and look at it, it's a sculpture.... You have to look at them either as images or as things. These are initially contradictory, so shut up and *look*; and then, once you have done that, both the image-ness and the object-ness can be co-present without contradictions."[5]

The Chair: a Prime Example

Chairs in particular have fascinated both artists and designers alike throughout the twentieth century. They serve as a prime example for the difference in attitude and approach between artists and designers

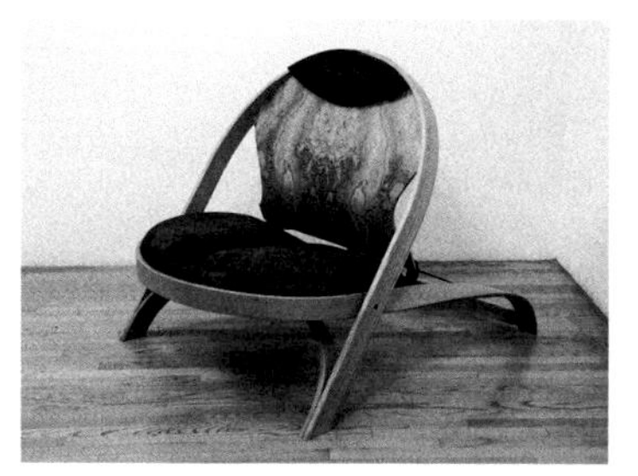

today. While certain artists, like Richard Artschwager, have principally approached the chair and other furniture elements from an aesthetic or sculptural perspective, other artists like Donald Judd and Franz West have developed chairs with a primarily functional aim. In both cases, the artists started to make furniture, in particular chairs, for their personal use.[6] Both artists decided to produce their furniture and offer it as such to the public. They build onto a tradition initiated by the avant-garde movements of the early twentieth century, when artists associated with such movements as Futurism (Giacomo Balla), De Stijl (Theo Van Doesburg), Russian avant-garde (Nicolai Suetin, Alexander Rodchenko), or Bauhaus (Joseph Albers) did not limit themselves to the fine arts, but also created furniture,

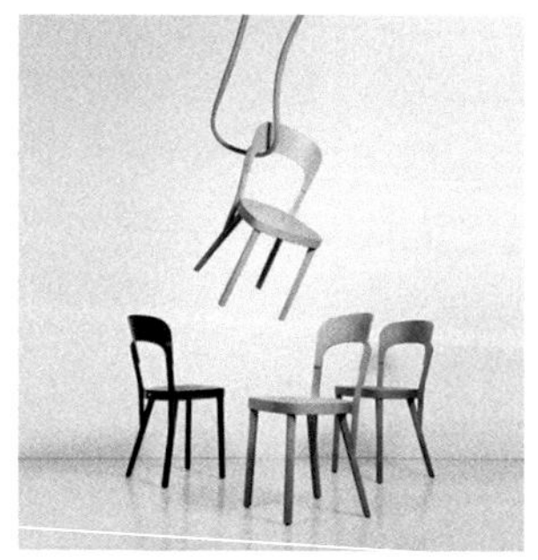

architectural, textile and/or graphic designs that were, especially in the case of the Russian and Soviet avant-garde, commissioned and realized with industrial partners.[7]

The chair is no doubt the furniture piece that has stimulated the most diverse and innovative projects in design history, reflecting also fundamental changes in society. Take for example, Robert Stadler's bistro *Chair 107* (2011) for Thonet, the fruit of a typical "designer" thought process analyzing manufacturing, pricing, and product improve-

Diesen Standpunkt teilte einige Jahrzehnte später – wenngleich mit einer gewissen Ironie – der kürzlich verstorbene amerikanische Künstler Richard Artschwager, indem er proklamierte: „Kunst ist nutzlos; Möbel sind nützlich".[4] Als Vorreiter des hier diskutierten Trends hatte er jahrelang Möbel gebaut, bevor er sich in den 1960er Jahren der Kunst zuwandte. Er nutzte sein Fachkönnen als Schreiner, um Skulpturen zu schaffen, die an Möbel erinnern und offenkundig die Grenzen der Disziplinen verwischen und den Betrachter entscheiden zu lassen: „Wenn du darauf sitzt, ist es ein Stuhl, wenn du drum herumgehst und es anschaust, ist es eine Skulptur (...) Du musst sie entweder als Bilder oder als Objekte betrachten. Das ist ein grundsätzlicher Widerspruch, also halt den Mund und schaue; und wenn du das getan hast, können sowohl die Bildhaftigkeit als auch die Objekthaftigkeit ohne Widersprüche koexistieren."[5]

Der Stuhl als Paradebeispiel

Stühle haben sowohl Künstler als auch Designer über das 20. Jahrhundert hinweg gleichermaßen fasziniert. Sie sind ein Paradebeispiel für die unterschiedlichen Vorstellungen und Ansätze von zeitgenössischen Künstlern und Designern. Während Künstler wie Richard Artschwager Stühle und andere Möbelstücke hauptsächlich aus einer ästhetischen oder bildhauerischen Perspektive betrachtet haben, haben Künstler wie Donald Judd und Franz West Stühle unter vorwiegend funktionalen Gesichtspunkten entwickelt. In beiden Fällen haben die Künstler Möbel, insbesondere Stühle, zunächst für ihren persönlichen Gebrauch hergestellt.[6] Beide ließen die Möbel produzieren, um sie so der Öffentlichkeit anzubieten. Damit stehen sie in einer Tradition, die in den Avantgardebewegungen des frühen 20. Jahrhunderts wurzelt, als Künstler, die mit Bewegungen wie dem Futurismus (Giacomo Balla), De Stijl (Theo van Doesburg), der russischen Avantgarde (Nikolai Suetin, Alexander Rodtschenko) oder dem Bauhaus (Josef Albers) verbunden waren, sich nicht auf die freien Künste beschränkten, sondern auch Möbel-, Architektur-, Textil- und/oder Grafikdesignentwürfe schufen, die, besonders im Fall der russischen und sowjetischen Avantgarde, von Industriepartnern beauftragt und produziert wurden.[7]

Der Stuhl ist zweifelsohne das Möbelstück, das die vielfältigsten und innovativsten Projekte der Designgeschichte inspiriert und dabei auch grundlegende gesellschaftliche Veränderungen reflektiert hat. Robert Stadlers Bistrostuhl *Chair 107* (2011) für Thonet ist zum Beispiel das Ergebnis eines typischen „Designer"-Denkprozesses, in dem Herstellung, Preisgestaltung und Produktverbesserung analysiert

ment. "My starting point was the fact that today *Chair 214* ... is rather expensive, which represents a certain break in regards to Thonet's history. ... The manufacturing of the back part is still rather traditional. With *Chair 107* I focused on a new design of that element which is now being produced in an almost totally automated process."[8] With *Chaos Side Chair* (2001), on the other hand, Konstantin Grcic wanted to produce a "dysfunctional" chair. At first glance, the object seems closer to a sculpture than a chair, due to its oddly proportioned, relatively small seating surface. However, this was intentional: Grcic wanted to make an uncomfortable chair for short rests, in which a user feels ill at ease and fidgets.[9] Ultimately, Grcic's chair is fully inscribed in the "form follows function" design tradition.

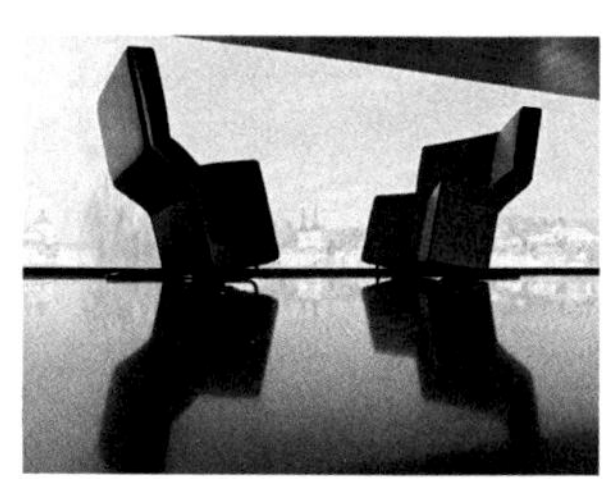

These designer chairs were born out of a typical progress-oriented, inventor-attitude that characterizes the designer; however, certain designers criticize this very attitude, pointing to its not-always-positive consequences. The highly conceptual installation *Stop Discrimination of Cheap Furniture* (Frac Nord-Pas de Calais, 2004) by Spanish designer Marti Guixé pinpoints the consequences of the trickle-down effect in which good design can lead to bad design, with catastrophic consequences for the world.[10] Modernism's authoritarian stance on "good design" has for example "inspired" the anonymous, repetitive low-income housing towers that have proliferated around the world — in the east and the west — since the nineteen-sixties, a far cry from Le Corbusier's *unités d'habitations*. Have these utopian, progress-oriented, technology-fascinated attitudes associated with modernism ultimately failed? In the late nineteen-sixties, designers (and architects) and movements emerged, which criticized and distanced themselves with the modernist heritage: from Joe Colombo's *Antidesign* concept, to the Italian Radical Design movement and design groups like Superstudio, Archizoom, followed by Memphis and postmodernism in the nineteen-seventies and eighties. Like their predecessors, designers today are also attacking modernism's core principles, in particular rationalism, and the canons "Form Follows Function" (Louis Sullivan) and "Ornament is a Crime" (Adolf Loos).

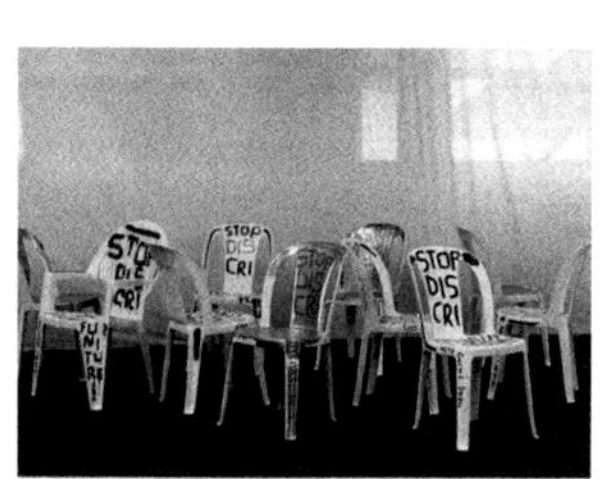

While today's designers don't share the utopian, "improve the world" attitude of the first anti-design protagonists, nor the aggressive, kitschy aesthetic of postmodernism, they utilize the technologies available today to question the role of the designer and the identity of objects within today's socioeconomic context. The resulting objects

werden: „Mein Ausgangspunkt war die Tatsache, dass der *Stuhl 214* heute (...) recht teuer ist, was im Hinblick auf die Geschichte Thonets einen gewissen Bruch darstellt. (...) die Herstellung der Rückenlehne ist noch immer ziemlich traditionell. Für den *Chair 107* habe ich dieses Element so gestaltet, dass es jetzt in einem fast vollkommen automatisierten Prozess produziert werden kann."[8] Konstantin Grcic hingegen wollte mit dem *Chaos Side Chair* (2001) einen „dysfunktionalen" Stuhl herstellen. Auf den ersten Blick wirkt das Objekt eher wie eine Skulptur, was an der seltsam proportionierten, relativ kleinen Sitzfläche liegt. Das war jedoch beabsichtigt: Grcic wollte einen unbequemen Stuhl für kurze Sitzpausen machen, auf dem der Benutzer sich ungemütlich fühlt und herumrutscht.[9] Letztlich steht Grcics Stuhl vollkommen in der Designtradition des „form follows function".

Diese Designerstühle entstanden unter für den Designer so typischen fortschritts- und innovationsorientierten Gesichtspunkten; einige Designer kritisieren jedoch gerade diesen Ansatz, indem sie auf seine nicht immer positiven Ergebnisse hinweisen. Die konzeptuelle Installation *Stop Discrimination of Cheap Furniture* (2004, Frac Nord-Pas de Calais) des spanischen Designers Marti Guixé verdeutlicht die Konsequenzen des Fahrstuhleffekts, bei dem gutes Design zu schlechtem Design führen kann, was katastrophale Konsequenzen für die Welt zur Folge hat.[10] Das autoritäre Beharren der Moderne auf „gutes Design" hat zum Beispiel die anonymen, immer gleichen Wohntürme für die niedrigen Einkommensklassen „inspiriert", die sich seit den 1960er Jahren auf der ganzen Welt, in Ost und West, ausgebreitet haben, ein müder Abklatsch von Le Corbusiers *unités d'habitations*. Sind also diese mit der Moderne verbundenen utopischen, fortschrittsorientierten, technologieverliebten Ansätze letztlich gescheitert? In den späten 1960ern traten Designer (und Architekten) und Bewegungen hervor, die das Erbe der Moderne kritisierten und sich von ihm distanzierten. Sie reichten von Joe Colombos Antidesign-Konzept über die italienische Radical-Design-Bewegung und Designergruppen wie Superstudio, Archizoom bis hin zu Memphis und der Postmoderne der 1970er und 1980er Jahre. Wie ihre Vorgänger greifen auch die heutigen Designer die Kernprinzipien der Moderne an, besonders deren Rationalismus und die Grundsätze „form follows function" (Louis Sullivan) und „Ornament ist Verbrechen" (Adolf Loos).

Wenngleich die Designer heute weder die utopistische Weltverbesserungsattitüde der ersten Vertreter der Antidesign-Bewegung noch die aggressive, kitschige Ästhetik der Postmoderne teilen, so benutzen sie doch die heute zur Verfügung stehende Technologie, um die Rolle des Designers und die Identität des Objekts im aktuellen sozio-ökono-

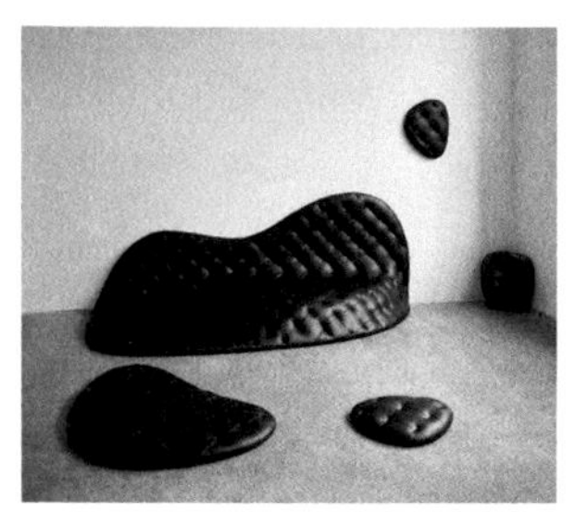

and projects can be apprehended through different angles, including numerous references to the history of design and the decorative arts, and are often filled with a sense of humor. A good example is Robert Stadler's take on a Chesterfield sofa, *Pools & Pouf!*. Many examples of seemingly dysfunctional, sculpture-like furniture or objects discussed in this paper illustrate how designers have defied "good design" and modernist laws.

Art = Design = Art?

Since the early nineteen-nineties, a new phenomenon has surfaced in which the borders separating art from design seem to have dissipated. Artists have moved onto a turf previously reserved for architects and interior or product designers. It is no longer exceptional for museums and biennials to invite participating artists to make "usable art" — functional spaces and objects — for their exhibitions or sites:

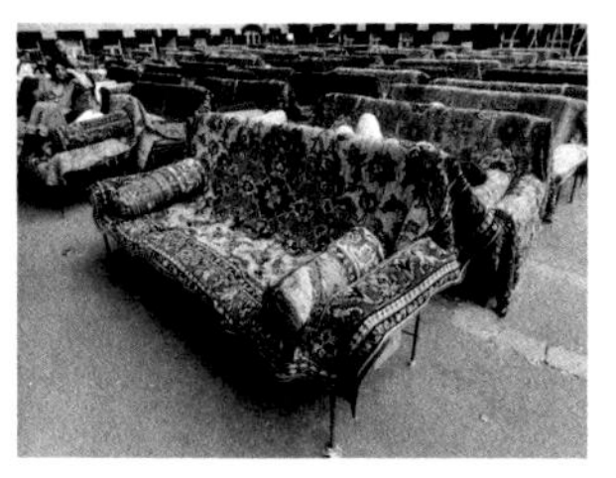

from Franz West's divan installation, *Auditorium,* for the documenta IX (1992) right up to Tobias Rehberger's *Biennial Pavilion Cafeteria,* which was awarded the Golden Lion at the 2009 Venice Biennial. However, these types of commissions are not exclusively limited to the art world: Atelier van Lieshout, for example, created the medical practice for Dr. Van Sint Fiet (2004), and Dominique Gonzalez-Foerster's redesign of Balenciaga boutiques worldwide (2002–2012). Joep van Lieshout's *Shaker* furniture line for Moooi (1999), illustrates the extent to which artists today infringe directly upon a territory previously reserved nearly exclusively to architects and designers.

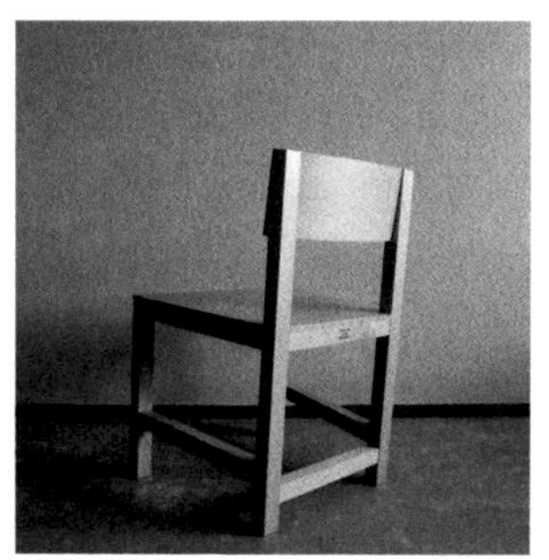

Have the terms artist and designer come to signify the same thing? Have these two disciplines merged into one? A look at the 2012 Design Miami/Designer of the Year Award seems to confirm this hypothesis: the recipient of the award was Acconci Studio, founded in 1988 by Vito Acconci — a recognized and influential protagonist of performance, video and installation art since the nineteen-sixties.

A parallel phenomenon has developed simultaneously within the design world. Since the early nineteen-nineties, a new generation of designers has emerged focused on elaborating highly conceptualized projects and seemingly dysfunctional products, at the edge of art. The Dutch Design label Droog Design, created in 1993, was no doubt an important catalyst in the development of this trend, proposing "handmade" design pieces produced in small editions or made to order,

mischen Kontext zu hinterfragen. Die daraus resultierenden Objekte und Projekte können aus verschiedenen Blickwinkeln heraus begriffen werden (darunter zahllose Referenzen auf die Geschichte des Designs und der dekorativen Künste) und zeugen häufig von Sinn für Humor. Ein gutes Beispiel ist *Pools & Pouf!,* Robert Stadlers Auseinandersetzung mit einem Chesterfield-Sofa. Viele der hier erwähnten, scheinbar dysfunktionalen, skulpturalen Möbel oder Objekte zeigen, wie Designer den Begriff des „guten Designs" und die Gesetze der Moderne herausfordern.

Kunst = Design = Kunst?

Seit den frühen 1990er Jahren ist ein neues Phänomen aufgetreten: die scheinbare Auflösung der Grenzen zwischen Kunst und Design. Künstler haben sich in einen Bereich vorgewagt, der bis dahin Architekten und Interior- oder Produktdesignern vorbehalten war. Es ist längst keine Ausnahme mehr, dass Museen und Biennalen Künstler einladen, für ihre Ausstellungsbereiche „nutzbare Kunst", also funktionale Räume und Objekte zu schaffen: von Franz Wests Diwan-Installation *Auditorium* für die documenta IX (1992) bis hin zu Tobias Rehbergers *Biennial Pavilion Cafeteria,* die 2009 mit dem Goldenen Löwen der Biennale in Venedig ausgezeichnet wurde. Derlei Aufträge sind jedoch nicht allein auf die Kunstwelt beschränkt: Zum Beispiel entwickelte Atelier van Lieshout eine Arztpraxis für Dr. Van Sint Fiet (2004) und Dominique Gonzalez-Foerster die Neugestaltung der Balenciaga-Boutiquen weltweit (2002–2012). Joep van Lieshouts *Shaker*-Möbellinie für Moooi (1999) zeigt, wie weit Künstler heutzutage direkt in Bereiche eindringen, die zuvor fast ausschließlich Architekten und Designern vorbehalten waren.

Bezeichnen die Begriffe „Künstler" und „Designer" mittlerweile dasselbe? Sind diese beiden Disziplinen zu einer verschmolzen? Die Verleihung des Designer of the Year Award auf der Design Miami/2012 scheint diese Hypothese zu bestätigen: Der Preis ging an das Acconci Studio, gegründet 1988 von Vito Acconci, einem seit den 1960er Jahren anerkannten und richtungsweisenden Protagonisten im Bereich der Performance-, Video- und Installationskunst.

Parallel dazu hat sich in der Welt des Designs ein ähnliches Phänomen entwickelt. Ein wichtiger Katalysator bei der Entwicklung dieses Trends war zweifelsohne das 1993 gegründete niederländische Designlabel Droog Design mit seinen in kleinen Editionen oder auf Bestellung hergestellten „handgefertigten" Designobjekten, die eher an Skulpturen als an nutzbare Möbelstücke erinnerten, wie etwa Tejo Remys *Chest of Drawers* (1991) oder Jurgen Beys *Kokon Furniture* (1997). Anstatt die Produkte auf der Möbelmesse in Mailand zu präsentieren,

resembling sculptures more than usable furniture — such as Tejo Remy's *Chest of Drawers* (1991) or Jurgen Bey's *Kokon Furniture* (1997). Instead of presenting their products in Milan at the furniture fair itself, Droog organizes thematic exhibitions in off-spaces, including abandoned hotels; a trend followed by other designers, manufacturers, and even design schools in Milan. Installations and performative events by designers have also become commonplace both at and beyond trade fairs, and have contributed to launching the careers of several of today's most hyped designers, including Front Design, Pieke Bergmans, and Maarten Baas. While the Swedish female design collective Front attracted attention in 2005 at the Milan Furniture Fair's Satellite section — dedicated to emerging designers — for their installation *A Story of Things,*[11] the two Dutch designers attracted attention around the same time through their respective, live "performances" of either adding onto (Bergmans' amorphous, sculptural *Design Virus Light Bulbs*) or destroying (Baas' *Smoke* burnt series) existing furniture.

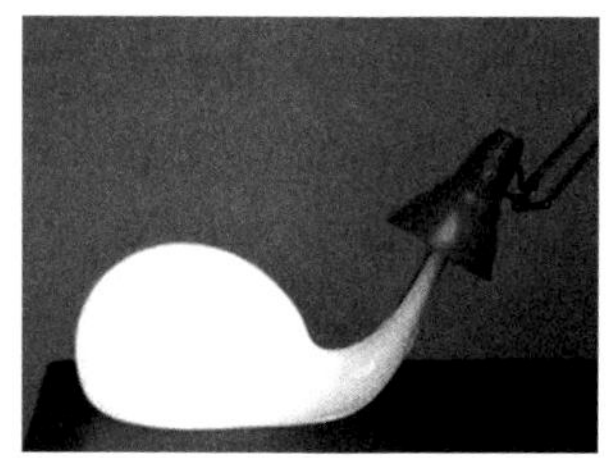

However, as is the case with artists, designers have transcended beyond their "natural environment and habitat" in the design world and have penetrated into the art world. Traditional distribution channels have become blurred. Baas' *Smoke* series illustrates this perfectly: it is produced and distributed not only by a design manufacturer (Moooi), but also by a New York gallery (Moss). Just as design labels today propose products developed by artists, designers develop exclusive limited editions and installations for galleries. Their work is not only represented by one of the numerous design galleries that have sprung up around the world since the nineteen-nineties — such as Kreo or Carpenter's Workshop Gallery — but also by major art galleries. It has become a must for any serious player in the art market to have a designer among its repertoire of artists, as can be illustrated by Larry Gagosian (Marc Newson), Thaddeus Ropac (Matali Crasset), and Emmanuel Perrotin (Robert Stadler), to name but a few. Auction houses like Artcurial or Phillips (formerly Phillips de Pury) have developed a strong niche in design sales, while design galleries are invited to participate alongside art galleries at certain art fairs (Fiac from 2004–09), or have created their own fairs, which run parallel to art fairs, (Design Miami/, founded in 2005). The high prices commanded by designers, like Jean Prouvé to Marc Newson, rival contemporary art and are similarly fueled by collectors from the art world.[12]

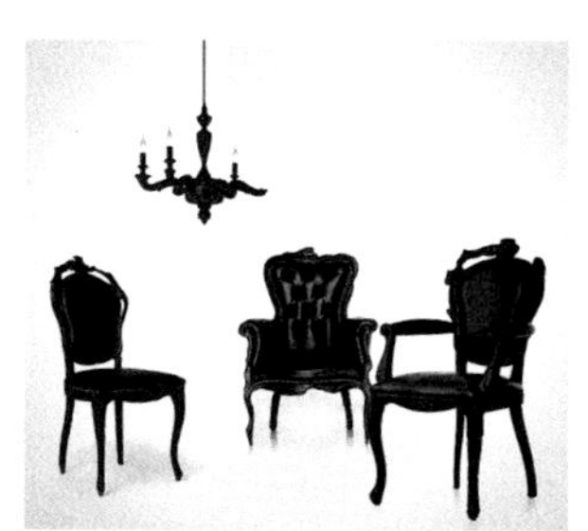

organisiert Droog thematische Ausstellungen an ungewöhnlichen Orten wie zum Beispiel verlassenen Hotels; diesem Trend folgen auch andere Designer, Hersteller und sogar Designschulen in Mailand. Installationen und performanceartige Events von Designern sind sowohl auf Messen als auch abseits davon alltäglich geworden und haben dazu beigetragen, die Karrieren von einigen der heute populärsten Designer anzustoßen, darunter Front Design, Pieke Bergmann und Maarten Baas. Während das schwedische Designerinnenkollektiv Front in dem aufstrebenden Designern gewidmeten *Salone Satellite* der Mailänder Möbelmesse 2005 mit ihrer Installation *A Story of Things* auf sich aufmerksam machte,[11] erregten die zwei niederländischen Designer ungefähr zur gleichen Zeit mit ihren jeweiligen Live-„Performances" Aufmerksamkeit, bei denen vorhandene Objekte entweder weiterentwickelt (Bergmanns amorphe, skulpturale *Design Virus Light Bulbs*) oder zerstört wurden (Baas' Serie *Smoke* aus verbrannten Möbeln).

Auf jeden Fall haben die Designer ebenso wie die Künstler die Grenzen ihres „natürlichen Lebensraums" überschritten und sind in die Welt der Kunst vorgedrungen. Auch die traditionellen Vertriebskanäle vermischen sich langsam. Baas' *Smoke*-Serie illustriert das perfekt: Sie wird nicht nur von einem Designhersteller (Moooi), sondern auch von einer New Yorker Galerie (Moss) produziert und vertrieben. Für jeden ernsthaften Akteur auf dem Kunstmarkt ist es unabdingbar geworden, einen Designer unter den vertretenen Künstlern zu haben, wie man an – um nur einige zu nennen – Larry Gagosian (Marc Newson), Thaddeus Ropac (Matali Crasset) und Emmanuel Perrotin (Robert Stadler) sehen kann. Auktionshäuser wie Artcurial oder Phillips (früher: Phillips de Pury) haben durch den Verkauf von Designstücken eine lukrative Marktlücke entdeckt, während Designgalerien eingeladen werden, gemeinsam mit Kunstgalerien an Kunstmessen teilzunehmen (Fiac 2004–09) oder eigene Messen zu installieren, die parallel zu den Kunstmessen laufen (Design Miami/seit 2005). Die hohen Preise von Designern, von Jean Prouvé bis hin zu Marc Newson, konkurrieren mit der Gegenwartskunst und werden von Kunstsammlern gleichermaßen in die Höhe getrieben.[12]

Künstler = Designer = Künstler?

Bis jetzt haben wir das Phänomen vom Blickwinkel des Betrachters/ Konsumenten aus untersucht. Wie sieht es jedoch mit den Autoren aus? Reflektieren sie über Status oder Identität eines Objekts oder Raums? Wie würden sie sich selbst charakterisieren: als Künstler, Designer, beides oder weder noch? Bei näherer Betrachtung wird klar, dass die Autoren sich entweder als Designer oder als Künstler be-

Artist = Designer = Artist?

Up until now, we have considered the end results, from the vantage point of the viewer/consumer. What about the author or creator? Does he/she confer a status or identity to the object or space? How would he qualify himself: as artist, designer, both or neither? A closer look reveals that the author considers himself as either a designer or an artist. A key protagonist of the so-called Design Art phenomenon, Tobias Rehberger serves as a perfect example. He defines himself as a sculptor: "My work is about differentiating between art and design, trying to define their differences."[13] Rehberger works in a conceptual manner, examining the very nature and identity of art and the role of the artist in its production, developing projects that illustrate or convey a deeper meaning or story, from the vantage point of our consumer and product-driven society — as illustrated by his *Vasenporträts* (since 1995).

According to designer Konstantin Grcic, "As an industrial designer, it's not about art!"[14] His general affinity for art is no doubt influenced by his personal background: his mother is a contemporary art gallerist, his sister Tamara a recognized artist. Perhaps this insider knowledge of the art field has helped forge his adamant stance on the difference between artist and designer. Grcic rarely makes pieces for design galleries, preferring to work for industry: "That's where my creativity and my freedom are born."[15] Grcic's remark may seem surprising and even contradictory, because working on industrial commissions or projects is both complex and strenuous. However, it highlights the fundamental difference in attitude between artist and designer. The designer does not create in a vacuum with full creative freedom: he receives a commission to develop a certain type of product for a specific usage and market niche. His creative process has to function within a series of constraints; he has to take into account factors such as production feasibility and costs, as well as product positioning, corporate image, etc. It can take years of work — numerous discussions, sketches, prototypes, etc. — to achieve a perfected, finalized product. The artist, on the other hand, is ultimately much freer and independent — especially regarding the content — while the realization is contingent on budgets. He usually develops projects he initiates, or answers to exhibition invitations from curators that enable him to explore self-determined issues. The creative process and artistic "line" determines the result, which does not need to be commercially or functionally viable as, for example, Tobias Rehberger's *Seascapes* (2000): a fully functioning, yet virtual sea resort that the artist freely developed for his exhibition at the Frac Nord-Pas de Calais (2000) in Dunkirk.[16]

trachten. Eine Schlüsselfigur des sogenannten Design-Art-Phänomens, Tobias Rehberger, ist dafür ein perfektes Beispiel. Er definiert sich selbst als Bildhauer: „Bei meiner Arbeit geht es darum, zwischen Kunst und Design zu differenzieren, ich versuche, die Unterschiede zu definieren."[13] Rehberger arbeitet konzeptuell, indem er das Wesen und die Identität von Kunst und die Rolle des Künstlers bei ihrer Produktion untersucht und Projekte entwickelt, die im Hinblick auf unsere konsum- und produktbesessene Gesellschaft eine tiefere Bedeutung oder Geschichte transportieren, wie zum Beispiel seine *Vasenporträts* (seit 1995).

Der Designer Konstantin Grcic konstatiert: „Einem Industriedesigner darf es nicht um Kunst gehen!"[14] Seine Affinität zur Kunst speist sich sicherlich aus seinem persönlichen Hintergrund: Seine Mutter ist Galeristin für zeitgenössische Kunst, seine Schwester Tamara eine anerkannte Künstlerin. Vielleicht hat dieses Insiderwissen des Kunstbetriebs zu seiner unerbittlichen Haltung bezüglich der Differenzierung zwischen Künstler und Designer geführt. Grcic produziert kaum für Designgalerien, sondern arbeitet lieber für die Industrie: „Da haben meine Kreativität und meine Freiheit ihre Wurzeln".[15] Grcics Bemerkung könnte überraschend und sogar widersprüchlich erscheinen, da die Arbeit an industriellen Aufträgen oder Projekten sowohl komplex als auch anstrengend ist. Sie bringt jedoch den grundlegenden Unterschied zwischen Künstler und Designer auf den Punkt. Designer gestalten nicht in einem Vakuum vollkommener kreativer Freiheit: Sie werden beauftragt, einen bestimmten Produkttypus für einen speziellen Zweck und eine spezielle Marktlücke zu entwickeln. Ihr kreativer Prozess wird durch eine Reihe von Zwängen bestimmt; sie müssen Faktoren wie produktionstechnische Machbarkeit und Kosten ebenso wie Marktposition, Firmenimage etc. beachten. Ein perfektioniertes Endprodukt kann jahrelange Arbeit – unzählige Diskussionen, Zeichnungen, Prototypen etc. – beanspruchen. Der Künstler hingegen ist sehr viel freier und unabhängiger, besonders was den Inhalt angeht, während die Umsetzung vom Budget abhängt. Er entwickelt für gewöhnlich selbstinitiierte Projekte oder nimmt Ausstellungsbeteiligungen von Kuratoren an, die es ihm ermöglichen, eigene Themen zu verwirklichen. Der kreative Prozess und die künstlerische „Linie" bestimmen das Ergebnis, das weder kommerziell noch funktional tragfähig sein muss, wie zum Beispiel Tobias Rehbergers *Seascapes* (2000), ein voll funktionsfähiges, jedoch virtuelles Seebad, das der Künstler für seine Ausstellung an der Frac Nord-Pas de Calais in Dünkirchen (2000) frei entwickelt hat.[16]

Die Unterschiede in den Denkprozessen werden besonders deutlich, wenn Künstler und Designer gleichzeitig eingeladen werden, neue

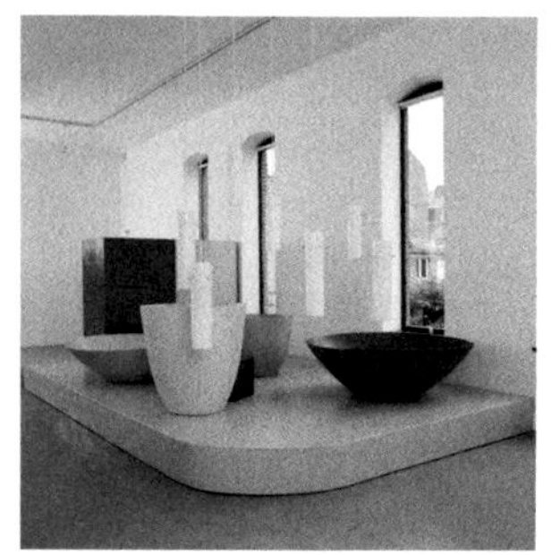

The difference in thought process becomes especially apparent when artists and designers are simultaneously invited to develop parallel to each other new projects or prototypes with the same industrial partner for a shared exhibition context, affected by minimal constraints. For the exhibition I curated at the Porzellanikon in Selb 2010, we selected a dozen designers and artists to develop porcelain projects with either Nymphenburg or Kahla.[17] The resulting objects oscillate between the sculptural and the functional, making it difficult to pinpoint the identity of the authors as designer or artist. A closer look reveals a fundamental difference in approach and goals, specific to each category. Several of the artists used the opportunity to give form to an idea they already had in mind. Thus, for example, Rehberger developed a particularly idiosyncratic project with Nymphenburg: he used its exclusive, high-end porcelain to

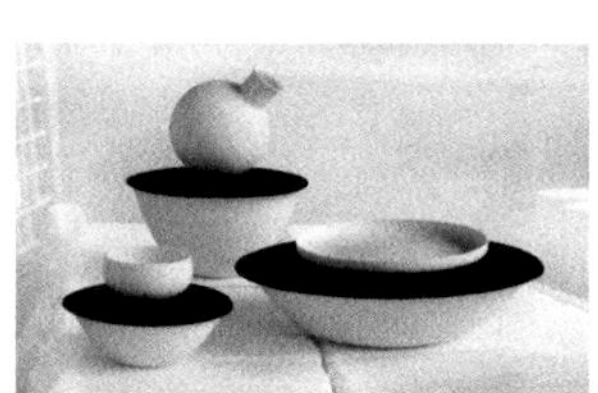

create shot glasses, beer glasses, tumblers, and various other objects for a friend's bar in Frankfurt *(Conny Plank)*. The designers, on the other hand, tended to develop projects inspired by the analysis of the company, its context or products, as Wieki Somers *Black Velvet* dinnerware design based on the velvety "Touch!" surface developed by Kahla.

This difference in approach and attitude between artist and designer is no doubt also influenced by the diverging education systems. Artists and designers are not trained or prepared for their future career choices in the same manner. Some of today's leading programs are exclusively devoted to either the fine or the applied arts, such as the Design Academy Eindhoven or the Staatliche Hochschule für Bildende Künste Städelschule in Frankfurt. Interestingly enough, some of the key protagonists of the art-design crossover phenomenon have studied and/or teach in these programs, such as Maarten Baas, Jurgen Bey, Hella Jongerius, Wieki Somers, Marcel Wanders — all Eindhoven graduates and teachers — or Tobias Rehberger, who is a Städelschule graduate and teacher, and his influential professor Martin Kippenberger. Even in schools that offer both programs, the course load and teaching methodologies differ — as I experienced firsthand as director of the Ecole supérieure des arts décoratifs (Esad) in Strasbourg (2004–07). In Strasbourg, the design and communications departments proposed a very structured study path filled with back-to-back classes to help the students learn and master a "trade," while the fine arts department privileged a much freer approach, with less classes and more time for group discussions and working sessions to develop a personal body of work. Contrary to the "l'art pour

Projekte oder Prototypen für eine Firma und einen gemeinsamen
Ausstellungskontext zu entwickeln und dabei nur minimalen Ein-
schränkungen unterliegen. Für die von mir kuratierte Ausstellung
am Porzellanikon in Selb 2010 haben wir ein Dutzend Designer und
Künstler ausgewählt, die Objekte aus Nymphenburg- oder Kahla-
Porzellan entwickeln sollten.[17] Die entstandenen Objekte oszillieren
zwischen Skulpturalität und Funktionalität, wodurch es schwierig
wird, auszumachen, ob die Autoren Designer oder Künstler sind. Bei
näherer Betrachtung entdeckt man einen grundlegenden Unterschied
in Ansatz und Zielsetzung. Einige Künstler nutzten die Gelegenheit,
eine zuvor entwickelte Idee oder einen Projektkontext wieder aufzu-
greifen. So schuf etwa Rehberger ein idiosynkratisches Projekt: Aus
dem exklusiven, hochwertigen Porzellan schuf er Schnaps-, Bier-
und Wassergläser sowie verschiedene andere Objekte für die Bar
eines Freundes in Frankfurt (Conny Plank). Die Designer hingegen
entwickelten Projekte, die durch die Analyse des Unternehmens,
seines Kontextes oder seiner Produkte inspiriert waren, wie zum
Beispiel Wieke Somers Service *Black Velvet:* Ausgangspunkt für das
Design war die von Kahla entwickelte Glasur „Touch".

Die Unterschiede in Ansatz und Haltung von Künstlern und
Designern werden zweifelsohne auch durch die unterschiedlichen
Ausbildungssysteme beeinflusst. Künstler und Designer werden nicht
auf gleiche Weise auf ihre zukünftigen Karrieremöglichkeiten vorbereitet oder dafür ausgebildet. Einige der heute führenden Institutionen
widmen sich ausschließlich entweder der freien oder der angewandten
Kunst, wie etwa die Design Academy Eindhoven oder die Staatliche
Hochschule für Bildende Künste Städelschule in Frankfurt. Interes-
santerweise haben einige der Schlüsselfiguren des Crossover-Phäno-
mens zwischen Kunst und Design an diesen Institutionen studiert und/
oder lehren dort, wie zum Beispiel die Eindhoven-Absolventen und
-Lehrer Maarten Baas, Jurgen Bey, Hella Jongerius, Wieki Somers,
Marcel Wanders oder Tobias Rehberger, ein Absolvent und Lehrer der
Städelschule, und sein einflussreicher Professor Martin Kippenberger.
Sogar an Schulen, die beide Richtungen anbieten, unterscheiden sich
die Kursprogramme und Lehrmethoden, wie ich es als Direktorin der
Ecole supérieure des arts décoratifs (Esad) in Straßburg (2004–07)
selbst erleben konnte. In Straßburg boten die Fachbereiche für Design
und Kommunikation einen sehr strukturierten Studiengang mit aufei-
nander aufbauenden Kursen an, die den Studenten ein „Gewerbe" und
den Umgang damit vermitteln sollten, während der Fachbereich für
freie Kunst einen sehr viel offeneren Ansatz mit weniger Kursen und
mehr Zeit für Gruppendiskussionen und Arbeitszeiten zur Entwicklung

l'art" attitude of their art colleagues, design students regularly worked on life-like situations, case studies and simulated commissions in which — as Grcic described above — the students' creativity had to deploy itself within the framework of constraints. This fundamentally different approach towards teaching made it difficult to develop porosity between the disciplines within the teaching program; it was mainly achieved through joint exhibition projects or commissions, with a specific objective, in which the students participated within the framework of their field.[18]

A prerequisite to a successful border crossing is the artist or designer's recognition among peers. These channels of recognition and networks are principally branch specific. An artist's reputation and recognition is determined by the critical reception of the work by the art press, its presentation in acclaimed art galleries and fairs, museums, contemporary art institutions and biennials, its presence in recognized public and private collections, its art market value. The designer's reputation is determined by actors in the design world: commissions by leading design manufacturers and industry, distribution networks, critical reception of products by peers and the design press, presence of products and projects at leading furniture fairs (in particular Milan), etc. Even in today's crossover context, artists and designers continue to operate and evolve principally in different networks.

Existential Crisis or Self-analysis?

What has motivated artists and designers in recent years to cross the border? What characterizes these objects and projects? A closer examination seems to show that in many cases, the issue of identity is at stake: one's own identity and positioning as artist or designer, as well as the positioning of the resulting object within a larger, historical context and tradition.

To what extent is the statute of an artwork or functional object affected by the presentation context? When design is presented out of

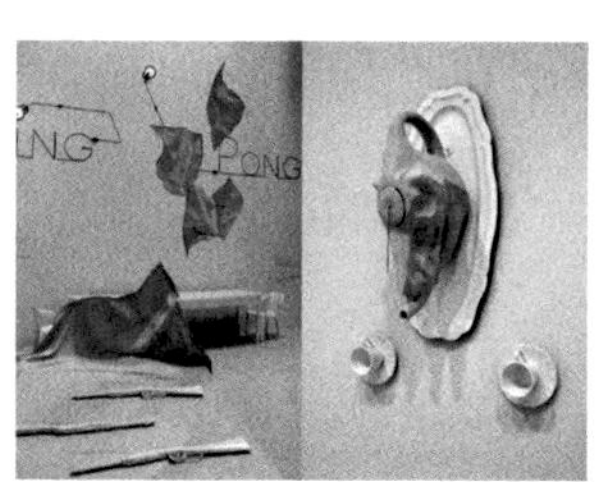

(usage) context, in an exhibition, it plays on art's turf. A good illustration of this is Chris Kabel and Wieki Somer's exhibition *Ping Pong* (2006, Esad), in which the student's exhibition design presented the products in unexpected ways: transforming for example Somer's pig skull shaped *High Tea Pot* (2003) into a sculptural wall relief. While design tolerates free interpretation, it would be more problematic in an art context where such parameters are usually defined by the artist. Artists, on the other hand, question the white cube — or the museum space — (contemporary) art's natural

eines persönlichen Schaffenswerks bot. Im Gegensatz zu der l'art-pour-l'art-Attitüde ihrer Kollegen aus dem Kunstbereich arbeiteten die Designstudenten an lebensechten Situationen, Fallstudien und simulierten Aufträgen, bei denen – wie zuvor von Grcic beschrieben – der Schaffensprozess der Studenten durch Sachzwänge bestimmt wurde. Dieser grundlegend andere Lehransatz machte es schwierig, eine Durchlässigkeit zwischen den Disziplinen zu entwickeln. Eine Durchlässigkeit zwischen den Fachbereichen entstand hauptsächlich durch gemeinsame Ausstellungsprojekte oder Aufträge mit bestimmten Zielsetzungen, an denen die Studenten im Rahmen ihrer jeweiligen Disziplin teilnahmen.[18]

Die Grundvoraussetzung für eine erfolgreiche Grenzüberschreitung ist das Ansehen eines Künstlers oder Designers innerhalb der eigenen Berufsbranche mit ihren spezifischen Netzwerken. Die Reputation und Anerkennung eines Künstlers wird durch die kritische Rezeption seines Werks durch die Kunstpresse, seine Präsentation in anerkannten Kunstgalerien und auf Kunstmessen, in Museen, zeitgenössischen Kunstinstitutionen und auf Biennalen, seine Präsentation in öffentlichen und privaten Sammlungen sowie seinen Marktwert bestimmt. Die Reputation des Designers wird durch die Designwelt bestimmt: Aufträge von führenden Designherstellern und der Industrie, Vertriebsnetzwerke, die kritische Rezeption von Produkten durch Kollegen und die Designpresse, Präsentation der Produkte und Objekte auf führenden Möbelmessen (besonders in Mailand) etc. Sogar im Kontext des modernen Crossover arbeiten und entwerfen Künstler und Designer weiterhin in grundsätzlich unterschiedlichen Netzwerken.

Existenzkrise oder Selbstanalyse?
Was hat Künstler und Designer in den letzten Jahren dazu motiviert, die Grenzen zu überschreiten? Was charakterisiert die dadurch entstandenen Objekte und Projekte? Eine nähere Untersuchung der Frage führt zu dem Schluss, dass in vielen Fällen das Thema der Identität zur Diskussion steht: sowohl die eigene Identität und Positionierung als Künstler oder Designer als auch die Positionierung des entstehenden Objekts innerhalb eines größeren Kontexts von Geschichte und Tradition.

Inwiefern wird der Status als Kunstwerk oder funktionales Objekt durch den Kontext der Präsentation beeinflusst? Wenn Design außerhalb seines (Anwendungs-) Kontexts in einer Ausstellung präsentiert wird, bewegt es sich in den Gefilden der Kunst. Ein gutes Beispiel hierfür ist die Ausstellung „Ping Pong" (2006, Esad) von Chris Kabel und Wieki Somers. Das von Studenten gestaltete Ausstellungsdesign präsentierte Designerobjekte auf überraschende Weise: Somers

home, by eliminating the shrine-like barriers that traditionally separate a passive public from the artwork within the exhibition space, or by leaving the museum altogether. French painter Franck Bragigand "restores the everyday" and grants new life to discarded objects, industrial products or spaces — commissioned by art institutions and companies alike, including Droog Design. While he pays homage to

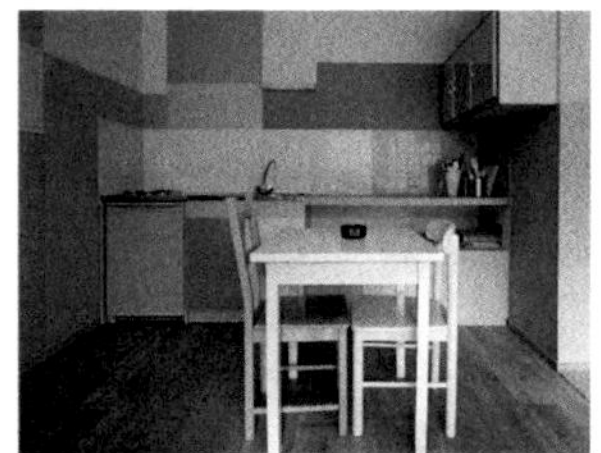

Theo Van Doesburg's site-specific, architectural interventions (cf. *Aubette,* 1928, Strasburg), his attitude is more generally inscribed in a painting tradition. Since Antiquity, and notably in the avant-garde movements (from Arts and Crafts to the De Stijl), painters have stretched beyond the autonomous canvas and work of art and have flirted with the decorative and applied arts, in particular within the context of architectural subordination.

The cross issue of bringing art into everyday life and everyday life into the white cube is central to many artists linked to the art-design phenomenon — using furniture as a catalyst — in particular those linked to relational aesthetics.[19] Perhaps no artist illustrates this better than Rirkrit Tiravanija, whose installations transform the white cube into a space for living and socializing — to cook, share meals, play music, or simply relax — often integrating references linked to modernism in architecture and design. Tiravanija builds upon the Readymade tradi-

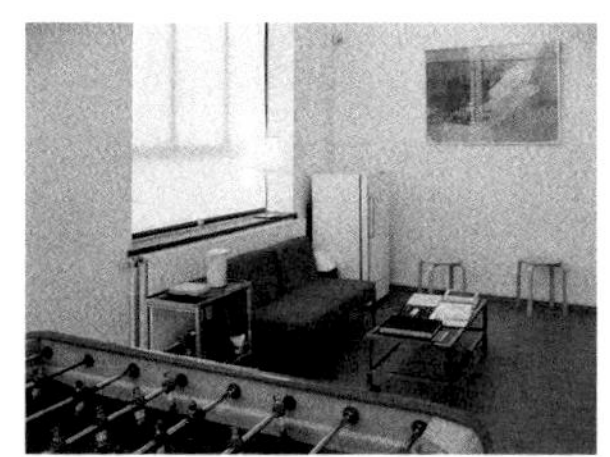

tion: that of displacing the industrial household product into a museum. However, while Duchamp alienated the object from its function, transforming it into a sculpture to be contemplated, Tiravanija simply displaces the object — functionality intact — in a new environment. The Duchampian Readymade continues to inspire projects today in art (Bragigand, Tiravanija), as well as in design (cf. Bey, Remy, Guixé, etc.). However, while Duchamp's appropriation and subversion of industrial products reflected modernism's fascination with the machine and the industrial age — a fascination also underlining artist and designer's readymade-inspired works and products of the nineteen-fifties and sixties (cf: Raymond Hains, Castiglioni) — contemporary artists and designers often utilize existing or second-hand pro-ducts with a critical and disillusioned reflection on industrialism and mass-consumption, and its effects in terms of the environment and society.

Ultimately, just as one can't judge a book by its cover, it's not always immediately apparent today whether an object is a work of art or a design product. Even if artists and designers create objects or work on projects that seem similar, the conceptual and methodological paths

High Tea Pot (2003) in Form eines Schweineschädels wurde zu einem skulpturalen Wandrelief. Eine solch freie Interpretation ist in einer Designausstellung möglich, im Kunstkontext – besonders im Fall von Installationen –würde sie schon schwieriger, da die Parameter dort vom Künstler geschaffen und umgesetzt werden. Auf der anderen Seite stellen Künstler den White Cube oder Museumsraum als natürliche Heimat der (zeitgenössischen) Kunst grundsätzlich infrage, indem sie die kultartigen Barrieren, die traditionell das passive Publikum von den Kunstwerken im Ausstellungsraum trennen, eliminieren oder das Museum gänzlich verlassen. Der französische Maler Franck Bragigand verfolgt eine „Wiederherstellung des Alltäglichen" (restauration du quotidien) und erweckt ausrangierte Gegenstände, industrielle Produkte oder Räume zu neuem Leben – beauftragt sowohl von Kunstinstitutionen als auch von Firmen wie zum Beispiel Droog Design. Während er Theo van Doesburgs ortsspezifischen Installationen eine Hommage erweist (vgl. *Aubette,* 1928, Straßburg), ist seine grundsätzliche Haltung eher in der Tradition der Malerei verwurzelt: Seit der Antike, insbesondere aber seit der Avantgarde (von der Arts-and-Crafts-Bewegung bis zu De Stijl) haben sich Maler über die autonome Leinwand und das Kunstwerk hinaus verwirklicht und sich von den dekorativen und angewandten Künsten verführen lassen – insbesondere im Bereich der Kunst am Bau.

Die themenübergreifende Frage, wie man Kunst ins alltägliche Leben und wie man das alltägliche Leben in den Museumsraum bringt, ist grundlegender Bestandteil der Praxis vieler mit dem Art-design-Phänomen befasster, Möbel als Katalysatoren nutzender Künstler, besonders jener im Kontext der relationalen Ästhetik.[19] Wohl kaum ein Künstler illustriert dies besser als Rirkrit Tiravanija, dessen Installationen den White Cube zu einem Raum sozialer Lebensformen machen: zum Kochen, gemeinsamen Essen, Musikmachen oder einfach Entspannen. Dabei werden oft Referenzen zu Architektur und Design der Moderne integriert. Tiravanija arbeitet in der Tradition des Readymade, bei dem industriell gefertigte Haushaltsgegenstände in ein Museum versetzt werden. Während Duchamp das Objekt seiner Funktion beraubte, indem er es in eine Skulptur verwandelte, verlagert Tiravanija einfach das funktionierende Objekt in eine neue Umgebung. Das Duchamp'sche Readymade hat bis heute Projekte sowohl in der Kunst (Bragigand, Tiravanija) als auch im Design (Bey, Remy Guixé etc.) inspiriert. Während jedoch Duchamps Anverwandlung und subversive Behandlung von Industrieprodukten die Faszination der Moderne für die Maschine und das Industriezeitalter widerspiegelt, benutzen zeitgenössische Künstler und Designer häufig gebrauchte Produkte,

they have taken differ, as does their objective or goal. Since the late nineteenth century, with the development of the Gesamtkunstwerk and the interdisciplinary avant-garde movements, border crossing and collaborations between protagonists from both the visual and applied arts have been recurrent. Today's artists and designers build upon this heritage, while inscribing their work within today's creative and intellectual context, reflecting on issues relating to contemporary society and their own discipline.

More essential than the identity issue, is the question of quality. Is it a good work or product? Does it add something meaningful to the art or design field, and to society as a whole, or reflect upon it in a pertinent manner? The main challenge, for artists and designers alike, is not to fall into the lure of creating simply a beautiful or spectacular product or installation, an empty shell with no deeper significance beneath the surface, or they will share in the fate of the sailors lured by the Loreley's lovely song.[20]

Figures

p.042   Willi Baumeister, *Die Wohnung*, Stuttgart, 1927
p.044/1 Richard Artschwager, *Chair / Chair*, 1987–90
p.044/2 Robert Stadler, *Chair 107*, 2011
p.046/1 Konstantin Grcic, *CHAOS Side Chair*, 2001
p.046/2 Martí Guixé, *Statement Chair, Stop Discrimination of Cheap Furniture*, 2004,
         Collection Frac Nord-Pas de Calais, Dünkirchen
p.048/1 Robert Stadler, *Pouls And Poof!*, 2004,
         Collection Frac Nord-Pas de Calais, Dünkirchen
p.048/2 Franz West, *Auditorium*, documenta IX, Kassel, 1992
p.048/3 Joep Van Lieshout, *AVL Shaker Chair*, 1999
p.050/1 Pieke Bergman, *Light Bulbs*, since 2008
p.050/2 Maarten Baas, *Smoke*, 2002
p.054/1 Tobias Rehberger, *Seascapes*, 2000, Sammlung Frac Nord-Pas de Calais,
         Dünkirchen
p.054/2 Wieki Somers, *Black Velvet*, 2010
p.056   Chris Kabel & Wieki Somer, *Ping Pong*, 2006, La Chaufferie, Esad, Strassburg
p.058/1 Franck Bragigand, *Interior design of an artist in residence studio*, 2005, Photo:
         Pierre Filliquet
p.058/2 Rirkrit Tiravanija, *Untitled (Recreational Lounge)*, 1994, Sammlung Frac
         Nord-Pas de Calais, Dünkirchen

anhand derer sie einen kritischen, desillusionierten Blick auf Industrialismus und Massenkonsum und deren Auswirkungen auf Umwelt und Gesellschaft werfen.

Da man die Dinge nicht nur anhand ihrer äußeren Erscheinung beurteilen kann, ist es heute nicht immer offensichtlich, ob ein Objekt ein Kunstwerk oder ein Designprodukt ist. Auch wenn Künstler und Designer Objekte oder Projekte schaffen, die ähnlich wirken, sind die von ihnen gewählten konzeptuellen und methodischen Wege sowie die Zielsetzung unterschiedlich. Seit der im späten 19. Jahrhundert beginnenden Entwicklung des Gesamtkunstwerks und den interdisziplinären Avantgardebewegungen hat es immer wieder Grenzüberschreitungen und Kollaborationen zwischen den schönen und den angewandten Künsten gegeben. Zeitgenössische Künstler und Designer bauen auf dieser Tradition auf, indem sie ihre Arbeiten in den kreativen und intellektuellen Kontext der Jetztzeit einschreiben und sich mit der gegenwärtigen gesellschaftlichen Situation und ihrem eigenen Metier auseinandersetzen.

Wichtiger als die Frage nach der Identität ist die nach der Qualität. Ist es eine gute Arbeit oder ein gutes Produkt? Bringt sie etwas Bedeutungsvolles in den Bereich der Kunst oder des Designs oder die Gesellschaft insgesamt ein und reflektiert sie dies auf relevante Weise? Die größte Herausforderung für Designer und Künstler ist es, sich nicht dazu verführen zu lassen, einfach ein schönes oder spektakuläres Objekt oder eine Installation zu schaffen, eine leere Hülle ohne tiefere Bedeutung. Andernfalls werden sie das Schicksal der Schiffer teilen, die von den betörenden Gesängen der Lorelei verführt wurden.[20]

Abbildungen

S.042   Willi Baumeister, *Die Wohnung*, Stuttgart, 1927
S.044/1 Richard Artschwager, *Chair / Chair* 1987–90
S.044/2 Robert Stadler, *Chair 107*, 2011
S.046/1 Konstantin Grcic, *CHAOS Side Chair*, 2001
S.046/2 Martí Guixé, *Statement Chair, Stop Discrimination of Cheap Furniture*, 2004,
         Sammlung Frac Nord-Pas de Calais, Dünkirchen
S.048/1 Robert Stadler, *Pouls And Poof!*, 2004,
         Sammlung Frac Nord-Pad de Calais, Dünkirchen
S.048/2 Franz West, *Auditorium*, documenta IX, Kassel, 1992
S.048/3 Joep Van Lieshout, *AVL Shaker Chair*, 1999
S.050/1 Pieke Bergman, *Light Bulbs*, seit 2008
S.050/2 Maarten Baas, *Smoke*, 2002
S.054/1 Tobias Rehberger, *Seascapes*, 2000, Sammlung Frac Nord-Pas de Calais,
         Dünkirchen
S.054/2 Wieki Somers, *Black Velvet*, 2010 (Projekt mit Kahla)
S.056   Chris Kabel & Wieki Somer, *Ping Pong*, 2006 Ausstellungsinstallation,
         La Chaufferie, Esad, Strassburg
S.058/1 Franck Bragigand, Innengestaltung einer Artist in Residence Wohnung,
         2005, Foto: Pierre Filliquet
S.058/2 Rirkrit Tiravanija, *Untitled (Recreational Lounge)*, 1994, Sammlung Frac
         Nord-Pas de Calais, Dünkirchen

Notes

1 Willi Baumeister: "Neue Typographie," in: *Die Form,* 1926, p. 215. Original quote translated by Lucinda Rennison

2 Cf. Karin Kirsch: *Die Weissenhofsiedlung,* Stuttgart 1987. The mentioned architects collaborated regularly with artists; Le Corbusier was also a painter, and made numerous murals

3 "Typography and Commercial Design" in: www.willi-baumeister.com (last access 15.4.2013). For more on Baumeister's role in the Werkbund exhibition, cf. Wolfgang Kermer (Ed.): *Willi Baumeister und die Werkbund-Ausstellung "Die Wohnung" Stuttgart 1927,* Staatliche Akademie der Bildende Künste, 2003

4 Quoted in: Barbara J. Bloemink (Ed.): Design ≠Art: Functional Objects from Donald Judd to Rachel Whiteread, New York 2004, p.85

5 Ibid., p. 89

6 Cf. Katia Baudin: "Art is Useless; Furniture is Useful. Über die Frage der Nutzung im Werk von Franz West," in: Kasper König, Mario Codognato, Peter Pakesch (Ed.): *Franz West. Autotheater,* Köln 2009, p. 138

7 Cf. Katia Baudin: *Utopias of the Everyday: Artists and Designers Experiment with Porcelain* and *Christina Kiaer: Imagine No Possessions: The Socialist Object of Russian Constructivism,* Cambridge 2005

8 Robert Stadler in: http://www.robertstadler.net/all/unlimited/Chair-107/ (last access: 28.6.2013)

9 Konstantin Grcic, in: http://www.konstantin-grcic.com/projects/chaos (last access: 28.6.2013)

10 Cf. brochure (author Katia Baudin) "Trafic d'Influences: Art et Design" (op. cit.), and www.designboom.com/history/monobloc.html

11 The installation included a wall covered with shelves holding red plastic duplicates of banal, everyday objects taken from real homes, with the owner's story relaying the significance of the object printed on the surface.

12 Newson's *Lockheed Lounge* (1988) sold for $2.1 Million at Phillips de Pury (2010), Prouvé's Maison tropical prototype sold for nearly $5 Million at Christies (2007). Ironically, Prouvé stands for prefabricated products for the masses, produced as economically as possible. Major contemporary art collectors, like Francois Pinault and Marcel Brient, also collect contemporary design, advised by Didier Krentowski—founder of Kreo, one of the first and most influential design galleries—who was initially himself an avid contemporary art collector.

13 Tobias Rehberger in an interview with Leontine Coelewij, "the chicken-and-egg-no-problem wall painting," in: Uta Grosenick (Ed.): *Tobias Rehberger* 1993–2008, Cologne 2008, p. 15

14 Konstantin Grcic in an interview published in *A+W Magazin,* 1/ 2007. Cf. also: http://www.awmagazin.de/design-style/aw-designer-des-jahres/artikel/konstantin-grcic. (last access 5.7.2013)

15 Konstantin Grcic, quoted in: Pierre Doze: "Towards New Sounds," in: Florian Böhm (Ed.): *Konstantin Grcic Industrial Design,* London 2005, p. 216

16 Exhibition "Seascapes and other Portraits," Frac Nord-Pas de Calais, Dunkirk (Curator: Katia Baudin). Cf. also Katia Baudin: "You Can't Judge a Book by its Cover (Or Can You After All)?: Stratégies du Portrait chez Tobias Rehberger," *Tobias Rehberger: Apples and Pears,* Galerie für zeitgenössische Kunst Leipzig, Frac Nord-Pas de Calais Dunkiek, Westfälischer Kunstverein Münster, Cologne 2001

17 Cf. Katia Baudin: *Utopias of the Everyday: Artists and Designers Experiment with Porcelain,* Porzellanikon, Selb und Hohenberg a.d. Eger 2010

18 The *Objet département,* focused on traditional techniques and crafts (glass, porcelain) encouraged projects at the interstice of art and design.

19 The term was coined by Nicolas Bourriaud. See his book *Esthéthique relationnelle,* Dijon 1998

20 Cf. Heinrich Heine's famous poem, "Die Loreley", 1824. According to legend, a siren on the Loreley cliff lures sailors with her beauty and song to crash into the cliff.

Anmerkungen

1 Willi Baumeister: „Neue Typographie", in: *Die Form* 1926, S. 215.

2 Vgl. Karin Kirsch: *Die Weißenhofsiedlung,* Stuttgart 1987. Die erwähnten Architekten haben regelmäßig mit Künstlern zusammengearbeitet; Le Corbusier war auch Maler und fertigte viele Wandgemälde.

3 Typographie und Werbegestaltung in: http://www.wili-baumeister.org/index.php?menuid=41. (letzter Zugriff 15.4.2013). Zu Baumeisters Rolle bei der Werkbund-Ausstellung vgl.: Wolfgang Kermer (Hg.): *Willi Baumeister und die Werkbund-Ausstellung „Die Wohnung" Stuttgart 1927,* Staatliche Akademie der Bildenden Künste, 2003

4 Zitat in: Barbara J. Bloemink (Hg.): Design≠Art: *Functional Objects from Donald Judd to Rachel Whiteread* New York 2004, S. 85

5 Ebd., S. 89

6 Vgl. Katia Baudin: „Art is Useless; Furniture is Useful. Über die Frage der Nutzung im Werk von Franz West", in: Kasper König, Mario Codognato, Peter Pakesch (Hg.): *Franz West. Autotheater,* Köln 2009, S. 138

7 Vgl.: Katia Baudin: *Utopias of the Everyday: Artists and Designers Experiment with Porcelain* S. 14 und Christina Kiaer: *Imagine No Possessions: The Socialist Object of Russian Constructivism,* Cambridge 2005

8 Robert Stadler, in: http://www.robertstadler.net/all/unlimited/Chair-107/ (letzter Zugriff: 28.6.2013)

9 Konstantin Grcic, in: http://konstantin-grcic.com/projects/chaos (letzter Zugriff: 28.6.2013)

10 Vgl. Broschüre (Autorin Katia Baudin) zur Ausstellung „Trafic d'Influences: Art et Design" (op.cit.) sowie www.designboom.com/history/monobloc.html

11 In der Installation war die Wand mit Regalen voller roter Plastikduplikate von banalen, echten Haushalten entnommenen Alltagsgegenständen bedeckt, auf die ihre von den Besitzern übermittelte Geschichte aufgedruckt war.

12 *Newsons Lockheed Lounge* (1988) wurde bei Phillips de Pury für $ 2,1 Mio. verkauft (2010), Prouvés Prototyp des *Maison tropical* für fast $ 5 Mio. bei Christies (2007). Ironischerweise steht Prouvé für vorfabrizierte Massenprodukte, die so günstig wie möglich hergestellt wurden. Führende Sammler zeitgenössischer Kunst, wie Francois Pinault und Marcel Brient, sammeln auch zeitgenössisches Design (Prouvé) und folgen Didier Krentowski, dem Begründer von Kreo, einer der ersten und wichtigsten Designgalerien. Krentowski war ursprünglich selbst begeisterter Kunstsammler.

13 Rehberger in einem Interview mit Leontine Coelewij: „the chicken-and-egg-no-problem wall painting", in: Uta Grosenick (Hg.), *Tobias Rehberger 1993–2008,* Köln 2008, S. 15

14 Konstantin Grcic zitiert in: *Architektur & Wohnen,* Ausgabe 1/2007 und http://www.awmagazin.de/design-style/aw-designer-des-jahres/artikel/konstantin-grcic. (letzter Zugriff am 5.7.2013).

15 Ebd. Konstantin Grcic zitiert in Pierre Doze: „Towards New Sounds", in: Florian Böhm (Hg.): *Konstantin Grcic Industrial Design,* Phaidon, London 2005, S. 216

16 Ausstellung „Seascapes and Other Portraits", Frac Nord-Pas de Calais, Dünkirchen (Kuratorin: Katia Baudin). Vgl. auch Katia Baudin: „You Can't Judge a Book by Its Cover (Or Can You After All)?: Stratégies du Protrait chez Tobias Rehberger", in: *Tobias Rehberger: Apples and Pears,* Galerie für zeitgenössische Kunst Leipzig, Frac Nord-Pas de Calais Dünkirchen, Westfälischer Kunstverein Münster, Köln 2001

17 Weitere Informationen in: Katia Baudin: *Utopias of the Everyday: Artists and Designers Experiment with Porcelain,* Porzellanikum, Selb und Hohenberg a.d.Eger 2010

18 Das *Objet département* mit einem Schwerpunkt auf traditionellen Techniken und Handwerkskünsten (Glas, Porzellan) förderte Projekte im Grenzbereich zwischen Kunst und Design.

19 Der Begriff wurde von Nicolas Bouriaud geprägt. Siehe seine *Esthétique relationnelle,* Dijon 1998.

20 Vgl. Heinrich Heines berühmtes Gedicht „Die Loreley", 1824. Der Legende nach betört eine Sirene auf dem Loreleyfelsen die Schiffer durch ihre Schönheit und ihren Gesang so, dass sie am Felsen zerschellen.

Wolfgang Ullrich

Überdruss an der Autonomie?
Zu neuen Formen angewandter Kunst
—
Weary of Autonomy?
New Forms of Applied Art

When seventeen works by Jeff Koons were exhibited in the historical rooms of the Palace of Versailles in autumn 2008, one could have got the impression that they had arrived home at last. After having toured — or should one say aimlessly wandered — through museums and *white cubes* for as much as two decades in some cases, they could now be seen in a place in which they seemed to fit perfectly. In some chambers, one even had to look twice before noticing what had been created by court artists at the time of Louis XIV, and what originated from Jeff Koons. And so the spectacle was not without risk for the latter, since his works suddenly appeared as part of a lavish interior design: they had turned into art and crafts — applied art.

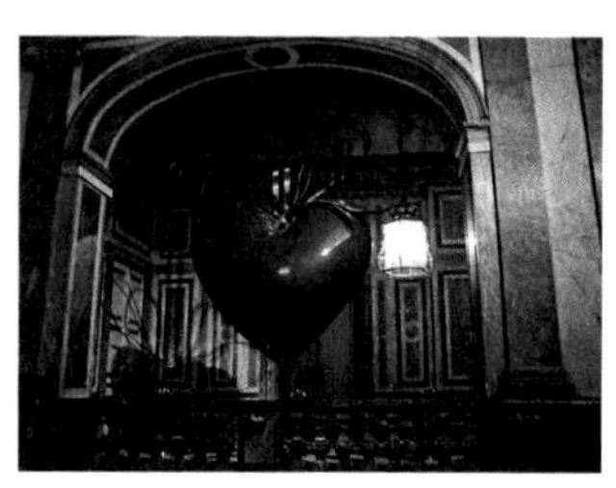

Rather than appreciating the porcelain, glass, aluminum, or wooden sculptures as obscene orgies of kitsch, as demonstrations of the evils of banality, or as concept art in the succession of Duchamp's ready-mades — as had happened with Koons' exhibitions as a rule until that date — now his work could be conceived as an accumulation of the effects of courtly amusement and luxury aesthetics. And it seemed as if Koons was applying with this exhibition for the job of a commissioned, even a court artist — as if he were weary of the necessity to understand himself as an autonomous artist.

But is such an attitude even symptomatic of today's art world, perhaps? Many artists, surely, have long preferred to produce commissioned works, site-related pieces, and design editions? Or perhaps they no longer have any other choice? As early as 1998, Hans-Ulrich Obrist commented that "even in the eighties, 90 per cent of artworks were still accepted as quasi finished objects," whereas a decade later, by contrast, it was "only 10 per cent that we take on finished — the rest are made especially."[1] It seems likely that this trend has increased even more since then. It became obvious in summer 2012 at the latest, when the following could be read on almost every exhibit label at the *documenta*: "Commissioned and produced by dOCUMENTA (13)." In this context, the artist is no more than a commissioned service provider, subordinated to a curator's concept, which would even allow last-minute omission of works, or alterations to their placement or presentation form.

Above all, the astonishing thing here is that so very little resistance is evident, despite such neo-courtly conditions in the art business. This is an indication of how strongly the idea of the autonomous artist is being — already has been — eroded in the meantime. Some artists even flirt with this circumstance: in particular, of course, the most

Als im Herbst 2008 siebzehn Werke von Jeff Koons in den historischen Räumen von Schloss Versailles ausgestellt wurden, konnte man den Eindruck gewinnen, sie seien endlich zu Hause angekommen. Nachdem sie davor zum Teil zwei Jahrzehnte lang durch Museen und *white cubes* gezogen – soll man sagen: geirrt? – waren, sah man sie nun an einem Ort, an dem sie wie angegossen passten. In manchen Gemächern musste man sogar zweimal hinschauen, bis man erkannte, was die Hofkünstler zu Zeiten von Ludwig XIV. geschaffen hatten und was von Jeff Koons stammte. Ohne Risiko für letzteren war das Spektakel also nicht, erschienen seine Arbeiten doch auf einmal als Teil eines aufwendigen Innenraumdesigns: Sie waren Kunstgewerbe – angewandte Kunst – geworden.

Statt die Porzellan-, Glas-, Aluminium- oder Holzskulpturen als obszöne Kitschorgien, als Demonstrationen des Bösen der Banalität oder als Konzeptkunst in der Nachfolge von Duchamps Readymades zu würdigen, wie es bei Koons-Ausstellungen bis dahin regelmäßig geschah, konnte man sie jetzt als Ansammlung von Effekten einer höfischen Amüsement- und Luxusästhetik wahrnehmen. Und es wirkte, als wollte Koons sich mit der Ausstellung als Hof- und Auftragskünstler bewerben – so, als habe er genug davon, sich weiter als autonomer Künstler begreifen zu müssen.

Ist eine solche Haltung aber vielleicht sogar symptomatisch für die heutige Kunstwelt? Ziehen es nicht längst viele Künstler vor, Auftragswerke, ortsbezogene Arbeiten und Design-Editionen zu machen? Oder bleibt ihnen vielleicht auch gar nichts anderes übrig? Hans-Ulrich Obrist bemerkte bereits 1998, „noch in den achtziger Jahren" seien „neunzig Prozent der Kunstwerke als quasi fertige Objekte übernommen" worden, ein Jahrzehnt später hingegen seien „es nur noch zehn Prozent, die wir fertig übernehmen – der Rest wird eigens angefertigt".[1] Dieser Trend dürfte sich seither nochmals verstärkt haben. Spätestens im Sommer 2012 wurde er offensichtlich, als auf der *documenta* auf fast jedem Exponatschild zu lesen war: „Commissioned and produced by dOCUMENTA (13)". Hier ist der Künstler nur noch Auftragnehmer, einem kuratorischen Gesamtkonzept untergeordnet, das sogar zuließ, Arbeiten kurzfristig auszuschließen oder hinsichtlich ihres Ortes oder ihrer Präsentationsform zu verändern.

Vor allem erstaunt daran, dass sich kaum einmal Widerstand bemerkbar macht angesichts solcher neohöfischer Verhältnisse im Kunstbetrieb. Dies ist ein Indiz dafür, wie stark die Idee des autonomen Künstlers mittlerweile erodiert – schon erodiert ist. Einige Künstler – natürlich vor allem die erfolgreichsten, die ihren Namen längst durchgesetzt haben – kokettieren sogar damit. So ließ sich Gerhard

successful, who have long since made their name. For example, at the 2010 presentation of his photo portrait of the former Lord Mayor of Cologne, Fritz Schramma, Gerhard Richter is cited as saying that he had consciously abandoned the role of the autonomous, free artist due to his "weariness with modernity": "Permanent provocations have simply become tedious."[2]

Now, it is difficult not to attribute the characteristic of *tedium* to Richter's representative portrait in particular, but this is by no means

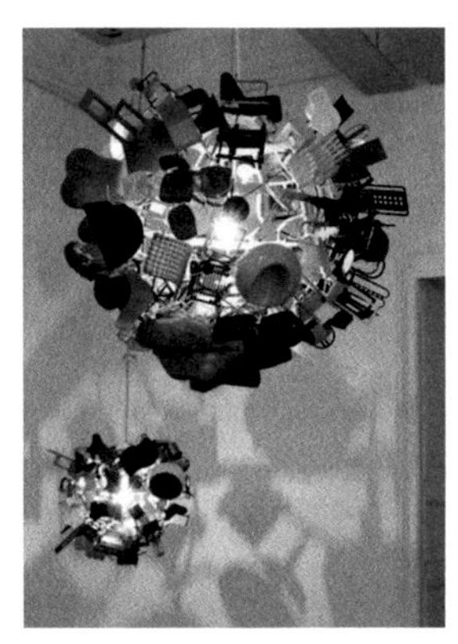

true of the majority of non-autonomous art produced on commission in recent years. By contrast, its significance often comes from its moments of provocation. Let us think, for example, about much that can be seen on art *parcours* in public space in many cities each summer. Artists like Paola Pivi, Olaf Metzel, or Hans Schabus are invited to these events because it is well known and desired that the commissioned works will lead reliably to some tensions. Readers' letters and other expressions of displeasure from the legendary taxpayer attract media attention and replace advertising as a result. And the city in question develops the image of being modern — not allowing itself to be intimidated by Philistines and petit bourgeois attitudes. (It is even quite common for city marketing to be the client behind such an art *parcours*.)

While there is still a tendency in these cases to operate with the clichéd image of autonomous art — this is absolutely not true, however, for the works are *site specific* and therefore evolve in response to a given situation — often artists do not even shy from demonstratively crossing the boundary to applied art. Here, the devaluation of the concept of autonomous art is revealed even more clearly. After all, one then has to accept those conditions imposed by objects with a functional value and so cannot act completely freely, solely according to

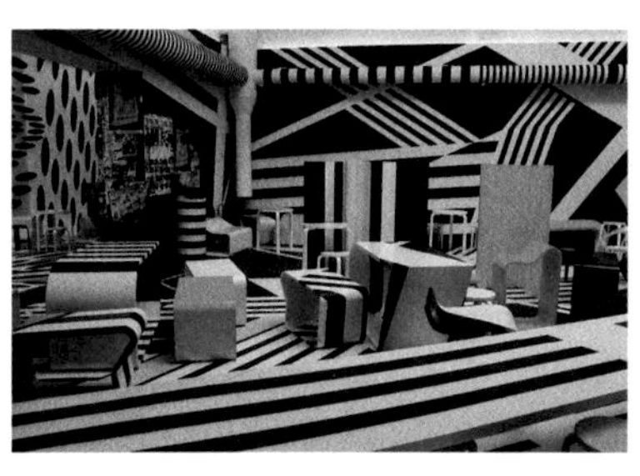

one's own requirements. An astonishingly large number of artists, meanwhile, allow themselves to be hired as interior designers or release market editions of lamps, furniture, or clothing. But most remarkably, this is not judged a major issue or a seen as a reason to resent those who do it. On the contrary, they may even — like Tobias Rehberger and his café design at the Venice Biennial in 2009 — receive prestigious art awards for it. This shows how little interest remains on the art scene itself in the traditional distinction between free and applied art, and how much this is clearly about something else.

Richter 2010 – bei der Präsentation seines Fotoporträts des ehemaligen Kölner Oberbürgermeisters Fritz Schramma – mit den Worten zitieren, er habe aus „Überdruss an der Moderne" die Rolle des autonomen, freien Künstlers bewusst aufgegeben: „Die ewigen Provokationen, das ist doch langweilig."[2]

Nun wird man zwar kaum umhin kommen, erst recht Richters repräsentativem Porträt das Attribut „langweilig" zu verpassen, doch gilt das keineswegs für den Großteil der nicht-autonomen, im Auftrag stattfindenden Kunst, die in den letzten Jahren entstanden ist. Sie lebt im Gegenteil sogar oft von Momenten des Provokativen. Man denke nur an vieles, was bei Parcours von Kunst im öffentlichen Raum in zahlreichen Städten allsommerlich zu sehen ist. Hier lädt man Künstler wie Paola Pivi, Olaf Metzel oder Hans Schabus ein, weil man weiß und will, dass die in Auftrag gegebenen Arbeiten zuverlässig für einige Aufregung sorgen werden. Leserbriefe und andere Unmutsäußerungen des legendären Steuerzahlers bringen Medienaufmerksamkeit und ersetzen insofern die Werbung. Und die jeweilige Stadt bekommt das Image, modern zu sein – sich von Banausen und Spießern nicht einschüchtern zu lassen. (Nicht selten ist das Stadtmarketing sogar Initiator und Auftraggeber der Kunst-Parcours.)

Operiert man in solchen Fällen noch gerne mit dem Klischee-Bild autonomer Kunst, das freilich gar nicht stimmt, weil die Arbeiten ja *site specific* und damit in Reaktion auf eine vorgegebene Situation entstehen, schrecken Künstler häufig auch nicht davor zurück, die Grenze zur angewandten Kunst demonstrativ zu überschreiten. Die Entwertung des Begriffs autonomer Kunst zeigt sich daran noch deutlicher. Immerhin muss man sich dann auf jene Bedingungen einlassen, die Objekte mit Gebrauchswert stellen, kann also nicht mehr ganz frei, nur nach eigenen Vorgaben agieren. Erstaunlich viele Künstler verdingen sich mittlerweile als Raumausstatter oder bringen Editionen von Lampen, Möbeln oder Kleidung auf den Markt. Am bemerkenswertesten ist jedoch, dass auch das nicht zu einem großen Thema erklärt oder den Betreffenden gar übel genommen wird. Vielmehr können sie dafür sogar – wie Tobias Rehberger für seine Cafégestaltung auf der Venedig-Biennale 2009 – die angesehensten Kunstpreise bekommen. Das zeigt, wie wenig sich die Kunstszene selbst noch für die traditionelle Unterscheidung von freier und angewandter Kunst interessiert – und wie sehr es offenbar um anderes geht.

Man begreift das am besten, wenn man sich klar macht, mit welchen Argumenten in den beiden letzten Jahrhunderten das Ideal der autonomen Kunst so engagiert – und durchaus ideologisch – propagiert wurde. Immer wieder wurde der Kunst ein Sonderstatus

This can be understood best when we clarify the arguments with which the ideal of autonomous art was engaged, certainly ideologically as well, and propagated over the last two centuries. Again and again, art has been granted a special status so that it could develop a counter world to the prevailing conditions. At first in Romanticism, and later in the avant-gardes, it was seen alternately as a breeding ground for utopias, as compensation for the molestations of everyday life, as the culmination point of every effort to eliminate the alienation of modernity. And people elected to see something in art that could offer comfort, promise spirituality, allow elevation, offer catharsis, provide new strength, but also practice criticism, present resistance, and prepare a revolution. But all of this is valid only because and as long as artists are not corrupted by existing factors and conditions enforced on them from the outside; indeed, when they don't peep at demand or allow themselves to be driven by commercial interests or everyday imperatives. In other words: autonomous art was, as the great other, a comprehensive therapy measure.

The fact that such grandiose ideas have now become rare, or are at least no longer defended vociferously, evidences a change in many people's understanding of self and the world. They obviously no longer feel so alienated and in need of redemption that they cling to art like clutching at the famous straw. When they are not feeling too great, they book a long weekend in a spa hotel or do some *fun* shopping. As members of a prosperous society, the money is available. And they are accustomed to satisfying various needs through consumerism, to compensating for their current emotional needs by purposefully purchasing products. Even socially critical, oppositional, or cultural-pessimistic feelings can find some confirmation in the product ranges of several brands — and are to this extent fully integrated into consumerism. This means that all worlds and counter worlds belong to the same system; there is no further need for a postulate of radical difference like that raised by art in the age of autonomy. Instead, art is perceived in turn as a consumer product — as a very specific one, it must be said. There is very little that is more exclusive than art, as often it is more expensive than almost every other product. The most spectacular price developments on the art market have led to the people primarily interested in art no longer being — as in the spirit of modernism — those with particular need of comfort and salvation, but those who can and wish to try out and demonstrate their buying power. But this means that art has shifted from a rather therapeutic to a more representative role. Its purpose is to reveal something of the status and character of its owners. But they not only impress us with the fact

zugewiesen, damit sie eine Gegenwelt zu den herrschenden Zuständen ausbilden kann. Zuerst in der Romantik, dann in den Avantgarden galt sie abwechselnd als Brutstätte von Utopien, als Kompensation der Molesten des Alltags, als Fluchtpunkt aller Bemühungen, die Entfremdung der Moderne aufzuheben. Und man sah in ihr wahlweise etwas, das Trost spenden, Spiritualität verheißen, Erhebung gewähren, Läuterung bieten, neue Kraft geben, aber auch Kritik üben, Widerstand leisten, eine Revolution vorbereiten kann. Das alles gilt aber nur, weil und solange die Künstler nicht korrumpiert sind von Vorgaben und Bedingungen, die von außen an sie herangetragen werden, ja wenn sie weder nach der Nachfrage schielen noch sich von kommerziellen Interessen oder Geboten des Alltags treiben lassen. Mit anderen Worten: Autonome Kunst war, als das große Andere, ein umfassendes Therapeutikum.

Dass solch hochtrabende Vorstellungen mittlerweile selten geworden sind oder zumindest nicht mehr laut verteidigt werden, zeugt von einem Wandel im Selbst- und Weltverständnis vieler Menschen. Sie fühlen sich offenbar nicht mehr so entfremdet und erlösungsbedürftig, dass sie sich an die Kunst klammern müssten wie an den berühmten Strohhalm. Wenn es ihnen mal nicht so gut geht, buchen sie ein verlängertes Wochenende in einem Wellness-Hotel oder machen einen Lustkauf. Als Mitglieder einer Wohlstandsgesellschaft haben sie das Geld dazu. Und sie sind es gewöhnt, unterschiedliche Bedürfnisse durch Konsum zu befriedigen, momentane emotionale Notlagen durch gezielt gekaufte Produkte auszugleichen. Selbst gesellschaftskritische, oppositionelle oder kulturpessimistische Empfindungen finden ihre Bestätigung in den Produktpaletten einzelner Marken – und sind insofern voll in den Konsumismus integriert. Damit gehören alle Welten und Gegenwelten in dasselbe System; ein Postulat radikaler Andersheit, wie es die Kunst im Zeitalter der Autonomie erhob, hat sich erübrigt. Dafür wird die Kunst ihrerseits als Konsumprodukt wahrgenommen – als ein ganz spezielles wohlgemerkt. So gibt es kaum Exklusiveres als die Kunst, ist sie doch oft teurer als fast alle anderen Produkte. Die spektakulären Preisentwicklungen auf dem Kunstmarkt haben dazu geführt, dass sich primär nicht mehr für sie interessiert, wer – im Geist der Moderne – besonders trost- und heilsbedürftig ist, sondern wer Kaufkraft unter Beweis stellen will und kann. Das aber heißt: Von einer eher therapeutischen Rolle ist die Kunst in eine eher repräsentative Rolle gewechselt. Sie soll etwas über Status und Charakter ihrer Besitzer verraten. Die machen jedoch nicht nur Eindruck damit, dass sie sich etwas sehr Teures leisten können, sondern umso mehr dann, wenn sie ihr Geld für etwas ausgeben,

that they are able to afford something so expensive; they do so all the more when they spend their money on something that the majority do not like, or even consider an impertinence. The acquisition then gains something of a potlatch — a demonstrative waste of money — and creates an intimidating sense of surprise and inferiority in others. And indeed, many of the lamps, tables, and chairs that artists as designers — and also designers appearing as artists — design do not

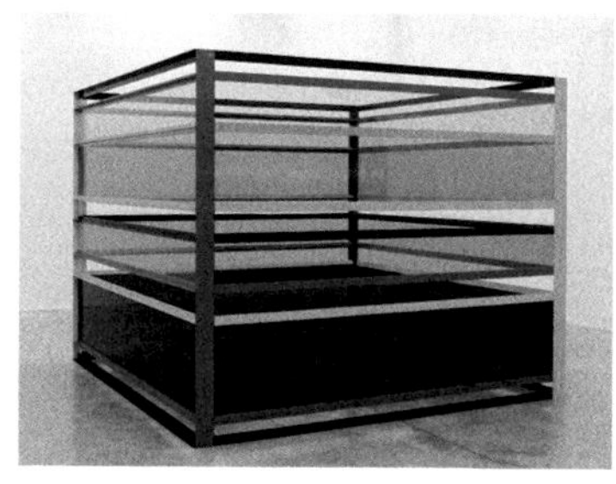

fit among any of the standard living room furnishings that can be found in the shops. In addition, these pieces are often not even functional and certainly not comfortable; they are characterized by awkwardness and complicated usage. They even make a mockery of practical value and suggest alternative functions. Much draws from — and will probably continue to do so for a long time, just like that aforementioned art in public space — the aesthetic repertoire and expression of autonomous art, which never sought to please in any way. But now the abrasive, garish, or alienating is being applied without compromise to functional objects and specifically staged in this way. Or who is able to work with the shelf-like, built-in features by Angela Bulloch or Liam Gillick? And who sits comfortably on a stool from the van Lieshout studio or an Uncle chair by Franz West?

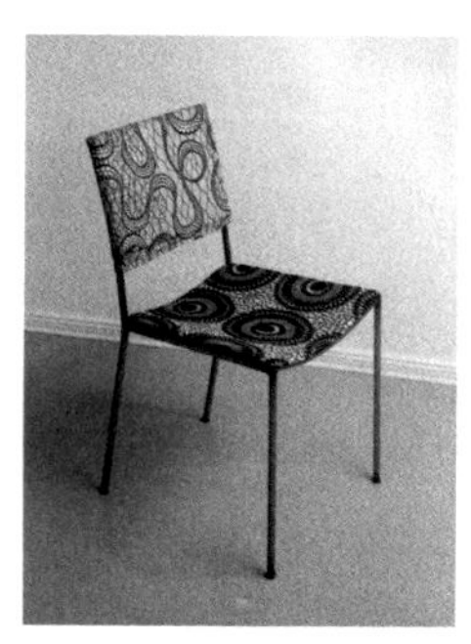

All these objects, therefore, demonstrate not only the wealth of those who own them but also, and above all, their idiosyncratic taste and strength: those who can tolerate such troublesome objects in their direct environment must be especially cool, or have a great sense of self-irony. This calls for more, even, than someone hanging a garish, disharmonious, or defiantly painted picture. While the latter can be blanked out to some extent, a piece of applied art is always involved in everyday life and must be borne afresh every day. Precisely in this way, however, it becomes a trophy with which the victors of society — the rich, successful, and sappy — can dress themselves better than with anything else that is either not as expensive and exclusive or as rebellious and cool. Basically, however, this means no more than this: such inapplicable applied art embodies luxury in the best sense of the word. For anyone who associates luxury merely with comfort and an easy life falls short of the mark. Instead, luxury always also — or even primarily — represents a challenge. There is a tendency to connect it with particular energy and a capacity for achievement: you have to be able to afford it, have to be strong enough to cope with it. In the original meaning of the word, *luxury* signified something like *excessive fertility*;

das einer Mehrheit gerade nicht gefällt, ja ihr gar als Zumutung erscheint. Dann bekommt der Kauf etwas von einem Potlatsch – von einer demonstrativen Geldverschwendung – und erzeugt bei anderen einschüchterndes Befremden und Unterlegenheitsgefühle. Tatsächlich passen viele der Lampen, Tische und Stühle, die Künstler als Designer – und genauso als Künstler auftretende Designer – entwerfen, zu keiner handelsüblichen, normierten Wohnzimmereinrichtung. Zudem sind die Stücke oft nicht einmal funktional und schon gar nicht komfortabel, sondern zeichnen sich eher durch Sperrigkeit und komplizierte Handhabung aus. Sie persiflieren sogar den Gebrauchswert oder suggerieren alternative Funktionen. Vieles lebt – vermutlich noch lange Zeit und genauso wie jene Kunst im öffentlichen Raum – vom ästhetischen Repertoire und Gestus autonomer Kunst, die gar nicht erst in den Verdacht kommen wollte, gefällig zu sein. Doch wird das Ruppige, Grelle, Verfremdende nun kompromisslos auf Gebrauchsobjekte angewendet und damit eigens inszeniert. Oder wer kann schon gut umgehen mit regalähnlichen Einbauten von Angela Bulloch oder Liam Gillick? Und wer sitzt bequem auf einem Stuhl aus dem Atelier van Lieshout oder auf einem Kodustuhl von Franz West?

All diese Objekte demonstrieren also nicht nur den Reichtum derer, die sie besitzen, sondern vor allem auch eigenwilligen Geschmack und Stärke: Es muss schon besonders cool sein oder über viel Ironie verfügen, wer selbst in seiner unmittelbaren Lebenswelt so anstrengende Gegenstände aushält. Das verlangt sogar noch etwas mehr, als wenn jemand sich ein grell, disharmonisch oder rotzig gemaltes Bild aufhängt. Während dieses sich noch halbwegs ausblenden lässt, mischt sich ein Stück angewandter Kunst nämlich immer in den Alltag ein und muss jedes Mal von Neuem ertragen werden. Genau damit aber wird es zur Trophäe, mit der sich die Sieger der Gesellschaft – die Reichen, Erfolgreichen, Vitalen – besser als mit allem anderen schmücken, das entweder nicht so teuer-exklusiv oder nicht so widerständig-cool ist. Das heißt aber nichts anderes, als dass die unanwendbar angewandte Kunst im besten Sinne Luxus verkörpert. Es greift nämlich zu kurz, wer diesen nur mit Komfort und leichtem Leben assoziiert. Vielmehr stellt Luxus immer auch – oder sogar zuerst – eine Herausforderung dar. Gerne wird daran besondere Vitalität und Leistungsfähigkeit geknüpft: Man muss ihn sich leisten können, muss stark genug sein, um ihm gewachsen zu sein. Schon in seiner ursprünglichen Wortbedeutung heißt „Luxus" so viel wie „üppige Fruchtbarkeit"; gemeint ist ein Strotzen, und es geht um die Demonstration von Kraft, Potenz, Überlegenheit. Luxus ist somit das Recht des Stärkeren. Das aber nimmt durchaus verschiedene Formen an, wobei Magazine, die

meaning abundance, and it is all about demonstrating strength, potency, superiority. Luxury is the right of the strongest, therefore. But this certainly adopts various forms, whereby magazines devoted to luxury articles provide information about the variations of superiority. Products are popular, for example, which are available only in a *limited edition* and thus difficult to obtain — indeed, they can only be acquired by those who are quicker or more persistent, who have better connections or more money than the rest. But originally, the phrase *limited edition* came from the field of art — which therefore, or so it seems, provides the model and standard for luxury products. Just as often products appear that, according to traditional taste, are ugly — even forbidding. In a "Luxury Index" by *Time Magazine* in 2008, for example,

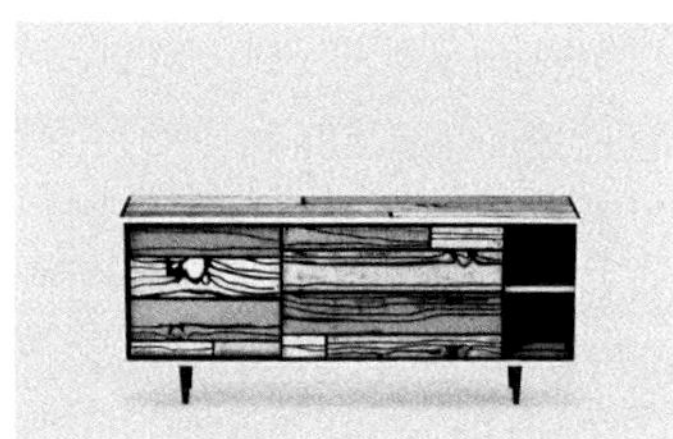

there was a dresser by the company Wrongwoods, the only point of which was its intensely grained laminates. So here, real wood was being imitated badly, quite deliberately. But those who are brave enough to buy such an obvious fake declare their coolness: indifference towards dominant tastes and thus independence. Those of us who are more sensitive, by contrast, often want things warm and cozy. Luxury, therefore, not only means having something that other people cannot afford: to the same extent, it means being able to do without something that other people need. And luxury consists in enjoying this abstinence because it demonstrates one's superiority and independence. In extreme cases, people can even be intimidated by luxury, as they wonder how anyone can tolerate being with an object that is cold, ugly, brash, or uncomfortable. In place of that dresser, examples include chairs that look unusual and chic but can be used as such only if one's back is extremely robust. Or one might imagine hole-punchers and staplers that are embellished with diamonds and therefore glitter seductively but are almost impossible to use.

All this shows that luxury is often quite the opposite of comfort. Only inasmuch as a luxury article is impractical can it also represent its owner's strength and superiority — resembling an insignia of power. Otherwise, it will only arouse envy at the most. As far as luxury creates comfort, everyone wishes to participate — in order to make life a little easier or more pleasant. Thus, luxury that spoils people is copied and adapted so quickly, according to the trickle-down principle, that it rapidly becomes something that is no longer special. Champagne is available at discount stores, and even those who don't have very much money can hire a Ferrari occasionally. We can rely upon event agencies and the tourist industry to arrange such things. But if

Luxusartikeln gewidmet sind, Aufschluss über Spielarten der Überlegenheit geben. Beliebt sind etwa Produkte, die nur als *limited edition* verfügbar und somit schwierig zu erreichen sind, ja die nur von denjenigen ergattert werden können, die schneller oder hartnäckiger sind, bessere Beziehungen oder mehr Geld haben als andere. Die Formulierung *limited edition* stammt aber ursprünglich aus dem Bereich der Kunst – sie liefert damit Muster und Maßstab für Luxusprodukte. Ähnlich oft tauchen Produkte auf, die nach herkömmlichem Empfinden hässlich – unwirtlich – sind. In einem „Luxury Index" des *Time Magazine* fand sich 2008 etwa eine Kommode der Firma Wrongwoods, deren einzige Pointe in kräftig gemaserten Laminaten besteht. Echtes Holz wird hier also bewusst schlecht imitiert. Doch wer es wagt, ein so offensichtliches Fake zu erwerben, bekundet Coolness: Gleichgültigkeit gegenüber dem vorherrschenden Geschmack und damit Unabhängigkeit.

Wer zarter besaitet ist, will es hingegen warm und heimelig. Luxus bedeutet also nicht nur, etwas zu haben, was sich andere Menschen nicht leisten können, sondern meint gleichermaßen, auf etwas verzichten zu können, was andere Menschen brauchen. Und Luxus besteht darin, diesen Verzicht zu genießen, weil er die eigene Überlegenheit und Unabhängigkeit unter Beweis stellt. Im Extremfall kann man mit Luxus sogar einschüchtern, da andere sich wundern, wie jemand es mit etwas aushalten kann, das kalt, hässlich, spröde oder unbequem ist. Statt jener Kommode ließen sich als Beispiele hierfür etwa auch Stühle nennen, die zwar ausgefallen und schick aussehen, aber nur zu benutzen sind, wenn man über einen robusten Rücken verfügt. Oder man denke an Locher und Hefter, die mit Diamanten besetzt sind und daher verführerisch funkeln, jedoch kaum noch zu handhaben sind.

Das alles zeigt, dass Luxus oft geradezu das Gegenteil von Komfort bedeutet. Nur sofern ein Luxusartikel unpraktisch ist, kann er auch die Stärke und Überlegenheit seines Besitzers repräsentieren und als Machtinsignie wirken. Sonst weckt er hingegen höchstens Neid. Soweit Luxus Bequemlichkeit verschafft, will jeder daran teilhaben, um es ebenfalls ein wenig einfacher oder angenehmer im Leben zu haben. Verwöhn-Luxus wird daher auch gemäß des Trickle-Down-Prinzips so schnell nachgeahmt und adaptiert, dass er schon bald nichts Besonderes mehr ist. Champagner gibt es beim Discounter und wer nicht viel Geld hat, kann sich dennoch gelegentlich einen Ferrari mieten. Eventagenturen und die Tourismusindustrie sorgen zuverlässig dafür. Wenn Luxus, der wirklichen Distinktionsgewinn mit sich bringt, aber unbequem sein muss, dann ist eigentlich alles in bester Ordnung: Diejenigen, die ihn sich leisten können und wollen, haben so viel zu leiden oder zu entbehren, dass man ihnen das Überlegenheitsgefühl

luxury that brings any real increase in distinction needs to be uncomfortable, then actually all is well with the world: those who can and wish to afford it need to suffer or do without so much that we are quite willing to grant them their sense of superiority. And those who cannot or do not wish to afford it can enjoy the privilege of a cozier, more comfortable everyday life. In this way, luxury even contributes to social harmony: it restricts our envy of the rich to such a degree that it makes social unrest less probable.

And so the change in art's function is actually almost inconceivably dramatic. While the ideal of autonomy bestowed a social-revolutionary role on art, its current mixture of design and fashion evidences the fact that it has become — in the most literal sense of the word — conservative. That is, as a result of its representative role, it confirms or even pats the back of those who possess social status: the strong are able to feel even stronger because of it, enjoying their superiority, while everyone else is made to feel even more uncertain because it is materially and intellectually impossible for them to participate in a form of art that appears so exclusive, so strange, and so audacious. But they are also restrained in their uncertainty and are not motivated by envy to protest against the status quo.

Due to its system-stabilizing impact, the current union of free and applied art should not be confused by any means with tendencies that could be observed repeatedly in the avant-garde: when representatives of De Stijl or members of the Bauhaus were concerned with the design of furniture or crockery, this happened because they hoped that the social-revolutionary force of their — autonomous, and anything but merely pleasing — art had already developed sufficiently to be transferred from a utopia into everyday form. The radical change that had already begun in paintings was to be completed in design. Today, by contrast, it is simply easier to make an impression with art that has become design than with anything else. In the longer term, however, it may not be the present so much as the age of autonomous art that represents the historical exception. The idea that art could heal and make individuals and the whole of society better in some way only gained weight in the late eighteenth century, when the educated bourgeoisie directly opposed any attempt to obligate art to events or representative purposes: in other words, this was the counter program to an understanding of art shaped by the aristocracy. Across the centuries at the royal courts, art's primary purpose had been to amaze, to trigger astonishment with its superlatives of artisanal professionalism, to produce surprises and gags, but also to create a distance to others.

gerne zugesteht. Und wer ihn sich nicht leisten kann oder will, darf dafür das Privileg eines etwas heimeligeren und bequemen Alltags genießen. Damit trägt der Luxus sogar noch zum sozialen Frieden bei, er dämmt Neid auf die Reichen auf ein Maß ein, das gesellschaftliche Unruhen unwahrscheinlicher werden lässt.

Der Funktionswandel der Kunst könnte dramatischer also kaum denkbar sein. Ließ das Ideal der Autonomie ihr eine sozialrevolutionäre Rolle zukommen, so zeugt ihre heutige Vermischung mit Design und Mode davon, dass sie – im wörtlichsten Sinne – konservativ geworden ist, nämlich aufgrund ihrer repräsentativen Rolle bestätigt, ja festklopft, wer welchen gesellschaftlichen Status besitzt: Die Starken dürfen sich durch sie noch stärker fühlen und ihre Souveränität genießen, alle anderen hingegen werden weiter verunsichert, weil es ihnen sowohl materiell als auch mental unmöglich ist, an einer Kunst teilzuhaben, die so exklusiv, so befremdend, so frech auftritt. Aber sie werden in ihrer Verunsicherung auch ruhig gehalten und nicht durch Neid zu Protest gegen den Status quo motiviert.

Wegen ihrer systemstabilisierenden Wirkung darf man die aktuelle Vereinigung von freier und angewandter Kunst auch keinesfalls mit Tendenzen verwechseln, die in der Avantgarde immer wieder zu beobachten waren: Wenn Vertreter von De Stijl oder Mitglieder des Bauhauses sich um die Gestaltung von Möbeln oder Geschirr kümmerten, dann geschah dies aus der Hoffnung, die sozialrevolutionäre Kraft ihrer – autonomen, ebenfalls alles andere als gefälligen – Kunst sei bereits genügend entwickelt, um von einer Utopie in eine alltagsfähige Form überführt werden zu können. Im Design sollte sich die Umwälzung vollenden, die auf Gemälden begonnen worden war. Heute hingegen lässt sich mit zu Design gewordener Kunst einfach besser imponieren als mit allem anderen. Allerdings dürfte – auf längere Sicht weniger die Gegenwart als vielmehr das Zeitalter der autonomen Kunst eine historische Ausnahme darstellen. Die Vorstellung, Kunst könne heilen und Individuen sowie die gesamte Gesellschaft besser machen, gewann erst durch das Bildungsbürgertum im späten 18. Jahrhundert an Gewicht; sie stand in direkter Opposition zu allen Versuchen, Kunst auf Event oder Repräsentation zu verpflichten, war also das Gegenprogramm zu einem von der Aristokratie geprägten Kunstverständnis. So sollte Kunst an den Höfen über Jahrhunderte hinweg vornehmlich verblüffen, durch Superlative handwerklicher Professionalität Staunen erwecken, Überraschungen und Gags produzieren, aber ebenso gegenüber Dritten Distanz schaffen. Letzteres gelang auch damals schon dadurch, dass gerade Gebrauchsgegenstände demonstrativ aufwendig und unfunktional gestaltet wurden. Stuhllehnen mit üppi-

At that time, one reason for the success of the latter aim was that functional objects in particular were demonstratively lavish and designed in a nonfunctional manner. Common features of courtly culture included chair backs with sumptuous carving that pressed hard into one's back when sitting, immense upholstered chairs into which

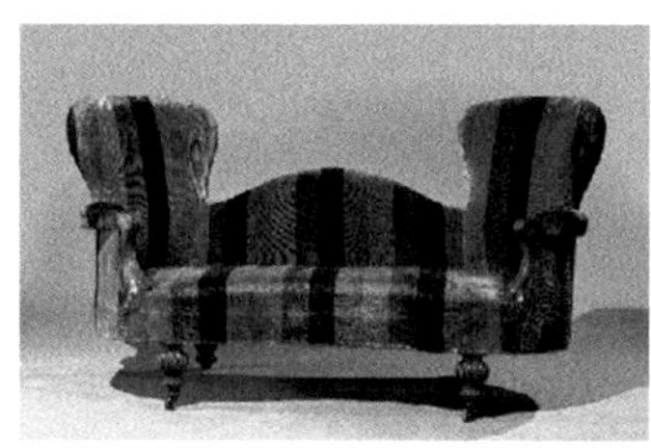

people sank completely, beds that were almost impossible to get into without help, and shoes in which it was almost impossible to walk — not to mention the rituals with which everyday activities were celebrated and staged in such complicated and strikingly garish ways. The intention was to demonstrate that one was so superior — so cool — that one could tolerate all the "dictates of ... design," as art historian Mimi Hellman put it in an essay about eighteenth-century aristocratic furnishing culture.[3] But even more than today, in those days the fact that people rejected comfort and coziness — although they could have afforded them — had a sociopolitical dimension as well: the aristocracy secured the peace of society this way; for the poor majority, who also had to manage without any form of comfort, were thus robbed of a reason for envy.

Therefore, the current union of art and design — the boom in objects that appear so brash, exclusive (and expensive) as art, but also lay claim to a role in everyday life — can be interpreted as indica-

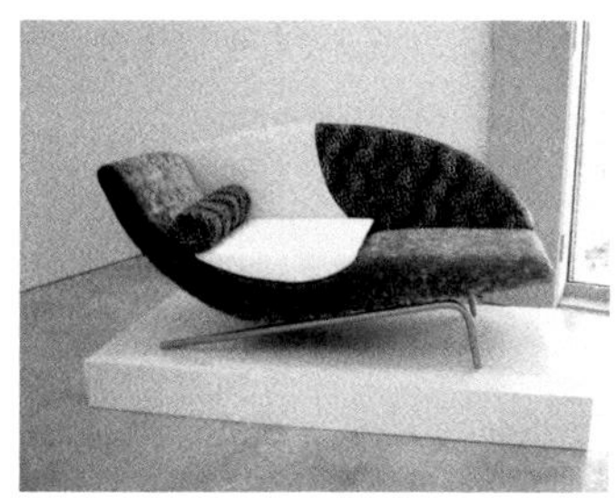

tive of a neo-aristocratic period. Art is once again placing itself on the side of the powerful, who may use it to stage, to experience their own strength and independence — and to go on developing them. They are permitted to provoke others with their taste and to challenge each other with the latest design gags and exclusive acquisitions. There are enough artists who are willing to comply. But as yet, not every Jeff Koons has found his Louis XIV.

gem Schnitzwerk, das beim Sitzen hart gegen den Rücken drückte, gewaltige Polstersessel, in denen man versank, Betten, die sich ohne Hilfe kaum besteigen ließen, und Schuhe, in denen es fast unmöglich war, zu gehen, gehörten zu den Üblichkeiten höfischer Kultur – ganz abgesehen von den Ritualen, mit denen alltägliche Tätigkeiten kompliziert zelebriert oder grell, aufdringlich in Szene gesetzt wurden. Damit sollte demonstriert werden, dass man so souverän – so cool – war, mit all den „Diktaten des Designs" („dictates of [...] design") zurechtzukommen, wie das die Kunsthistorikerin Mimi Hellman in einem Aufsatz über die aristokratische Möbelkultur des 18. Jahrhunderts formulierte.[3] Doch dass man auf Komfort und Gemütlichkeit verzichtete, obwohl man sie sich hätte leisten können, hatte damals wohl noch stärker als heute auch eine sozialpolitische Dimension: Der Adel sicherte auf diese Weise den sozialen Frieden, nahm man doch einer armen Mehrheit, die ihrerseits auf jeglichen Komfort zu verzichten hatte, immerhin einen Grund zu Neid.

Die aktuelle Vereinigung von Kunst und Design, ja der Boom an Objekten, die so spröde, exklusiv (und teuer) wie Kunst auftreten, aber zugleich den Anspruch erheben, in den Alltag hineinzuregieren, kann somit als Indiz einer neoaristokratischen Periode gedeutet werden. Kunst stellt sich wieder auf der Seite der Mächtigen, und diese können sie dazu nutzen, ihre Stärke und Unabhängigkeit in Szene zu setzen, auszuleben – und auch weiter auszubauen. Sie dürfen andere mit ihrem Geschmack provozieren und sich wechselseitig mit den neuesten Designgags und exklusiven Erwerbungen herausfordern. Künstler, die da mitmachen, gibt es genügend. Aber noch nicht jeder Jeff Koons hat seinen Ludwig XIV. gefunden.

Figures

Notes

[1] Quoted by: Hanno Rauterberg: "Shake the artist. A new generation of curators confused the art establishment – by adapting and the desire to experiment", in *Die Zeit* 17/1998 of 16 April 1998 (http://www.zeit.de/1998/17/Den_Kuenstler_schuetteln/komplettansicht)

[2] Christoph Driessen: How Schramma enters into the history of art, 2010, on: http://www.art-magazin.de/szene/27736/gerhard_richter_ex_ob_fritz_schramma (last accessed: March 28, 2013)

[3] Mimi Hellman, "Furniture, Sociability, and the Work of Leisure in Eighteenth-Century France", in: *Eighteenth-Century Studies* 32/4 (1999), pp. 415-445, here p. 428

Abbildungen

Anmerkungen

[1] Zit. nach: Hanno Rauterberg: „Den Künstler schütteln. Eine neue Generation von
   Ausstellungsmachern irritiert den Kunstbetrieb – durch Anpassung und die Lust am
   Experiment", in: *Die Zeit* 17/1998 vom 16. April 1998 (http://www.zeit.de/1998/17/Den_
   Kuenstler_schuetteln/komplettansicht)
[2] Christoph Driessen: „Wie Schramma in die Kunstgeschichte eingeht", 2010, auf: http://
   www.art-magazin.de/szene/27736/gerhard_richter_ex_ob_fritz_schramma (letzter
   Zugriff: 28. März 2013)
[3] Mimi Hellman: „Furniture, Sociability, and the Work of Leisure in Eighteenth-Century
   France", in: *Eighteenth-Century Studies* 32/4 (1999), S. 415–445, hier S. 428

Christine Hill

Do It Yourself Bauhaus
—
Do-It-Yourself Bauhaus

As an American long based in Berlin, I have encountered there is a thin line between fluency in the German language and occasional surprises or misunderstandings with respect to meaning and word usage. My studio's name, *Volksboutique*, aptly illustrates this circumstance.

The *Volksboutique* has been operating all sorts of traveling business projects since 1996, largely at the invite of museums and galleries. This has changed considerably since I assumed my teaching duties at the Bauhaus University in 2004, because long-term residencies in other cities are no longer viable. In 2009, I opened the current iteration of the *Volksboutique* in a Prenzlauer-Berg storefront, the first permanent site since the original clothing store in Berlin Mitte in 1996. *The Volksboutique Small Business* is open to the public on Fridays and by special appointment, and it houses my entire workshop in the back.

Since 2004, I have been teaching at the Bauhaus University in Weimar. In the United States, it happens quite frequently that when I am discussing my work, I end up explaining the name of the university, and clearing up misunderstandings. People are very impressed when I say that I am teaching at the Bauhaus University, to a point where I start to wonder if they think we are all hanging out with Kandinsky in the cafeteria, talking about the good old design days. Likewise, it delights me that the equivalent of the American Home Depot DIY chain is known here as Bauhaus. The idea that this name is shared by a range of institutions, some high and some low culture, with vastly different agendas falls squarely within the realm of investigation in my art production. Considering the name "Bauhaus" as an American also led me to wonder how the German home improvement store, Bauhaus, is permitted to use this name so freely.

In 2009, at the ninetieth anniversary of Bauhaus (which was founded in 1919) the three major Bauhaus institutions in Germany — the Stiftung Bauhaus Dessau, the Klassik Stiftung Weimar, and the Bauhaus Archive in Berlin — decided to put on a major exhibition. They commissioned me to produce a work for the Martin-Gropius-Bau in Berlin. I do not usually perform commissions, being more focused on the work that I have started with *Volksboutique*. But I was interested in this sort of collision between things I have been encountering while teaching at the Bauhaus: expectations of what you do at the Bauhaus, and being misunderstood as some sort of representative of an entire movement, given that I am not a Bauhaus historian.

My first meeting to discuss this commission was at the Bauhaus Archive in Berlin. I got in a taxi and asked to go to the Bauhaus Archive. The driver drove for a while before asking carefully, "Why does the Bauhaus need an archive?" I asked him which Bauhaus he thought I was

Als Amerikanerin, die seit vielen Jahren in Berlin lebt, ist für mich der Grat zwischen der Beherrschung der deutschen Sprache und Missverständnissen hinsichtlich der Bedeutung und des Gebrauchs von Wörtern recht schmal. Der Name meines Studios, *Volksboutique*, zeugt sehr treffend von diesem Umstand.

Die *Volksboutique* hat seit 1996 diverse mobile Geschäftsprojekte durchgeführt, meist auf Einladung von Museen oder Galerien. Dies hat sich beträchtlich geändert, seit ich 2004 meine Lehrtätigkeit an der Bauhaus-Universität aufgenommen habe. Dadurch sind längere Aufenthalte in anderen Städten nicht mehr möglich. 2009 eröffnete ich die aktuelle Version der *Volksboutique* in einem Laden in Prenzlauer Berg, die erste feste Adresse seit dem 1996 eröffneten Kleidergeschäft in Berlin-Mitte. Die *Volksboutique Small Business* ist jeden Freitag und nach Vereinbarung geöffnet und beherbergt im Hinterzimmer mein gesamtes Atelier.

Seit 2004 unterrichte ich an der Bauhaus-Universität in Weimar. In den Vereinigten Staaten enden Gespräche über meine Tätigkeit regelmäßig damit, dass ich den Namen der Universität erkläre und Missverständnisse aufkläre. Die Leute sind so beeindruckt davon, dass ich an der Bauhaus-Universität unterrichte, dass ich manchmal vermute, sie glauben, dass wir dort alle mit Kandinsky in der Cafeteria sitzen und über die guten alten Zeiten des Designs sprechen. Ich finde es äußerst amüsant, dass das Äquivalent der amerikanischen Baumarktkette Home Depot hier Bauhaus heißt. Die Idee, dass eine ganze Reihe von teils der Hochkultur, teils profaneren Sphären angehörenden Institutionen mit extrem unterschiedlichen Programmen diesen Namen teilt, steht in direktem Zusammenhang mit den Untersuchungen, die ich mittels meiner künstlerischen Produktionen anstelle. Als Amerikanerin frage ich mich, wie es möglich ist, dass eine Baumarktkette den Namen „Bauhaus" einfach so benutzen darf.

Für 2009 planten die drei wichtigsten deutschen Institutionen des Bauhauses – die Stiftung Bauhaus Dessau, die Klassik Stiftung Weimar und das Bauhaus-Archiv Berlin – eine große Ausstellung zum neunzigsten Jahrestag des 1919 gegründeten Bauhauses. Sie beauftragten mich mit einer Arbeit für den Martin-Gropius-Bau in Berlin. Normalerweise führe ich keine Auftragsarbeiten durch, da ich mich eher auf die Arbeit konzentriere, die ich mit der *Volksboutique* begonnen habe. Spannend daran fand ich jedoch das Zusammentreffen verschiedener Blickrichtungen, die im Zusammenhang mit meiner Lehrtätigkeit an der Bauhaus-Universität entstanden: die Erwartungen, was ich an der Bauhaus-Universität mache und die missverständliche Annahme, ich sei eine Art Repräsentantin einer ganzen Bewegung, dabei bin ich

talking about. He replied, "the home repair store?" Thus, it becomes clear that you can mention this name anecdotally in various groups of people and it will be understood differently depending on the context. A group of graduates of the university has been calling themselves and their project "My Bauhaus Is Better Than Yours" for years. They recently received legal correspondence from the home improvement chain telling them to cease using their name because the products were being used in a home-design context. Granted, those students were claiming "My Bauhaus Is Better Than Yours" ironically, and had been using their project to talk about exactly the topics the issue with the DIY chain highlighted. The group has now been rebranded New Tendency; they did not have sufficient resources to fight Bauhaus, the DIY chain.

When I was looking for information about the history of the Martin-Gropius-Bau, one of the first articles I found was a Berlin newspaper journalist discussing how many artists had tried to bring the atrium of the Martin-Gropius-Bau to life, and how many had failed. It was exactly this space that I had been invited to activate for the show. As part of the lead-up to the project, it was not particularly encouraging. It was the first major cooperation between these three institutions in recent times: they all have different points of view and different directors, and it was quite an ambitious project for everyone to be attempting to come together. On top of this, I was being introduced as the only non-Bauhaus, contemporary artist involved in the entire exhibition. While Bauhaus in itself was not really a topic for me, it became one as I started to think about the work that I have been doing recently, and the links that there might be to this kind of project. I have been keeping quite a pedantic record of almost every workspace, living space, and exhibition space I have been able to activate since I began working. It has been about twenty years now, so I have many series of drawings of this type. They are like the work of a hobby architect: isometric drawings showing just how things are arranged and how work comes about, viewed from above. The idea for the Bauhaus exhibition, therefore, was to merge these two apparently opposing pursuits — the design movement, the school, and pedagogic lessons of the Bauhaus movement together with the home depot or DIY chain. A further, as yet unmentioned entity I employed here was IKEA, as some of the most interesting research I did about Bauhaus was about Hannes Meyer, who was one of the more unpopular Bauhaus directors and had a very short tenure there. He was most interested in the idea of Bauhaus products being goods for daily use rather than luxury items. Not many people are fortunate enough to have a Freischwinger at home or original Wagenfeld lamps in the living room,

nicht einmal eine Bauhaus-Historikerin. Das erste Treffen zur Besprechung dieser Auftragsarbeit sollte im Bauhaus-Archiv in Berlin stattfinden. Ich stieg in ein Taxi und bat den Fahrer, zum Bauhaus-Archiv zu fahren. Der Chauffeur fuhr eine Weile, um dann vorsichtig zu fragen: „Wozu braucht denn das Bauhaus ein Archiv?" Also fragte ich, von welchem Bauhaus ich seiner Meinung nach gesprochen habe. Er erwiderte: „Von dem Baumarkt?" Durch diese Anekdote wird klar, dass dieser Name je nach dem Kontext, in dem man ihn nennt, unterschiedlich verstanden wird. Eine Gruppe von Universitätsabsolventen nannte sich und ihr Projekt jahrelang „My Bauhaus Is Better Than Yours". Kürzlich bekamen sie Post von den Anwälten der Baumarktkette, die ihnen die Benutzung ihres Namens untersagte, da ihre Produkte im Zusammenhang mit Innendesign stünden. Natürlich war die Aussage „My Bauhaus Is Better Than Yours" ironisch gemeint und ihr Projekt diente dazu, genau die Dinge zu thematisieren, die durch den Einspruch der Baumarktkette ins Zentrum der Aufmerksamkeit gerückt worden waren. Die Gruppe hat sich in „New Tendency" umbenannt. Sie hatte nicht genug finanzielle Ressourcen, um gegen das Bauhaus – die Baumarktkette – anzutreten.

Als ich nach Informationen über die Geschichte des Martin-Gropius-Baus suchte, stieß ich ziemlich bald auf den Artikel eines Berliner Journalisten, der beschrieb, wie viele Künstler schon versucht hatten, das Atrium des Martin-Gropius-Baus mit Leben zu füllen und wie viele daran gescheitert waren. Es handelte sich dabei um genau den Raum, den ich für die Ausstellung bespielen sollte. Als Einführung in das Projekt war das nicht sonderlich ermutigend. Hierbei handelte es sich um die erste größere Zusammenarbeit dieser drei Institutionen in jüngerer Zeit: Sie alle hatten unterschiedliche Ansatzpunkte und unterschiedliche Leiter, wodurch der Versuch, hier zu einer Übereinkunft zu kommen, für alle eine ziemliche Herausforderung darstellte. Darüber hinaus war ich als Nicht-Bauhaus-Künstlerin die einzige zeitgenössische Teilnehmerin der Ausstellung. Bis dahin war das Bauhaus an sich für mich eigentlich kein Thema gewesen. Es wurde jedoch dazu, als ich begann, über meine jüngsten Arbeiten und eventuelle Verbindungen zu diesem Projekt nachzudenken. Von Beginn meiner künstlerischen Arbeit an habe ich ziemlich pedantische Aufzeichnungen zu fast allen meiner gegründeten Arbeits-, Lebens- und Ausstellungsräume angefertigt. Das sind nun schon ungefähr 20 Jahre, sodass ich viele Serien von derlei Zeichnungen habe. Sie erinnern an die Arbeiten eines Hobby-Architekten: isometrische Zeichnungen, die einfach in der Aufsicht zeigen, wie die Dinge angeordnet sind und was dort geschieht. Die Idee für die Bauhaus-

but it is probably safe to say that what Hannes Meyer was aiming for with the Bauhaus, IKEA has achieved in contemporary society.

The Martin-Gropius-Bau in Berlin is an imposing building. The atrium commands considerable attention in itself, so putting something into it almost always seems superfluous. *Do It Yourself Bauhaus* was the central piece of the retrospective Bauhaus exhibition staged in sixteen peripheral galleries around this atrium. The exhibition, entitled "Modell Bauhaus or Bauhaus — A Contemporary Model", was one of the most comprehensive explorations ever of many of the Bauhaus works, from paintings and drawings to postcards from different Bauhaus

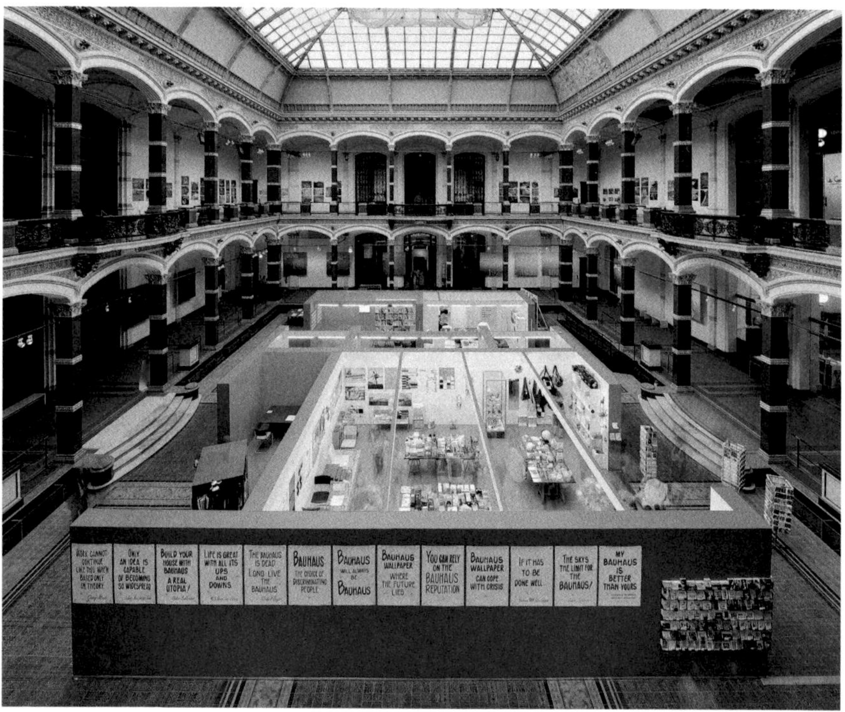

teachers to their students, weaving, household products, furniture designs, and architecture displays. It was possible to access my installation from all of these galleries. Formally, it resembled a trade fair. Anyone who has shopped at IKEA will know that you begin with a bag, a little strip of measuring tape, and a tiny, little pencil, and you embark on your own trip with a chance to take notes and do research while you are on the shop floor. This tenet was also implemented in my project. The piece was installed for four months, starting in June 2009, and the entire project was manned by twenty "explainers" — as they are called in the museum world — who were hired by *Volksboutique* to operate, explain, and represent the project throughout the exhibition duration. These people were dressed to echo employees at Bauhaus:

Ausstellung bestand daher in einer Verschmelzung dieser zwei augenscheinlich widersprüchlichen Felder: das Bauhaus als Designbewegung und Lehrstätte einerseits, die Heimwerker- oder Baumarktkette andererseits. Ein weiteres, bislang noch nicht erwähntes Element, das ich hier einbrachte, war IKEA, da einige der interessantesten Informationen, auf die ich während meiner Recherchen zum Bauhaus stieß, Hannes Meyer betrafen, einen der weniger populären Leiter des Bauhauses mit einer sehr kurzen Amtszeit. Er setzte sich dafür ein, dass Bauhausprodukte für den alltäglichen Gebrauch konzipiert werden sollten und nicht so sehr als Luxusgegenstände. Nicht viele Menschen haben das Glück, einen Freischwinger oder original Wagenfeld-Leuchten im Wohnzimmer zu haben, aber man kann wohl mit einiger Sicherheit sagen, dass IKEA das, was Hannes Meyer mit dem Bauhaus anstrebte, für die heutige Gesellschaft umgesetzt hat.

Der Martin-Gropius-Bau in Berlin ist ein imposantes Gebäude. Das Atrium an sich ist schon so beeindruckend, dass es fast überflüssig erscheint, dort etwas hineinzustellen. *Do It Yourself Bauhaus* stand im Zentrum der Bauhaus-Retrospektive, die in 16 das Atrium umrahmenden Räumen gezeigt wurde. Die Ausstellung mit dem Titel „Modell Bauhaus" war eine der umfassendsten Untersuchungen, die je zu Arbeiten des Bauhauses angestellt wurden, und reichte von Gemälden und Zeichnungen bis zu Postkarten, die verschiedene Bauhaus-Lehrer ihren Studenten geschickt hatten, sowie Webarbeiten, Haushaltsgegenständen, Möbeldesign und Architekturplänen. Meine Installation war von jedem der Ausstellungsräume aus erreichbar. Formal erinnerte sie an eine Warenmesse. Jeder, der einmal bei IKEA eingekauft hat, weiß, dass man sich mit einer Tasche, einem kleinen Maßband und einem winzigen Stift ausgerüstet auf seine ganz individuelle Einkaufstour begeben und sich auf dem Weg durch das Geschäft Notizen machen und Recherchen anstellen kann. Dieser Ansatz wurde auch Teil meines Projekts. Die Arbeit war ab Juni 2009 vier Monate installiert und wurde von 20 sogenannten „Vermittlern" umfassend begleitet. Diese wurden von der *Volksboutique* angeworben, um das Projekt während der Ausstellungsdauer zu betreiben. Die Kleidung dieser Leute spiegelte jene der Bauhaus-Angestellten wider: Sie trugen kleine Werkzeuggürtel und Kleidung in der einschlägigen Farbkombination und waren beauftragt, die *Volksboutique* zu repräsentieren, das Projekt zu erklären, aber auch persönliche Anekdoten zum Besten zu geben, um so ihr eigenes Interesse an der Teilhabe an dem Projekt zu vermitteln. Normalerweise bin ich diejenige, die für die Repräsentation zuständig ist. Für meine eigens gegründeten Läden und experimentellen Geschäftsmodelle habe ich immer persönlich

they had little tool belts and wore relevant color combinations; and they were encouraged not only to represent what *Volksboutique* was doing and explain the project, but also to include personal anecdotes, outlining their own interest in being part of the project. Generally, I am the person who does the representing; there are a lot of shop spaces, a lot of exploratory business models, and I have always felt compelled to generate and relate information. However, this is impractical if projects continue for months, and it has become an operative problem that I am expected to be the person visitors encounter when they come into any work of mine. In my estimation, therefore, this was a successful way to blend me out and have different *Volksboutique* representatives show the piece to museum visitors.

The hired explainers kept journals in which they recorded how the day went or the odd incidents they experienced. One woman reported euphorically "Lady Gaga was here today!" and so I had found a project where I could be effectively replaced, and my replacement got to meet Lady Gaga. It was interesting to see how the project developed and how people experienced it, and how they classified it alongside the other spaces in the museum as well.

A series of posters lining the entire perimeter showed a series of aphorisms and slogans. One side was in English and the other was in German, and they all originated from IKEA, from the Bauhaus masters, and from Bauhaus, the DIY chain; but few attributions were provided, so people could compare them without prejudice. It emerged that the slogans are all very similar in their salesmanship or in the way they refer to lifestyle design, or building design, or taking control of the life that you lead.

Anyone who has been to a contemporary art museum or any museum at all knows that today, the souvenir shop has become a homogenous place where paintings can be found reproduced on coffee mugs and you can buy Moleskine notebooks, all kinds of designer key rings, and many things one would not necessarily expect or need to access in a major museum. One of my most productive collaborations was with the Buchhandlung Walther König. Our aim was to try to make a functioning gift shop within the project, which would sell only Bauhaus-oriented souvenirs. This involved meeting with all manner of novelty salesmen — people who usually sell to these types of stores — to try to decide what made these objects Bauhaus-like. Instead of the bookstore or the souvenir shop being the entity that you sneak past when you walk out of the museum after you have had your cultural experience, the idea was to make it the first thing that grabbed you when you came in.

Informationen gesammelt und verknüpft. Dies ist jedoch nicht durchführbar, wenn die Projekte Monate andauern, und so wurde der Anspruch, dass stets ich den Besuchern meiner Arbeiten begegnen sollte, zu einem organisatorischen Problem. Daher hielt ich es für Erfolg versprechend, selbst in den Hintergrund zu treten und verschiedene Repräsentanten der *Volksboutique* damit zu beauftragen, den Museumsbesuchern meine Arbeit zu zeigen.

Die „Vermittler" führten Buch darüber, wie die Tage verliefen, und notierten ungewöhnliche Ereignisse. Eine Mitarbeiterin notierte euphorisch: „Heute war Lady Gaga hier!" und somit hatte ich ein Projekt geschaffen, in dem ich erfolgreich vertreten werde und meine Vertretung Lady Gaga begegnen konnte. Es war interessant zu beobachten, wie sich das Projekt entwickelte und vorankam, wie die Menschen es erlebten und wie sie es im Zusammenhang mit den anderen Räumen des Museums bewerteten.

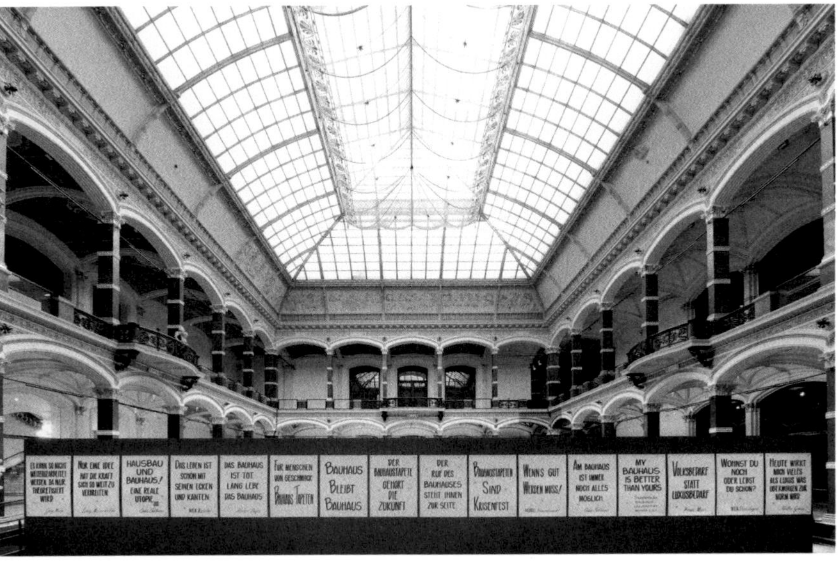

Auf einer Reihe von Plakaten, die den Ausstellungsraum umsäumten, waren zudem Aphorismen und Slogans zu lesen. Auf einer Seite standen sie auf Englisch, auf der anderen auf Deutsch. Sie stammten allesamt von IKEA, den Bauhausmeistern und aus dem Bauhaus, also der Baumarktkette. Es gab allerdings nur wenige Quellenangaben, sodass die Betrachter die Zitate vorurteilslos miteinander vergleichen konnten. Es wurde offenkundig, dass alle Slogans in Bezug auf ihre Verkaufsstrategie oder die Gestaltung des Lebensstils, des architektonischen Stils und das Eingreifen in die Lebensführung einander sehr ähnlich waren.

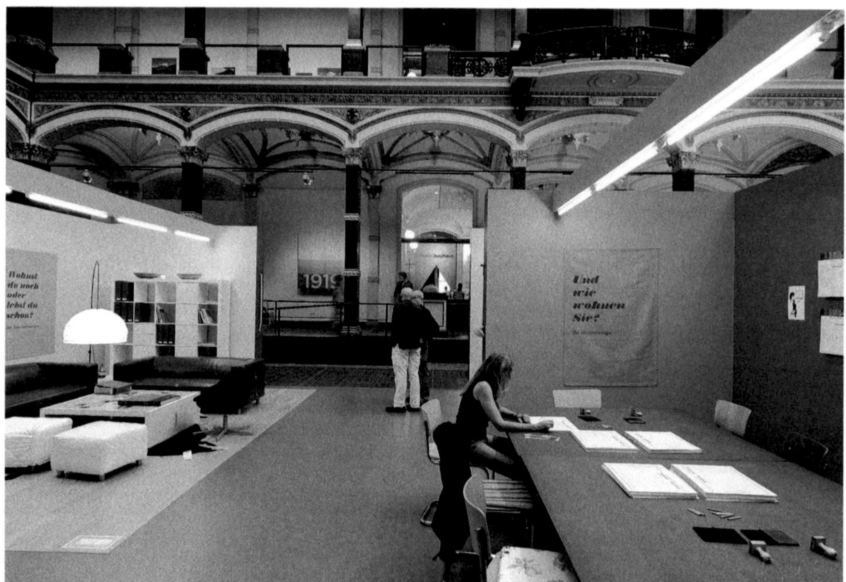

The main entry to my project was a kind of foyer: on the right was an IKEA living room. I was allowed "backstage" at IKEA Tempelhof in Berlin to talk to the CEO, who interestingly wears the exact same outfit that all IKEA staff wear: rather badly fitting jeans and an unfortunate yellow polo shirt emblazoned with IKEA logos. The IKEA world aims to omit hierarchy, all should be viewed equally. There is a fascinating website, unfortunately only accessible with a secret password, called *insid-eikea*. It shows all the IKEA employees supposedly managing their day-to-day operations, including setting up the IKEA display floors, where you see lots of living-room arrangements. The idea is to show how amazing life would be if you had this couch next to this lamp — there is absolutely nothing arbitrary about those selections. Those rooms have been planned down to the very last plastic plant in the corner. The room that we borrowed from IKEA for this exhibition is fittingly called *Modern*. It has a little cow rug, those little red leather sofas, of course, and a plastic television set. Everything in the room was predetermined. Our *Modern* room included a complete library of IKEA instruction manual printouts. Anyone who has ever bought anything from IKEA knows the ubiquitous pictograms enabling people to construct their furniture using a tiny key. We archived the entire set alphabetically. This created a type of bible or lexicon of the IKEA ways of putting things together. I also framed one of the tiny assembly keys in the room.

A lot of the pieces that I have made in museums also have a lot of office or seating arrangements; my presentation tends to be where people settle down immediately. It is where they can work on their

Jeder, der einmal ein modernes Kunstmuseum oder überhaupt ein Museum besucht hat, weiß, dass der Museumsshop heutzutage ein wiedererkennbarer Ort geworden ist, an dem man auf Kaffeebecher applizierte Gemälde findet oder Moleskine-Notizbücher kaufen kann, alle möglichen Designer-Schlüsselringe und viele andere Dinge, die man in einem namhaften Museum nicht unbedingt erwarten würde. Die Kooperation mit der Buchhandlung Walther König war eine der produktivsten im Rahmen dieses Projekts. Unser Ziel war es, einen funktionierenden Souvenirshop einzurichten, der ausschließlich Bauhaus-geprägte Souvenirs verkaufen sollte. Dies erforderte Treffen mit allen möglichen Handelsvertretern, die solche Souvenirs normalerweise an die entsprechenden Läden verkaufen, um zu entscheiden, was diese Dinge Bauhaus-ähnlich machte. Anstatt den Buchladen oder das Souvenirgeschäft als letzte Station zu platzieren, in die man nach dem kulturellen Erlebnis noch schnell hineinschlüpft, sollte in meinem Projekt der Laden die erste Attraktion sein, die Besucher anlockte.

Der Haupteingang zu meinem Projekt war eine Art Foyer: Zur Rechten befand sich ein IKEA-Wohnzimmer. Bei IKEA in Berlin-Tempelhof hatte ich Gelegenheit, den Geschäftsführer im „Backstage-Bereich" zu treffen. Interessanterweise trägt er genau dieselbe Kleidung wie alle anderen IKEA-Mitarbeiter: ziemlich schlecht sitzende Jeans und ein unvorteilhaft gelbes Polohemd mit IKEA-Logos. Die IKEA-Welt möchte Hierarchien abschaffen, alle sollen gleich behandelt werden. Es gibt eine faszinierende Website, auf die man leider nur mit einem geheimen Passwort zugreifen kann – sie heißt *insideikea*. Sie zeigt, wie diverse IKEA-Mitarbeiter vorgeben, alltägliche Arbeitsschritte zu verrichten, darunter den Aufbau der IKEA-Ausstellungsflächen mit vielen verschiedenen Wohnzimmereinrichtungen. Dahinter steht die Idee zu zeigen, wie toll das Leben wäre, wenn man diese Couch neben jene Lampe stellen würde – bei der Zusammenstellung dieser Dinge bleibt absolut nichts der Willkür überlassen. Diese Räume sind bis zur letzten Plastikpflanze in der Zimmerecke durchgeplant. Die Einrichtung, die wir von IKEA für diese Ausstellung ausgeliehen haben, hieß passenderweise *Modern*. Sie bestand unter anderem aus einem kleinen Kuhfellteppich, den unvermeidlichen kleinen roten Ledersofas und einem Plastikfernseher. Alles in diesem Raum war vorbestimmt. In unserer Version von *Modern* gab es eine vollständige Bibliothek mit Ausdrucken von IKEA-Aufbauanleitungen. Jeder, der einmal etwas bei IKEA gekauft hat, kennt die allgegenwärtigen Piktogramme, die es einem ermöglichen, seine Möbel mit Hilfe eines winzigen Schlüssels aufzubauen. Wir haben die gesamten Anleitungen alphabetisch archiviert. So entstand eine Art Bibel oder Lexikon über die IKEA-Methode zum

iPhone or the like, and so my contribution had a second function in this exhibition as the kind of lobby or place where people could catch up with each other or sit down and take a break from the exhibition. Some of these different spaces provided ways for people to participate in the project as a whole; for example, the shopping aspect was taken care of with the souvenir shop or they were given preprinted floor plans and invited to submit pen drawings of either an ideal space that they remembered: for instance, a childhood bedroom or the kitchen at home, or some sort of fantastic, future place where they would like to live. On the back wall we mounted archives of all the hundreds of detailed *Wohndesign* submissions that people contributed, and now my follow-up task is to go through them and try to figure out what can be done with them.

Opposite the *Wohndesign* table was a space we called the *Wohnberatung*, a quiet room with a library containing over 600 volumes of DIY-themed publications. The books were housed in a shelving unit made by Rafael Horzon, who is very well known in Berlin for his shelving business Möbel Horzon which offers a very upgraded, conceptual response to the IKEA shelving systems. In exchange for this shelving unit, I offered him free advertising in the Bauhaus exhibition: the Möbel Horzon logo was lit throughout the exhibition. This was one of the major discussions I had with the curators: do we really need to prominently advertise for Möbel Horzon? I felt that if we were advertising for IKEA and for Bauhaus, we might as well get the small business people in Berlin up there as well. Here was an opportunity for people to sit down and talk to a consultant who had been briefed but was not trained in interior design, who would solve design problems on the spot using this archive of do-it-yourself books, some quite outdated, many from the nineteen-seventies, many with very bizarre solutions for fixing something yourself. People could take away a little note that solved their problem for them.

Additionally, we featured a display case with an original dollhouse of Bauhaus furniture design from around 1920/21 and a customized production suitcase made by *Volksboutique* years earlier, which had been shown at the Venice Biennial in 2007. Here it was partnered with a Werkbund display case from the Museum der Dinge in Berlin. A personal favorite of mine from this project was a custom tool kit from Bauhaus. The home repair store will put together a little tool kit of everything you need to do things yourself, even though it is actually quite basic. All items bore the red and white Bauhaus logo. I liked this idea of having a box of empowerment on display in the museum.

Zusammenfügen der Dinge. Ich hängte auch einen gerahmten kleinen Montageschlüssel in dem Wohnzimmer auf.

In vielen Arbeiten, die ich für Museen konzipierte, habe ich Büro- oder Sitzanordnungen geschaffen; in meinen Installationen können die Leute unmittelbar zur Ruhe kommen. Sie können dort beispielsweise mit ihrem iPhone arbeiten und so bekam mein Beitrag zu dieser Ausstellung eine zweite Funktion: Er bot eine Art Lobby bzw. einen Ort, an dem die Besucher sich wiedertreffen oder hinsetzen konnten, um während des Ausstellungsbesuches zu pausieren. Einige der Bereiche boten den Besuchern auch die Möglichkeit, direkt an dem Projekt teilzunehmen. So wurde zum Beispiel der Shopping-Aspekt durch den Souvenirshop abgedeckt oder die Besucher bekamen vorgedruckte Grundrisse und wurden aufgefordert, entweder einen idealen Raum, an den sie sich erinnern, zum Beispiel ihr Kinderzimmer oder die Küche zu Hause, oder einen ausgedachten Raum, in dem sie in der Zukunft einmal leben möchten, einzuzeichnen. An der Rückwand befestigten wir ein Archiv mit all diesen detaillierten *Wohndesign*-Zeichnungen, die die Besucher eingereicht hatten, und meine Aufgabe ist es jetzt, sie durchzugehen und zu überlegen, was man mit ihnen tun könnte.

095

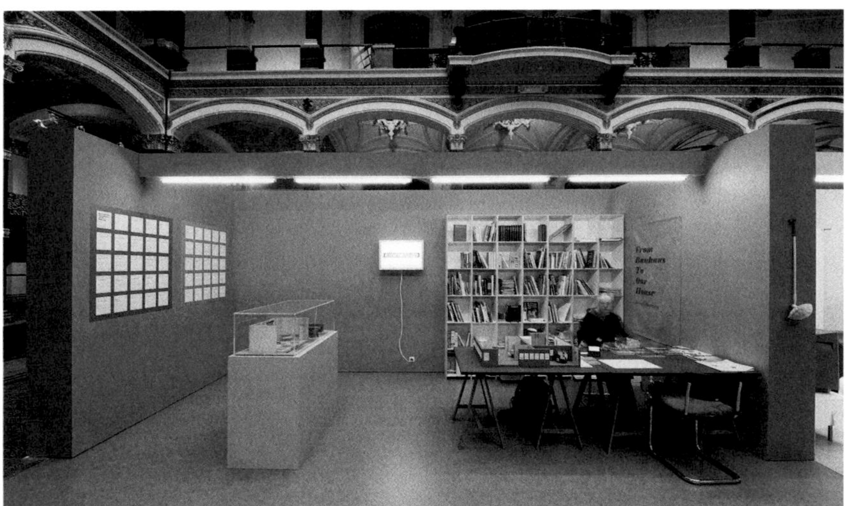

Gegenüber dem *Wohndesign*-Tisch gab es einen Bereich, den wir die *Wohnberatung* nannten, ein ruhiger Raum mit einer Bibliothek von über sechshundert Büchern zum Thema Heimwerkerarbeiten. Die Bücher standen in Regalen von Rafael Horzon, in Berlin bekannt durch sein Regalgeschäft Möbel Horzon, das eine elaborierte, konzeptuelle Antwort auf die IKEA-Regalsysteme bietet. Im Austausch für seine Regaleinheit bot ich ihm an, in der Bauhaus-Ausstellung gratis Wer-

There is an ongoing series of *Inventories* produced by *Volksboutique*. They are series of freestanding shelving systems or wagons with contents that relate to a similar theme. We included one that was themed *Bauhaus Trivialities*. As the entire exhibition in this museum was of retrospective devices — i.e., everything that was made in the Bauhaus name — this inventory is a collection of everything that slipped in under the wire. It includes a number of souvenirs and trinkets pulled from eBay that all advertise with the name *Bauhaus*. They are placed on an MDF construction that is a quasi-interpretation of a Bauhaus student design from the nineteen-twenties called *Kabinett für Junggesellen*. It is a beautifully made clothing cabinet, and we intended to make a cheap imitation but it ended up becoming quite solid and beautiful in its object quality. Inside, there is a funeral urn in Bauhaus style; there is also, a Bauhaus birdhouse, a *Klospresse* from Thüringen that stamps out dumplings in Bauhaus shapes, and material from the Gothic band, Bauhaus. Also included are works made by students at the Bauhaus University — e.g., a copy of the Wagenfeld lamp made entirely of wood. There is a Lego construction that is half in Corbusier, half in Bauhaus style — but I am not even sure what it was — still in the packaging. This is a growing archive of all kinds of trivia, curiosities, and souvenirs that are pitching themselves as being *"Bauhaus"* but would never have been selected by the actual Bauhaus curators.

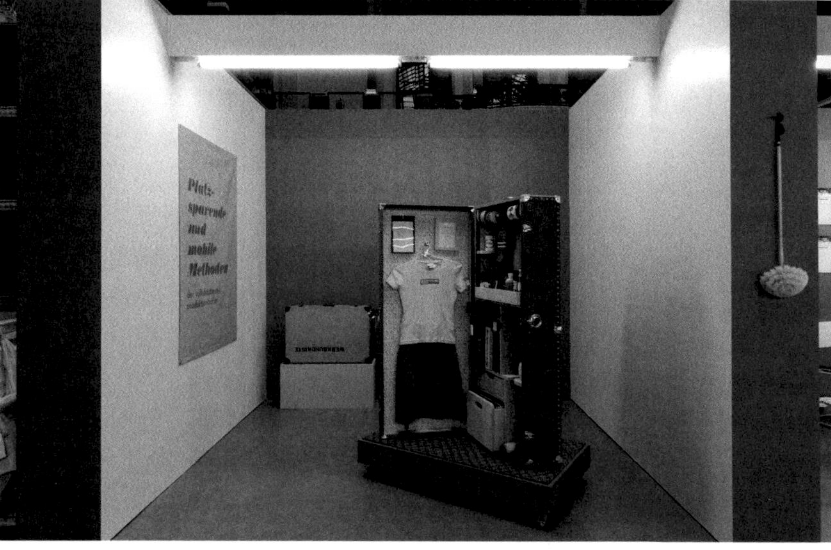

Something that became apparent to me after participating in the Venice Biennale is that no matter how many signs there are in the museum saying "No Photos," you cannot stop the iPhone and prevent people from using it. This is a fascinating aspect for me because I have

bung machen zu können: Das Möbel-Horzon-Logo leuchtete während der gesamten Ausstellungsdauer. Dies sollte zu einem der Hauptdiskussionspunkte mit den Kuratoren werden – müssen wir unbedingt so auffällig für Möbel Horzon werben? Ich fand, dass wir, wenn wir für IKEA und Bauhaus Werbung machten, ebenso gut die Berliner Kleinunternehmer etwas fördern könnten. Hier hatten die Besucher nun die Möglichkeit, sich zu setzen und mit einem Berater zu sprechen, der zwar vorbereitet, aber kein gelernter Innenarchitekt war. Er sollte vor Ort Designprobleme lösen, indem er unser Archiv von Büchern benutzte, die teilweise ziemlich altmodisch waren: Viele stammten aus den 1970er Jahren, viele hatten sehr bizarre Vorschläge für die Lösung von handwerklichen Fragen. Die Leute konnten dann eine Notiz zur Lösung ihres Problems mitnehmen.

Des Weiteren gab es eine Vitrine mit einem original Puppenhaus mit Bauhaus-Möbeln von 1920/21 sowie einen kundenspezifischen Produktkoffer, der vor Jahren in der *Volksboutique* hergestellt und 2007 auf der Biennale in Venedig gezeigt worden war. Beides wurde hier mit einer Werkbund-Vitrine aus dem Museum der Dinge in Berlin kombiniert. Mein persönliches Lieblingsobjekt auf dieser Ausstellung war ein kundenspezifischer Werkzeugkasten aus dem Bauhaus. Der Heimwerkermarkt stellt einem einen kleinen Werkzeugkasten zusammen mit allem, was man braucht, um Dinge selbst zu reparieren. Er ist recht einfach. Alle Werkzeuge tragen das rot-weiße Bauhaus-Logo. Ich mochte den Gedanken, dass ein Kasten, der zur Eigenständigkeit befähigt, Teil der Museumsausstellung wird.

Die *Volksboutique* produziert fortlaufend eine Reihe von *Inventories/Inventaren*. Das sind in freistehenden Regalsystemen oder Wagen untergebrachte Dinge mit Bezug zu einem bestimmten Thema. In die Ausstellung nahmen wir eine Auswahl zum Thema *Bauhaus-Trivialitäten* auf. Da die ganze Ausstellung in diesem Museum aus originalen Gegenständen bestand, die unter dem Namen Bauhaus entstanden waren, ist dieses *Inventory* eine Sammlung von Dingen, die sich gewissermaßen heimlich eingeschlichen hatten. Darunter war eine Reihe von Souvenirs, Kleinigkeiten, die bei eBay unter dem Namen *Bauhaus* angeboten und erworben worden waren. Sie wurden auf einem MDF-Möbel befestigt, einer Art Interpretation des Designstücks *Kabinett für Junggesellen*, das Bauhausstudenten in den 1920er Jahren geschaffen hatten. Das ist ein handwerklich sehr schön ausgeführter Kleiderschrank, von dem wir eigentlich eine billige Replik herstellen wollten, die am Ende aber recht solide und qualitativ hochwertig wurde. Darin befand sich eine Urne im Bauhaus-Stil. Hinzu kamen ein Bauhaus-Vogelhaus, eine Kloßpresse aus Thüringen, mit der

always taken a lot of pride in my work documentation, in keeping tight control over which images of a work I made get published. And suddenly the Internet is full of pictures of my work because someone just took a portrait of his girlfriend in a little corner of my installation and published it.

There is an iconic photograph showing the Bauhaus masters all standing in a line on a roof, I think in Dessau. It took two months of correspondence with the owner of this photograph's rights to get permission to alter the image, so that it could be fitted onto a board that we could install in the museum. There are cutouts, and the idea familiar from circuses, fairs, or game shows, that people can put their faces into the bodies of certain Bauhaus masters and have an in-museum photo session. We included a small model of my project as represented in the actual exhibition, and this adds a type of "mirroring" to create every possible perspective — looking down on the exhibition, and looking at a model of the exhibition, and looking into another model of the exhibition. This echoed the effect of viewing my actual installation from the second floor mezzanine of the museum: *Bauhaus — A Contemporary Model*.

The project *Do It Yourself Bauhaus* was an immense undertaking: it took two-and-a-half years. There were so many people involved, *Volksboutique* had so many employees and to-do lists all of a sudden, and I was constantly keeping an eye on so many things. I realized that the shop space was becoming a retreat where I went to relax and just have a few things to take care of, sometimes even very mundane things

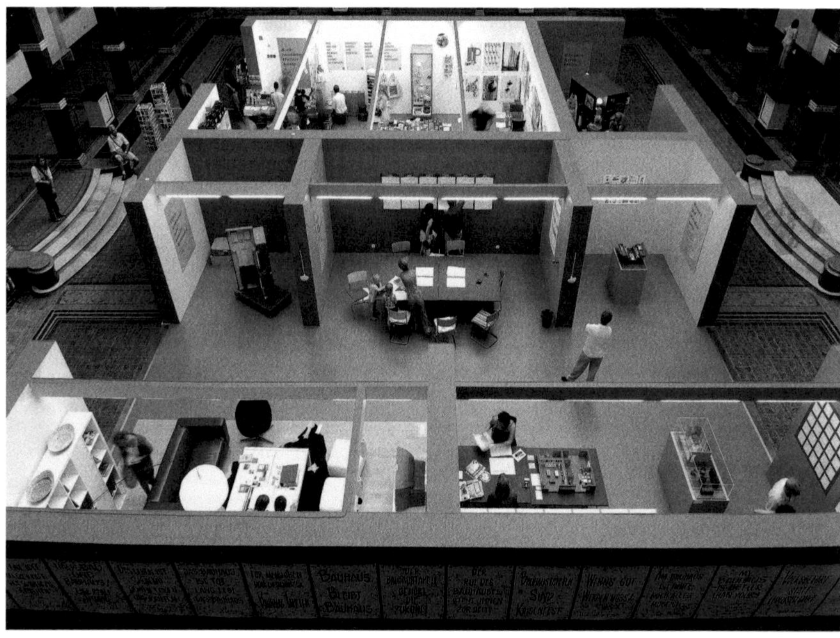

man Klöße in Bauhaus-Formen herstellen kann, und Material der Gothic-Band „Bauhaus". Es gab Arbeiten von Studenten der Bauhaus-Universität, wie zum Beispiel eine hölzerne Kopie der Wagenfeld-Leuchte, einen Lego-Baukasten, halb Le Corbusier- und halb Bauhaus-Stil, von dem ich nicht genau weiß, wie er eigentlich aussieht, da er sich noch in der Verpackung befand. Es handelte sich hier um ein

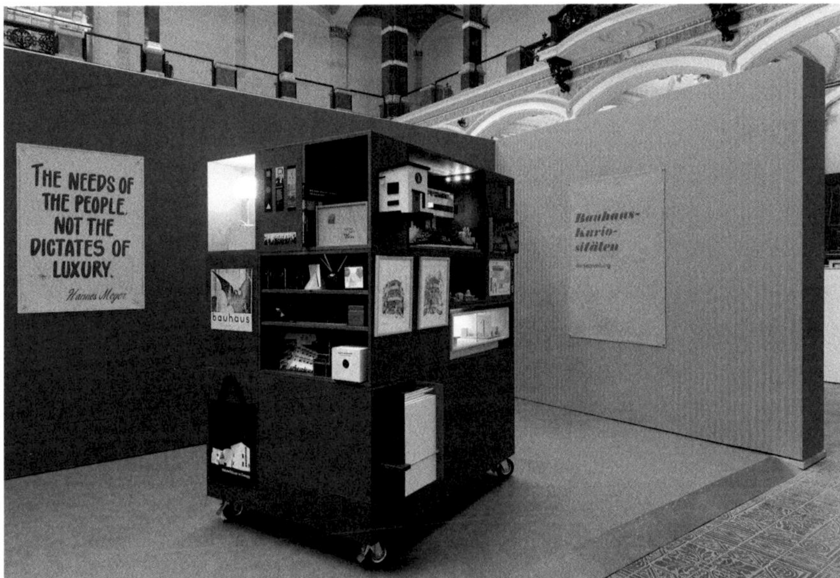

stetig wachsendes Archiv aller möglichen Kleinigkeiten oder Kuriositäten, die unter dem Namen „Bauhaus" firmieren, aber niemals von den eigentlichen Bauhaus-Kuratoren ausgewählt worden wären.

Aufgrund meiner Teilnahme an der Biennale von Venedig wusste ich, dass trotz unzähliger Schilder im Museum, die „Fotografieren verboten" fordern, das iPhone und seine Benutzung nicht verhindert werden können. Dieser Aspekt fasziniert mich, zumal ich immer sehr stolz auf die Dokumentationen meiner Arbeit gewesen bin und stets die Kontrolle über die Veröffentlichungen behalten wollte. Nun aber ist das Internet voll von Bildern meiner Arbeiten, weil ein Besucher seine Freundin in einer Ecke meiner Installation aufgenommen und ihr Bild veröffentlicht hat.

Es gibt eine berühmte Fotografie der Bauhaus-Meister, die alle in einer Reihe auf einem Dach stehen, ich glaube, in Dessau. Wir mussten zwei Monate mit dem Besitzer der Bildrechte dieser Fotografie korrespondieren, um die Erlaubnis zu bekommen, es so zu verändern, dass wir es auf eine Tafel aufbringen konnten, die wir im Museum aufstellen wollten. Die Tafel hatte Aussparungen und ähnlich wie beim Zirkus, auf Jahrmärkten oder bei Gameshows konnten die Besucher ihre

to manage, like sweeping, or tidying things. It became an important adjustment in scale. There is a continuum in the shop in that I work on projects of various sizes in museums, but there is this constancy in the fact that the shop is open on a regular basis. It is not primarily a retail project, although it does sell a few *Volksboutique* products. Mostly, it is there to function as a magnet or as an archive space and to attract like-minded people. I get quite a lot of visitors on the days that I am open, and it is usually people who come to talk shop: they want to talk about collections, or about small objects, about retail, or the way the neighborhood is developing. It is this aspect of *Volksboutique* projects that has interested me most since the start. A subsequent construction that profited from the visual look of the previous exhibition *Do It Yourself Bauhaus* is the *Small Business Model*. It is clearly recognizable as a *Kaufmannsladen* (toy shop) on a life-size scale. It was first shown at the Galerie EIGEN+ART in Leipzig last year, and is now a series. I like taking this established setting, where people can get behind the counter and take on the role of proprietor, experiencing a different kind of role-play, or a different kind of position in the exhibition. If you Google *Kaufmannsladen*, of course, you get many options, and my goal is to see how many of them can I make.

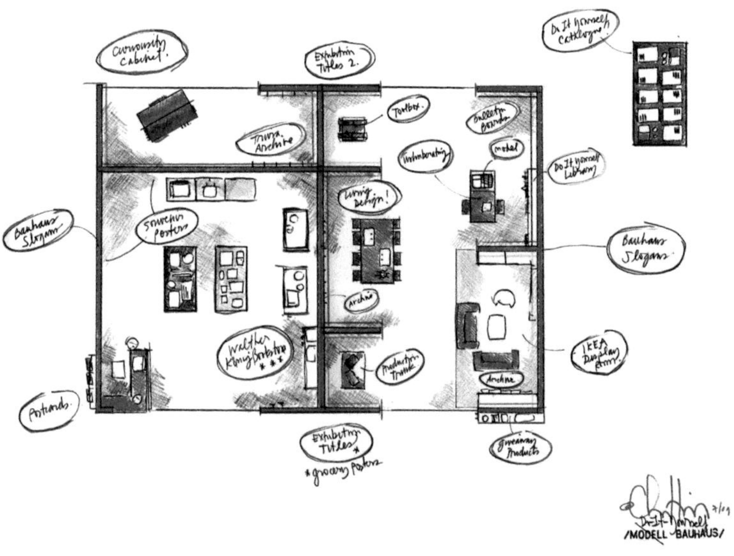

Gesichter in die Körper bestimmter Bauhaus-Meister stecken und sich so im Museum fotografieren lassen. Wir stellten ein kleines Modell auf, das das Projekt abbildete, um so eine Art „Spiegelung" zu schaffen, die jede mögliche Perspektive verdeutlichte: auf die Ausstellung herabzublicken, das Modell der Ausstellung anzuschauen und in ein anderes Modell der Ausstellung hineinzublicken. Dies gab den Effekt wieder, der entstand, wenn man aus dem ersten Geschoss des Museums auf meine Ausstellung hinabblickte: das *Modell Bauhaus*.

Das Projekt *Do It Yourself Bauhaus* war ein immenses Unternehmen, es erforderte zweieinhalb Jahre Vorbereitung und die Zusammenarbeit mit sehr vielen Menschen. Die *Volksboutique* hatte plötzlich sehr viele Angestellte, es gab unzählige To-Do-Listen und ich musste permanent sehr viele Dinge im Blick behalten. Ich realisierte, dass der Laden zu einem Rückzugsort wurde, an dem ich mich entspannen konnte und mich nur um einige wenige, manchmal sogar banale Dinge wie Fegen oder Saubermachen kümmern musste. Der Laden machte mir die Verhältnismäßigkeit der Dinge bewusst. Während ich in Museen an Projekten unterschiedlichen Umfangs arbeite, hat der Laden mit seinen regulären Öffnungszeiten eine gewisse Kontinuität. Er ist nicht in erster Linie ein Einzelhandelsprojekt, obwohl dort einige *Volksboutique*-Produkte verkauft werden. In der Hauptsache dient er als Magnet oder Archivraum, der gleichgesinnte Menschen anziehen soll. An den Öffnungstagen kommen ziemlich viele Besucher, für gewöhnlich Leute, die ein bisschen fachsimpeln wollen, also über Sammlungen oder alle möglichen Dinge sprechen, über den Handel damit oder über die Entwicklung des Bezirks. Dieser Aspekt der *Volksboutique*-Projekte hat mich von Anfang an am meisten interessiert. Eine Folgeinstallation, die von der Ästhetik der vorangegangenen *Do It Yourself Bauhaus*-Ausstellung profitiert hat, ist das *Small Business Model*. Man kann darin ganz eindeutig einen Kaufmannsladen in Lebensgröße erkennen. Letztes Jahr wurde er in der Galerie EIGEN + ART in Leipzig das erste Mal gezeigt und ist jetzt in Serie gegangen. Ich nutze gerne ein solch etabliertes Szenario, in dem die Leute hinter den Ladentisch gehen und die Rolle des Inhabers übernehmen können, um so eine neue Art des Rollenspiels zu erleben oder eine andere Position in der Ausstellung einzunehmen. Wenn man *Kaufmannsladen* googelt, bekommt man natürlich viele Optionen und mein Ziel ist es, in möglichst vielen vorzukommen.

Figures

p.088–100   Christine Hill & Volksboutique, *Do It Yourself Bauhaus*, 2009, Commissioned for "Modell Bauhaus/Bauhaus: A Contemporary Model", at the Martin-Gropius-Bau Berlin, Courtesy: Galerie EIGEN+ART Leipzig/Berlin and Ronald Feldman Fine Arts, New York, Photos: Uwe Walter Berlin

Notes

This essay is based on a transcription of the speech by Christine Hill, held on 5.12.2012 at the symposium Art and / or Design? at ABK Stuttgart.

103

Abbildungen

S.088– 100   Christine Hill & Volksboutique, *Do It Yourself Bauhaus,* 2009, Auftragsar-
              beit für die Ausstellung „Modell Bauhaus" im Martin-Gropius-Bau Berlin,
              Courtesy: Galerie EIGEN+ART Leipzig/Berlin und Ronald Feldman Fine
              Arts, New York, Fotografien: Uwe Walter Berlin

Anmerkung

Dieser Beitrag basiert auf einer Transkription des Vortrages von Christine Hill, gehalten
am 5.12.2012 im Rahmen des Symposiums Kunst und/oder Design? an der ABK Stuttgart.

Louise Schouwenberg

Design ≠ Kunst
—
Design ≠ Art

Functional things are old, ancient even. They refer to their archetypes, and to the meanings they've gathered over time. These layers of meaning reach far beyond the everyday use. Cultural and social differences, prevailing ideas about taste, aesthetics and morality; things tell us something about the era and context in which they were born, but also about the times in which we (re)assign value to them. Many artists involve existing objects in their work to play with their emotional and symbolic connotations. The ever-intended functionality plays only a marginal role as an idea. For designers, this balance is usually different, even though it is a very subtle difference. Designers work consciously with connotations and denotations, the concrete, functional significance of their products. Regardless of their products actually *functioning*, the bigger stories gain substance primarily within the margins of a functional setting.

In October 2012, I curated the exhibition "Elephant in the Room" for the modern art gallery Fons Welters, in Amsterdam. The exhibited works played with the notion of meaning versus functionality in objects we might recognize as familiar. Were they pieces of furniture? Utensils? The *things* in the exhibition were all located somewhere in the gray area between utility and meaning. They referred to a basic use, yet they were above all strange creatures that would not disappear in their servile functionality, as is usually expected from utensils. For this exhibition the context of the visual arts was consciously sought. Within the gallery these peculiar "Elephants in the Room" shared something essential about the relationship people have with things that surround them in daily life. As such, their main focus is meaning within and beyond functionality, or preceding functionality:

Tuomas Markunpoika Tolvanen created a tribute to human fragility. He covered pieces of existing furniture with a fine web of rings, made from steel pipes. After welding the rings he set fire to the original wooden items. The resulting objects resemble the fuzzy fading memories of

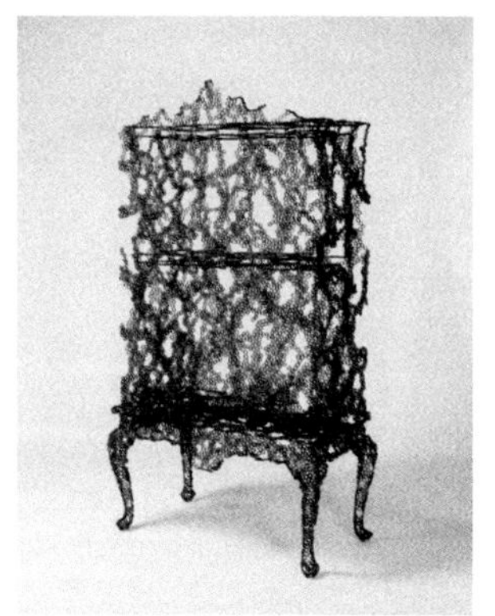

the originals. At the same time they represent a striking mix of old and new, industry and handcraft, steel and lace. Temporality reveals itself as the meaning of authentic care, according to the German philosopher Martin Heidegger.[1] In our caring relationship with the material world around us, we define who we are. Why then are design objects usually perfect and bear no relationship to our human nature, asks Tolvanen. For his remarkable answer, he took inspiration from his grandmother's disintegrating memories as she struggled with Alzheimer's disease. "Once a strong and bold woman, now only a fading image

Funktionale Dinge sind alt, wenn nicht sogar antik. Sie verweisen auf ihre Archetypen und Bedeutungen, die ihnen im Laufe der Zeit zugeordnet wurden. Diese Bedeutungsebenen weisen weit über den alltäglichen Gebrauch hinaus. Kulturelle und soziale Unterschiede, vorherrschende Vorstellungen von Geschmack, Ästhetik und Moral: Gegenstände erzählen uns etwas über die Epoche und den Kontext, aus denen sie stammen, aber auch über die Zeit, in der wir ihnen (neue) Werte zuordnen. Viele Künstler beziehen vorhandene Objekte in ihre Arbeit ein, um mit ihren emotionalen und symbolischen Bezügen zu spielen. Die ursprüngliche Funktion spielt nur noch eine ideelle Nebenrolle. Für Designer ist die Gewichtung hier für gewöhnlich eine andere, wobei der Unterschied sehr subtil ist. Designer arbeiten ganz bewusst sowohl mit Konnotationen und Bedeutungen als auch mit dem konkreten, funktionalen Charakter ihrer Produkte. Ganz unabhängig davon, ob ihre Produkte tatsächlich *funktionieren*, gewinnen die herausragenden Arbeiten doch meist innerhalb eines funktionalen Rahmens an Substanz.

Im Oktober 2012 habe ich die Ausstellung „Elephant in the Room" für die Galerie Fons Welters in Amsterdam kuratiert. Die ausgestellten Arbeiten spielten mit dem Kontrast zwischen Bedeutung und Funktionalität uns vertraut erscheinender Objekte. Handelte es sich bei den Ausstellungsstücken um Möbel? Um Gebrauchsgegenstände? Die *Dinge* in der Ausstellung befanden sich allesamt in einer Grauzone zwischen Nutzbarkeit und Bedeutungsgehalt. Sie dienten einem Zweck, waren jedoch vorrangig seltsame Schöpfungen, deren Sonderlichkeit nicht hinter ihrer zweckdienlichen Funktion verschwand, wie das von Gebrauchsgegenständen für gewöhnlich erwartet wird. Der Bezug zu den bildenden Künsten wurde in dieser Ausstellung bewusst gesucht. Denn im Kontext der Galerie verwiesen all diese merkwürdigen „Elefanten im Zimmer" auf jene Beziehungen, die Menschen zu den sie im alltäglichen Leben umgebenden Dingen haben. So war ein Hauptaugenmerk darauf gerichtet, ob die Bedeutung der gezeigten Objekte in oder hinter ihrer Funktionalität liegt bzw. dieser vorausgeht:

Tuomas Markunpoika Tolvanen kreiert in seinen Arbeiten beispielsweise eine Hommage an die Fragilität des menschlichen Daseins. Er überzog bereits existierende Möbel mit einem feinen Geflecht, das aus ringförmig geschnittenem Stahlrohr bestand. Nachdem er die Ringe verschweißt hatte, setzte er die ursprünglichen Holzmöbel in Brand. Das Resultat waren Objekte, die wie eine undeutlich schwindende Erinnerung wirkten, eine eindrucksvolle Mischung aus alt und neu, Industrie und Handwerk, Stahl und Spitze. Die Bedeutung der Zeitlichkeit bildet sich in der authentischen Sorge ab, gemäß dem

of her past. Her disease is unraveling the fabric of her life, knot by knot, and vaporizing the very core of her personality and life, her memories, and turning her into a shell of a human being."

The whimsical objects and installations of Mathieu Frossard have an unclear purpose and an unfamiliar beauty. Designers tend to speak about their works in terms of *functionality* or *concepts*, whereas in the end, beauty foremost seems to define their value, says Frossard. Which

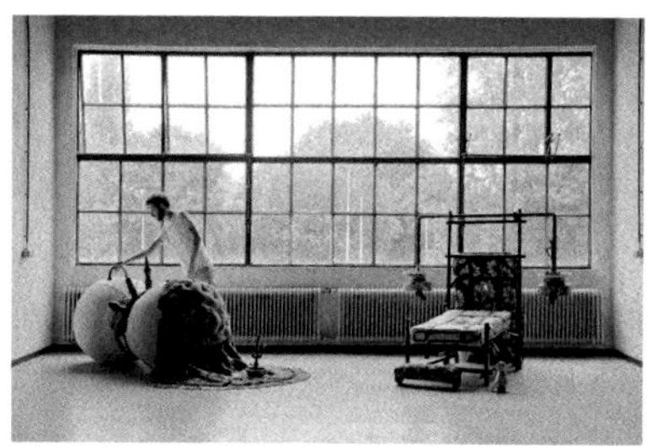

design will survive the test of time is probably less caused by its meaning or supposed functionality, and more by its aesthetic appeal. According to Frossard, beauty resists an easy definition, as the perception and evaluation of beauty are mainly based on subjectivity. Beauty is open. It leaves room for many interpretations and, consequently, can be appropriated by every individual viewer. In contrast, the notion of functionality seems to be an objective characteristic of a design object, usually not open for multiple ways of seeing and interpreting it. Frossard's installations represent this tension between function and beauty, between defined objectivity and fluctuating subjectivity. Some elements seem to evoke familiar references, but immediately escape a fixed definition once the viewer tries to grasp it. The imagination is triggered, and function becomes as open to appropriation and interpretation as beauty has always been.

In her work, Alicia Ongay Perez questions both the functional essence of existing objects, and their iconic, sculptural, and symbolic meanings. How do these aspects relate to each other within the closed

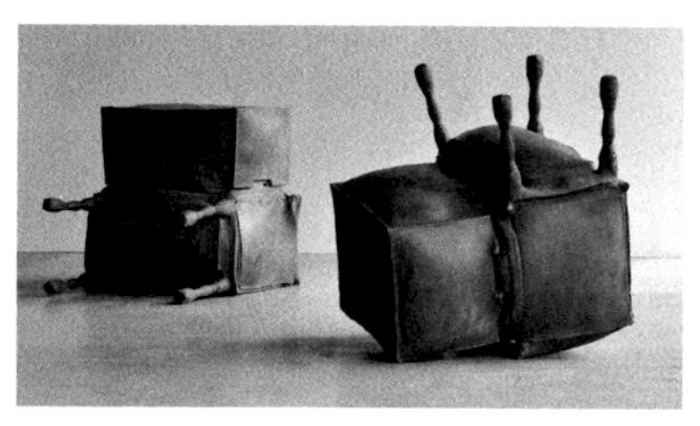

world of design, and what is their role in the outside world? Perez: "I am fascinated by the evolving urban plethora of people on the streets and all the trash culture and variety this includes. However, as much as I miss the rich diversity of London, as a British citizen in Holland I feel less distracted by social and political current affairs. This allows me to work in a more abstract and potentially introspective way. Sometimes I think conceptual work is like escapism for me — a space in which I am free from social atrocities I see all around me. Last night I watched a program about honor killings in Muslim communities in London; then I did a sculpture of a vase." Alicia Ongay Perez thinks conceptual design is an introspective discussion on what design is, similar to conceptual art examining the nature of art itself, according to Joseph Kosuth. She explored the hidden premises of contemporary design by creating a series of ceramic replicas of

Philosophen Martin Heidegger.[1] Über die sorgende Beziehung zu der uns umgebenden materiellen Welt definieren wir, wer wir sind. „Warum aber sind dann Designobjekte normalerweise perfekt und stehen in keiner Beziehung zu unseren menschlichen Natur?", fragt Tolvanen. Zu seiner außergewöhnlichen Antwort inspirierte ihn die durch eine Alzheimer-Erkrankung schwindende Erinnerungskraft seiner Großmutter. „Die ehemals starke und tapfere Frau ist heute nur noch ein verblassendes Bild ihrer Vergangenheit. Ihre Krankheit zerfasert das Gewebe ihres Lebens, Verknüpfung um Verknüpfung, zersetzt den wahren Kern ihrer Persönlichkeit und ihres Lebens, ihrer Erinnerungen, und verwandelt sie in die bloße Hülle eines menschlichen Wesens."

Die skurrilen Objekte und Installationen von Mathieu Frossard dienen hingegen einem undefinierbaren Zweck und sind von ungewöhnlicher Schönheit. Designer neigen dazu, in Bezug auf ihr Werk von *Funktionalität* oder *Konzepten* zu sprechen, jedoch bestimmt am Ende die Schönheit den Wert des Objektes, meint Frossard. Ob ein Designobjekt über die Zeiten bestehen kann, ist wahrscheinlich weniger durch dessen Bedeutungsgehalt oder Funktionalität bestimmt, sondern eher durch den ästhetischen Reiz. Laut Frossard ist es nicht einfach, Schönheit zu definieren, da die Wahrnehmung und Einschätzung von Schönheit recht subjektiv ist. Schönheit ist ein weites Feld. Sie lässt vielen Interpretationen Raum und kann folglich von jedem Betrachter individuell bestimmt werden. Im Gegensatz dazu scheint die Funktionalität objektives Merkmal eines Designobjektes zu sein, eine vielfältigere Betrachtungs- und Interpretationsweise wird demnach für gewöhnlich nicht zugestanden. Frossards Installationen repräsentieren diese Spannung zwischen Funktion und Schönheit, zwischen definierter Objektivität und fluktuierender Subjektivität. Einige Elemente scheinen vertraute Bezüge zu evozieren, entziehen sich jedoch sofort einer bestimmten Definition, wenn der Betrachter versucht, ihrer habhaft zu werden. Die Vorstellungskraft erwacht und die Funktion wird zu einem offenen Prinzip der Aneignung und Interpretation, so wie es die Schönheit immer gewesen ist.

Alicia Ongay Perez hinterfragt in ihrer Arbeit sowohl die funktionale Essenz bereits existierender Objekte als auch deren ikonische, skulpturale und symbolische Bedeutung. Welche Bezüge haben diese Aspekte innerhalb der Welt des Designs und welche Rolle spielen sie in der Welt außerhalb des Designs? Perez: „Ich bin fasziniert von den ständig wachsenden Menschenmassen auf den Straßen sowie all der Trashkultur und der ihr innewohnenden Vielfältigkeit. So sehr ich als Britin die enorme Londoner Vielfalt vermisse, fühle ich mich in Holland durch die aktuellen Ereignisse im sozialen und politischen Bereich

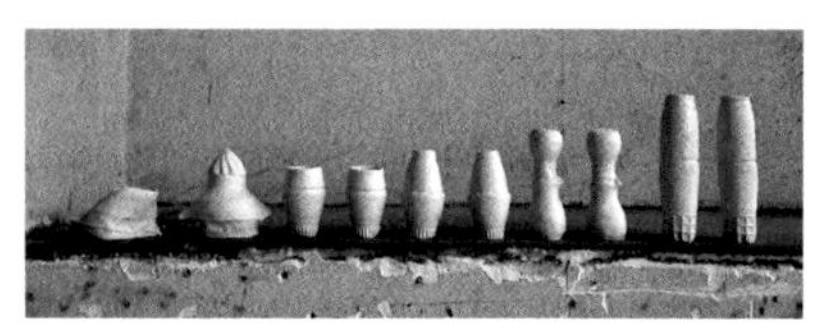

einfach weniger abgelenkt. Das gestattet mir, auf abstraktere und potentiell introspektive Art zu arbeiten. Manchmal glaube ich, dass konzeptuelle Arbeit für mich so etwas wie Eskapismus ist: ein Raum, in dem ich frei von all den sozialen Schrecklichkeiten bin, die ich um mich herum beobachte. Gestern Abend habe ich eine Sendung über Ehrenmorde in Londoner Muslim-Gemeinden angeschaut und dann eine Vase gemacht." Alicia Ongay Perez betrachtet konzeptuelles Design als eine introspektive Auseinandersetzung darüber, was Design ist, ähnlich wie, gemäß Joseph Kosuth, die konzeptuelle Kunst das Wesen der Kunst an sich untersucht. Verborgene Ursprünge zeitgenössischen Designs lotete sie aus, indem sie eine Serie von Keramikrepliken von alten Vasen und Schränken schuf, die schon lange keinen Marktwert mehr hatten. Sie experimentierte mit Hülle und Form sowie mit nach außen gestülpten Volumen, die dem leeren Inneren Gestalt geben, in dem ihre ursprüngliche Funktion verborgen ist. Diese kühnen Objekte verweisen auf den ausgeprägt skulpturalen Charakter der einfachen Dinge, die wir alltäglich benutzen, sowie den Kontext, in dem sie Bedeutung haben. Wo also gehören sie hin?

Die Arbeit von Tamar Shafrir bestand aus zwei auf die Wand des Ausstellungsraums geschriebenen Zeilen: „Die Idee der Neutralität muss permanent infrage gestellt werden, sogar bei Objekten, die keine Ideologie zu haben scheinen." Und: „Ist Design zu einem in sein eigenes Bild verliebten Narziss geworden?" Diese Zeilen stehen miteinander im Konflikt und repräsentieren so jenen Bruch, der die Welt des Designs momentan beschäftigt. Shafrir sagt im Grunde genommen, dass reine Funktionalität schlichtweg nicht existiert. Alle Dinge haben zwangsläufig mehr Bedeutungsebenen, Bezüge, Assoziationen, als wir es auf den ersten Blick annehmen würden. Es beginnt bereits damit, dass alle funktionalen Objekte immer auch skulptural sind; ließe ein Designer diese Tatsache jemals außer Acht, würde die Gestaltung wahrscheinlich darunter leiden. Shafrir macht aber auch eine interessante kritische Beobachtung: Während sich Designer zunehmend auf den Inhalt ihrer Arbeit und eine introspektive Infragestellung ihres Fachgebietes konzentrieren, scheinen einige von ihnen den Kern ihrer Disziplin, die Funktionalität, zu vergessen.

Warum sprechen wir heute über dieses Thema? Warum erscheint es wichtig, die Unterschiede zwischen Kunst und Design herauszuarbeiten? Weil während des letzten Jahrzehnts beide – die Welt der Kunst und die des Designs – im Bann des sogenannten *designart*-Phänomens standen. Verführt von den lukrativen Marktangeboten für Designobjekte, begannen immer mehr Designer den Aspekt der Brauchbarkeit außer Acht zu lassen, um kostspielige Unikate und

In my view, the following designs are significant experimental designs. You have to excuse me for using primarily Dutch designs; this is my main field of expertise.

The designs I show all shed an interesting light on the way we, human beings, deal with the daily world of objects that surround us. I consciously say *experimental*, because I assume some of them will eventually lead to functional objects in which meanings are hidden in an unobtrusive, almost coincidental way. A few of these designs started as striking designs with a powerful meaning, which due to the workings of the market changed in the course of time — for instance, traditional iconography, digital manipulation, and the combination of old and new creative techniques. These enabled a translation of the layered information on the computer screen onto the wooden layers of the table. When the limited wooden edition was sold out, the designers let themselves be convinced by a gallerist to recreate the iconic object in one piece of marble. It may have been a commercial success, but the meaning of the layered original piece vanished in the process.

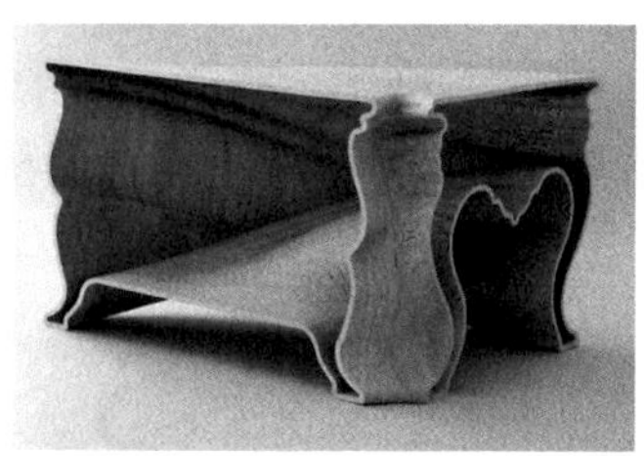

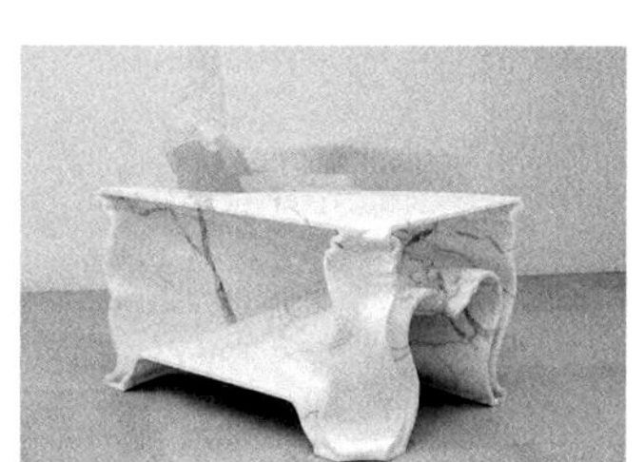

Remy's chair of old rags criticized the notion of newness and perfection, and empowered the user to create his own furniture and was one of the first conceptual designs that became known in the world for its simple yet important meaning. Implicitly, *Rag Chair* became a commercial success. In order to benefit from it even more, the designer created new versions made from expensive new fabrics. What he seemed to forget is that he actually ruined the original concept by doing so. One may then ask whether the new version's story has the same power as the original one. And one may ask if that is important.[3]

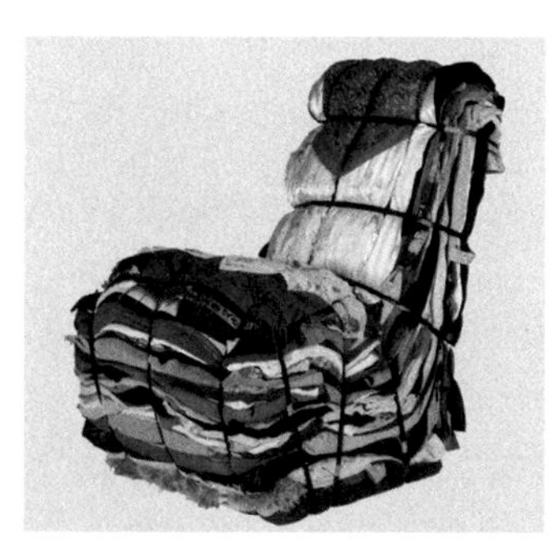

The meaning of the next designs I show has not weakened in the course of time. Experimental design works may offer a new perspective on functionality, on the past, and on the links between design and other cultural domains, like *Tree Trunk* and *Kokon Furniture* by Jurgen Bey, in which he questions the notion of conventions in design. The design of *Ear Chairs* is based on research of new perspectives on office design, working, and meeting. The chairs offer many possibilities but also speak in a new way about the relationship between furniture and architecture, between people and objects. Nacho Carbonell is interested in creating playful, communicative objects that can arouse one's sensations and imagination and change

Objekte in beschränkter Auflage zu schaffen. Diese Einzelstücke, die oft mittels arbeitsintensiver Handwerkstechniken entstanden, hatten nur noch einen vagen Bezug zur Funktionalität und einige ignorierten diese vollkommen. Derlei Ausschweifungen, denen aufgrund der ökonomischen Krise ein Ende bereitet wurde, hatten offensichtlich wenig mit Design zu tun. Dennoch warfen sie ein Thema auf, das einfach nicht ignoriert werden kann. Kunst und Design treffen und überschneiden sich auf vielfältige Art. Auf der Suche nach einer ausgewogenen Balance zwischen reiner Funktionalität und inhärentem Bedeutungsgehalt sehen einige Designer nicht nur in der Affirmation des skulpturalen und bedeutungstragenden Charakters jeglichen Designs eine Lösung, sondern auch in der Erweiterung der Grenzen ihres Fachs. Ihre Experimente werden nicht nur zu bedeutenden Veränderungen des Designs selbst führen, sondern auch nachhaltig die Art und Weise beeinflussen, wie wir über Design und Kunst denken.[2]

Ich werde im Folgenden Designstücke vorstellen, die meiner Ansicht nach zu den wichtigen experimentellen Designarbeiten gehören. Man verzeihe mir, dass ich hauptsächlich auf niederländisches Design verweise – aber dies ist mein Arbeitsschwerpunkt. Diese Designstücke beleuchten auf interessante Art und Weise, wie wir Menschen alltäglich mit den uns umgebenden Dingen umgehen. Ich sage bewusst *experimentell*, da ich annehme, dass einige von diesen Arbeiten letztendlich zu funktionalen Objekten mit einem unaufdringlichen, fast beiläufigen Bedeutungsgehalt weiterentwickelt werden. Einige dieser Designobjekte waren ursprünglich beeindruckend aufgrund ihrer intensiven Aussagekraft, die jedoch im Lauf der Zeit durch die Anforderungen des Marktes Veränderungen unterworfen wurden. Ein Beispiel dafür ist eine Arbeit, in der traditionelle Ikonografie, digitale Manipulation und die Kombination von alten und neuen Produktionsverfahren thematisiert wurden. In diesem Prozess wurden Informationsschichten vom Computerbildschirm auf die Holzschichten eines Tisches übertragen. Als die limitierte Auflage in Holz ausverkauft war, ließen sich die Designer von einem Galeristen dazu überreden, das ikonische Objekt mit einem Stück Marmor neu aufzu-legen. Dies mag ein kommerzieller Erfolg gewesen sein, aber die Bedeutung des geschichteten Originals ging dabei verloren.

Tejo Remys Stuhl aus alten Lumpen kritisiert implizit die Begriffe von Neuheit und Perfektion und ermöglicht es dem Benutzer, Möbel selbst zu gestalten und war einer der ersten konzeptuellen Entwürfe, der aufgrund seiner schlichten, jedoch grundsätzlichen Aussage bekannt wurde. *Rag Chair* wurde ein kommerzieller Erfolg. Um seinen Profit zu steigern, schuf der Designer neue Versionen aus teuren,

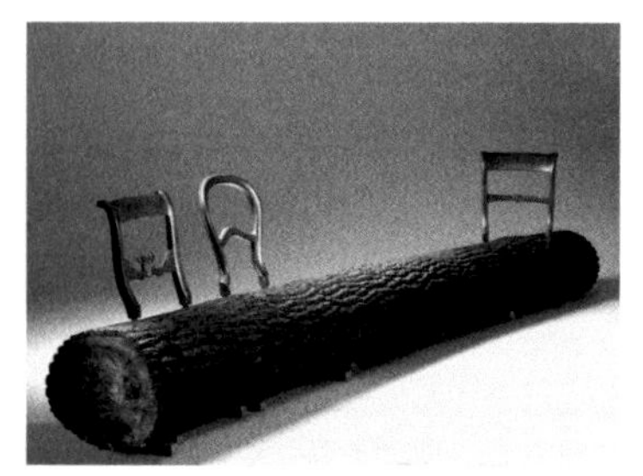

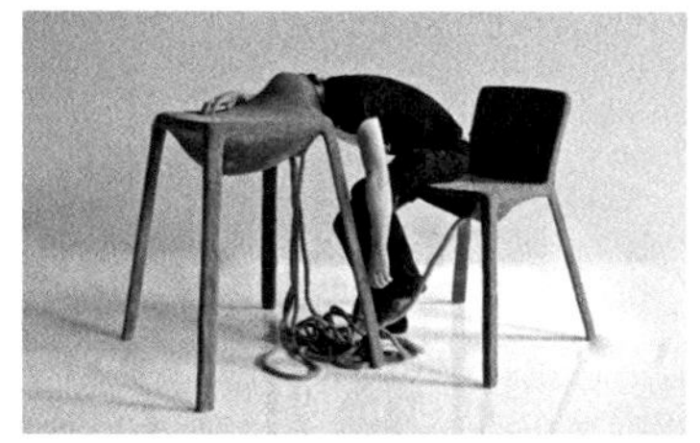

the perception of things. The objects of the *Skin Collection* apparently border on the edge of fine art, yet their importance lies foremost in the design world.

The producing machine *Collective Works* by mischer'traxler only works if people pay attention. Reacting to its audience by means of sensors, the process translates the flow of people into an object, by setting in motion more and more markers. The results vary in color and size, just like the level of interest varies during the time of production. One might consider the whole installation as an intriguing art installation, but at the same time it can also be viewed as a comment on consumption, on a society that has become used to throwing things away, on the necessity to revalue objects and reconsider the production process that is needed to create things.

The works of designer Hella Jongerius are collected by museums and are produced in large batches by the industry. In her oeuvre, one can see how almost all of her experimental works, in which she deals with themes like the close relationship of people and objects, eventually lead to products that are produced by the industry. In her first works, *Soft Urn* and *Big White Pot*, she researched the surface and meanings of various materials, as well as the traces of the making process. Jongerius's *Coloured Vases* are based on the research of varying perceptions of colors. Each vase displays both old glazes,

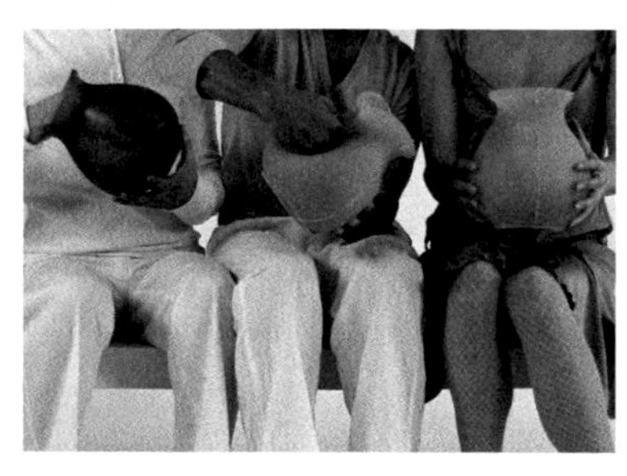

created from traditional recipes, and modern synthetic glazes. This installation might be considered an art installation. It can also be considered the experimental phase of a project. As a next step, Jongerius currently develops new colors for the industry, which are more varied and contain more layers than the synthetic colors the industry now produces. According to Jongerius, the beauty of crafted pieces lies foremost in the age-old knowledge and skills of the makers. Therefore, she decided to create pieces in which the many possibilities of the workshop surfaces. The underlying motive for researching this topic lies in her aim to create a stronger bond between users, objects, and makers. Decoration is usually a flat image added to the surface, with great communicative power. In the object *Frog Table*, decoration has become almost a living creature. A being that cannot be ignored at your table. This experimental piece has no industrial spin-off yet, but I am sure that will come.

neuen Stoffen und übersah dabei offensichtlich, dass er dadurch das ursprüngliche Konzept letztlich zerstörte. Man könnte fragen, ob die Geschichte der neuen Version die gleiche Kraft hat wie das ursprüngliche Konzept. Und man könnte fragen, ob das wichtig ist.[3]

Die folgenden Designstücke haben im Laufe der Zeit nicht an Bedeutungskraft verloren. Experimentelle Designarbeiten eröffnen neue Perspektiven auf die Funktionalität, die Vergangenheit und die Beziehungen zwischen Design und anderen kulturellen Bereichen, wie etwa *Tree Trunk* und *Kokon Furniture* von Jurgen Bey, mit denen er den Begriff der Konvention im Design hinterfragt. Mit der Gestaltung der *Ear Chairs* werden neue Perspektiven des Bürodesigns für die Ausstattung von Arbeits- und Konferenzräumen erschlossen. Die Sessel bieten viele Möglichkeiten, verweisen jedoch auch auf die Beziehung von Möbel und Architektur, von Mensch und Objekt und zeigen diese in einem neuen Licht. Nacho Carbonell interessiert sich für die Schaffung von verspielten, kommunikativen Objekten, die die Sinne und die Vorstellungskraft anregen und die Wahrnehmung der Dinge verändern können. Die Objekte der *Skin Collection* bewegen sich eindeutig an der Grenze zur Kunst, ihre Bedeutung liegt jedoch hauptsächlich im Bereich des Designs.

Die Produktionsmaschine *Collective Works* von mischer'traxler arbeitet nur, wenn Menschen ihr Aufmerksamkeit schenken. Auf das Publikum mittels Sensoren reagierend, übersetzt die Maschine den Menschenstrom in ein Objekt, indem sie mehr und mehr Markierstifte aktiviert. Die Ergebnisse variieren in Farbe und Größe, zumal sie der schwankenden Aufmerksamkeit während der Produktionszeit entsprechen. Man könnte die gesamte Installation als faszinierende Kunstinstallation betrachten, gleichzeitig kann man sie aber auch als einen Kommentar zum Konsumverhalten verstehen, zu einer Gesellschaft, die sich daran gewöhnt hat, Dinge wegzuwerfen, aber auch zu der Notwendigkeit, Objekte wieder aufzuwerten und den Produktionsprozess, der zur Herstellung von Dingen nötig ist, neu zu überdenken.

Die Arbeiten der Designerin Hella Jongerius werden sowohl von Museen gesammelt als auch von der Industrie in hohen Auflagen produziert. An ihrem Werk kann man sehen, wie fast alle ihre experimentellen Arbeiten, in denen sie Themen wie die enge Beziehung des Menschen zu Objekten behandelt, schließlich zu industriell gefertigten Produkten werden. Mit *Soft Urn* und *Big White Pot*, die zu ihren ersten Arbeiten gehören, untersuchte sie die Oberfläche und Bedeutung verschiedener Materialien sowie die Spuren, die der Produktionsprozess hinterlässt. Mit ihren *Coloured Vases* untersucht Jongerius die unterschiedliche Wahrnehmung von Farben. Jede Vase weist

I finish this sequence of images with two installations — one made by an artist, one made by designers — which deal with the same theme but with very different results. Both were shown in the entrance area of a museum of modern art. Both installations were inspired by an old

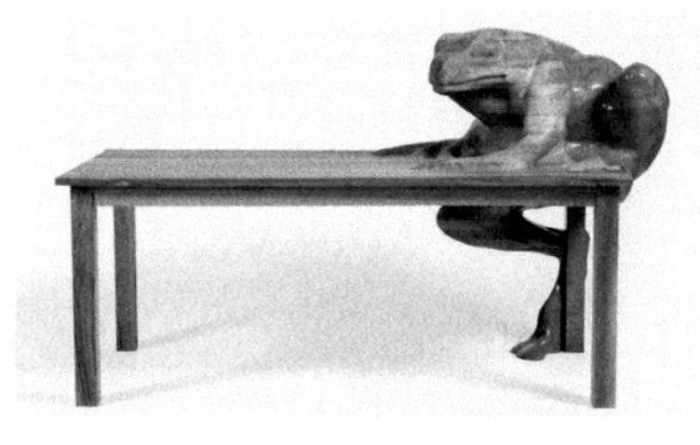

convention in the coalmines — the miners' wardrobe. The disused miners' wardrobe solved a basic problem in a clever way. To keep the coats clean and safe in such a dirty environment, each of them could be lifted from the ground. In 2008, the German artist Benjamin Bergmann [4] created an installation for the Pinakothek der Moderne in Munich, and called it *Tief Unten Tag Hell*. In the same year, Studio Wieki Somers (Wieki Somers and Dylan van den Berg) created the *Merry-Go-Round Coat Rack* for the entrance area of Museum Boijmans Van Beuningen in Rotterdam. A visitor to the museum can hang his or her coat on a coat hanger, lift it up, and put a lock on it. All coats

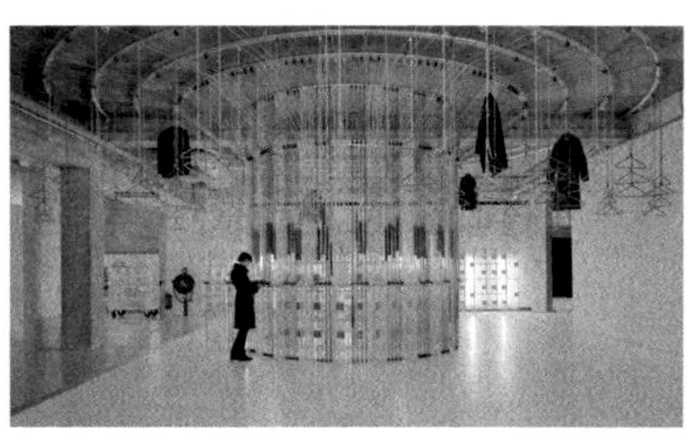

thus lifted up hang visible to everyone, dangling in the air safe and clean. Due to the interaction with the daily public, the merry-go-round constantly changes in form and color and, like a mirror, reflects what is going on in the museum. Are there many visitors or few? Are the visitors presumably old, wearing subdued colors, or are they presumably hip and young with flashy colorful coats?

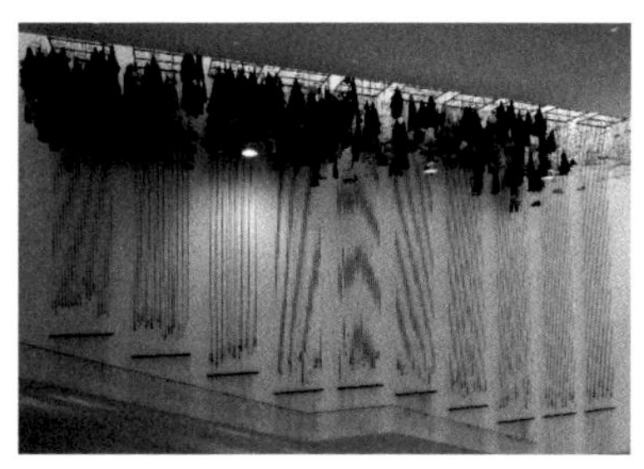

The main difference of the two works is the functionality. Bergmann's fixed selection of coats hangs still high in the air. The coats were probably once worn by people, but those people were obviously not visitors to the museum. In their current uselessness, they are reminiscent of people who probably experienced something dreadful. It's fair to conclude that, arisen from the catacombs of a mine shaft, the empty coats refer to death. Meanwhile, the coats in Museum Boijmans Van Beuningen refer to life, to the here and now. Is one installation more successful, more beautiful or interesting than the other one? No, definitely not. They represent different meanings and interpretations. The meaning of the instal-lation by Studio Wieki Somers rises beyond its functionality and mirrors the identities of the visitors to the museum, whereas Bergmann's interpretation of the old miners wardrobe finds its striking meaning in its current uselessness, somewhere in the twilight zone between entrance and museum halls. Is it important to know that one of the installations was created by an

sowohl althergebrachte Glasuren auf, die nach traditionellen Rezepten hergestellt wurden, als auch moderne, synthetische Glasuren. Diese Installation könnte man als Kunstinstallation betrachten. Sie kann auch als experimentelle Phase eines Projekts gesehen werden. Jongerius setzt diese Arbeit zurzeit fort, indem sie neue Farben für die Industrie entwickelt, die variantenreicher und vielschichtiger sind als die bislang produzierten. Laut Jongerius liegt die Schönheit von handwerklichen Produkten hauptsächlich in dem alten Wissen und Können der Handwerker. Deshalb entschied sie sich, Stücke zu schaffen, in denen die vielfältigen Möglichkeiten der Werkstatt zutage treten. Dies geschieht in der Absicht, eine direktere Verbindung zwischen dem Benutzer, dem Objekt und dem Produzenten zu schaffen. Dekoration ist für gewöhnlich ein flaches, nachträglich auf die Oberfläche aufgetragenes Bild von nicht allzu großer kommunikativer Kraft. Bei dem Objekt *Frog Table* hingegen ist die Dekoration fast zu einem lebendigen Wesen geworden. Ein Wesen, das sich am Tisch kaum ignorieren lässt.

Zum Abschluss dieser Reihe möchte ich zwei Installationen vorstellen, die beide dasselbe Thema behandeln, allerdings mit sehr unterschiedlichen Resultaten – die eine von einem Künstler, die andere von Designern geschaffen. Beide Installationen wurden in den Eingangsbereichen von Museen für moderne Kunst gezeigt und beide wurden durch eine tradierte Einrichtung in den Kohleminen inspiriert: die Garderobe der Bergleute – sogenannte Püngelhaken in der Kaue [Anmerkung des Herausgebers]. Diese heute nicht mehr gebräuchlichen Garderoben lösten ein grundsätzliches Problem auf intelligente Weise: Um die Mäntel in einer solch schmutzigen Umgebung sauber und sicher aufzubewahren, konnten sie emporgezogen werden. 2008 schuf der deutsche Künstler Benjamin Bergmann[4] eine Installation für die Pinakothek der Moderne in München und nannte sie *Tief Unten Tag Hell*. Im selben Jahr schuf das Studio Wieki Somers (Wieki Somers und Dylan van den Berg) den *Merry-Go-Round Coat Rack* für den Eingangsbereich des Museums Boijmans Van Beuningen in Rotterdam. Die Museumsbesucher können ihre Mäntel auf Bügel hängen, sie hochziehen und mit einem Schloss sichern. So hängen alle Mäntel für jeden sichtbar dort, baumeln aber sicher und sauber über ihren Köpfen. Dank der Interaktion mit dem Publikum verändert sich das Karussell permanent in Form und Farbe und reflektiert wie ein Spiegel das, was im Museum geschieht. Sind viele Besucher da oder wenige? Sind die Besucher vielleicht alt und tragen gedeckte Farben oder sind sie hip und jung, worauf auffallend farbenfrohe Mäntel hinweisen würden?

Der Hauptunterschied zwischen den beiden Arbeiten liegt in ihrer Funktionalität. Bergmanns festgelegte Auswahl von Mänteln hängt

artist and the other by a designer? I think it's not important for the viewer. However, for the creation process it's very important. Most likely both installations could only have been born in their respective disciplines.

DESIGN ≠ ART ≠ CRAFT

In 1905, Paul Cézanne wrote a letter to his friend Emile Bernard, in which he said: "Je vous dois la vérité en peinture, et je vous la dirai." ("I owe you the truth in painting, and I will tell it to you.") That was a rather ambitious plan: to reveal the truth in painting! Apparently Cézanne saw it as his artistic obligation to reveal the truth in painting, not via words, but via his paintings. It inspired French philosopher Jacques Derrida to deal with important notions from art history. In *La Vérité en Peinture*, he deconstructed those notions in order to reveal their underlying assumptions, implications, and consequences. "… I am occupied with folding the great philosophical question of the tradition (*'What is art?' 'the beautiful?' 'representation'? 'the origin of the work of art?' etc.*) onto the insistent atopics of the *parergon*: neither work (*ergon*) nor outside the work [*hors d'oeuvre*], neither inside nor outside, neither above nor below …" Here Derrida asks: "What is the work itself, the *ergon*? Is it the painted canvas only? Would then the frame be merely an addition to the work? A *parergon*, an outside of the work? Or is the frame part of the work itself?"[5]

According to the philosopher Immanuel Kant, an overly decorated frame of a painting would distract too much from the work itself. According to Derrida, this implies that some frames can distract from the content, others less or not at all. Then he starts to prove that any frame has an influence on the reading of the work, regardless of whether it is ornamented or simple[6] "… The parergon is a form which has as its traditional determination not that it stands out but that it disappears, buries itself, effaces itself, melts away at the moment it deploys its greatest energy."[7]

We have grown accustomed to the idea that there's a clear division and hierarchy between *work* and "those aspects that are outside the work." At the very moment it deploys its greatest energy by showing the work inside the frame at its best, the frame seems to disappear from our awareness. As if it no longer exists. This is not true, says Derrida. "A parergon comes against, beside, and in addition to the ergon … but it does not fall to one side…. Neither simply outside nor simply inside. Like an accessory that one is obliged to welcome on board, on the border[8]…. It (parergon) is no longer merely around the work. That which it (parergon) puts in place — the instances of the frame, the title, the

statisch in der Luft. Die Mäntel sind wahrscheinlich einmal von Menschen getragen worden, aber diese Menschen waren offensichtlich nicht die Besucher dieses Museums. Angesichts ihrer gegenwärtigen Nutzlosigkeit assoziiert man Personen, denen möglicherweise etwas Schreckliches widerfahren ist. Der Schluss liegt nahe, dass die leeren, aus den Katakomben einer Mine aufgestiegenen Mäntel auf den Tod verweisen. Im Gegensatz dazu beziehen sich die Mäntel im Museum Boijmans Van Beuningen auf das Leben und das Hier und Jetzt. Ist die eine Installation gelungener, schöner oder interessanter als die andere? Nein, bestimmt nicht. Sie repräsentieren jeweils andere Bedeutungen und Interpretationsmöglichkeiten. Die Bedeutung der Installation von Studio Wieki Somers sprengt die Grenzen der Funktionalität, indem sie die Identitäten der Museumsbesucher spiegelt, während Bergmanns Interpretation der alten Bergarbeitergarderobe – irgendwo in der Grauzone zwischen Eingang und Museumsräumen – durch den Verlust ihrer Funktion tief beeindruckt. Ist es wichtig, zu wissen, dass eine der Installationen von einem Künstler, die andere von Designern geschaffen wurde? Ich glaube, für den Betrachter ist es nicht wichtig. Für den Schaffensprozess ist es jedoch sehr wichtig. Beide Installationen konnten aller Wahrscheinlichkeit nach nur in ihrer jeweiligen Disziplin entstehen.

DESIGN ≠ KUNST ≠ HANDWERK

1905 schrieb Paul Cézanne in einem Brief an seinen Freund Emile Bernard „Je vous dois la vérité en peinture, et je le vous dirai" („Ich schulde Ihnen die Wahrheit in Malerei und ich werde sie Ihnen sagen"). Das war ein recht ehrgeiziger Plan: Offensichtlich sah Cézanne seinen künstlerischen Auftrag darin, die Wahrheit in Malerei, und nicht etwa in Worten, zu offenbaren. Das inspirierte den französischen Philosophen Jacques Derrida dazu, sich mit zentralen Begriffen der Kunstgeschichte zu befassen. In *La Vérité en Peinture* dekonstruierte er diese Begriffe, um die ihnen innewohnenden Annahmen, Implikationen und Konsequenzen freizulegen. „(...) ist damit beschäftigt, die große philosophische Frage der Tradition (‚Was ist Kunst?', ‚das Schöne?', die Repräsentation?', der Ursprung des Kunstwerkes?' und so weiter) auf die insistierende Atopik des *Parergons* zurückzubiegen: Weder Werk (*ergon*) noch Beiwerk (*hors d'oeuvre*), weder innen noch außen, weder unten noch oben (...)."Hier fragt Derrida „Was ist das Werk selbst, das *Ergon*? Ist es nur die bemalte Leinwand? Wäre dann der Rahmen ein bloßer Zusatz zu dem Werk? Ein *Parergon,* ein Außerhalb-des-Werks? Oder ist der Rahmen Teil des Werks selbst?". [5]

signature ... — does not stop disturbing the internal order of discourse on painting, its works, its commerce, its evaluations, its surplus-values, its speculation, its law, and its hierarchies."[9] All the aspects that are apparently outside of the work itself matter. The parergon is the frame around the painting. And the parergon is also the title of the painting, the title of the sculpture, the installation. It's the signature of the artist. It's the spatial and philosophical context in which the work is shown, etc. We need only to think of Marcel Duchamps' *Fountain* and Andy Warhol's *Brillo Box*. "Parerga have a thickness, a surface which separates them not only from the integral inside, from the body proper of the ergon, but also from the outside, from the wall on which the painting is hung ... then, step by step, from the whole field of historical, economic, political inscription in which the drive to signature is. No *theory*, no *practice*, no *theoretical practice* can intervene effectively in this field if it does not weigh up and bear on the frame, which is the decisive structure of what is at stake ..."[10]

Whether we like it or not: the notion of value in art is not defined by some mysterious objective quality. The meaning of art depends on a set of external factors as well. The context of a work defines how we view, experience, and read it.

DESIGN ≠ ART

Naturally, this is not only true for art — it's also true for any design. As a consequence, any designer needs to take into account the *hors d'oeuvre*, the outside of the work, the parerga of design. As we have seen in recent decades, art objects, crafted objects, and designs often appear to have similar traits. They can even look the same. Due to this sameness, a division between Design, Art, and Craft seems to have become obsolete, unnecessary. It is widely welcomed that disciplines merge, that borders vanish. But is this helpful for a designer or an artist when creating new steps in design, new steps in art? I think not. In my view, it is certainly not helpful to deny the differences, as this merging of fields tends to deny the differences between the parerga in the various fields. The parerga in art are different from the parerga in design, which are different from the parerga in craft. I will address this with the next work, the only example I give of works I am personally very critical about: Studio Job, consisting of the designers Job Smeets and Nynke Tynagel created a plan for a private fence. It was inspired by the gate at Buchenwald, a German concentration camp during World War II. The gate features a hanging bell, two chimneys joined by a billow of smoke — a nod to crematoriums — as well as the same inscription found on the Buchenwald Gate. The inscription and

Dem Philosophen Immanuel Kant zufolge lenkt der übermäßig geschmückte Rahmen eines Gemäldes zu sehr vom Werk selbst ab. Daraus folgert Derrida, dass einige Rahmen vom Inhalt ablenken können, andere hingegen weniger oder gar nicht. Dann weist er nach, dass jeder Rahmen einen Einfluss auf die Interpretation des Werks hat, gleichgültig, ob er verziert oder schlicht ist.[6] „… das *Parergon* ist eine Form, deren traditionelle Bestimmung es ist, sich nicht abzuheben, sondern zu verschwinden, zu versinken, zu verblassen, in dem Augenblick zu zerfließen, wo es seine größte Energie entfaltet."[7] Wir haben uns daran gewöhnt, dass es eine klare Unterscheidung und Hierarchie zwischen „Werk" und „jenen Aspekten außerhalb des Werkes" gibt. Gleichzeitig wird alle Energie darauf gerichtet, das Werk in seinem Rahmen möglichst gut zur Geltung kommen zu lassen, der Rahmen selbst entschwindet unserer Wahrnehmung. Als ob er nicht mehr existierte. Das ist nicht wahr, sagt Derrida. „Ein *Parergon* tritt dem *ergon* (…) entgegen, zur Seite und zu ihm hinzu, aber es fällt nicht beiseite (…) weder einfach außen noch einfach innen; wie eine Nebensache, die man verpflichtet ist, am Rande, an Bord aufzunehmen…)."[8] „Es [das *Parergon*] ist nicht mehr allein um das Werk herum angesiedelt. Das, was es aufstellt – die Instanzen des Rahmens, des Titels, der Signatur (…) und so weiter – hört nicht mehr auf, die *interne* Ordnung des Diskurses über Malerei, ihre Werke, ihren Handel, ihre Aufwertungen, ihren Mehrwert, ihre Spekulationen, ihr Recht und ihre Hierarchien durcheinanderzubringen."[9] Alle Aspekte, die offensichtlich außerhalb des Werkes selbst liegen, sind wichtig. Das Parergon ist der Rahmen um das Bild. Und das Parergon ist auch der Titel des Bildes, der Titel der Skulptur, der Installation. Es ist die Signatur des Künstlers. Es ist der räumliche und philosophische Kontext, in dem das Bild gezeigt wird et cetera. Man denke nur an Marcel Duchamps *Fountain* oder Andy Warhols *Brillo Box*. „Die *Parerga* haben Dichte, eine Oberfläche, die sie nicht allein (…) vom ganzheitlichen Inneren, vom eigentlichen Körper des Ergon, sondern ebenso vom Außen trennt, von der Mauer, an der das Bild angebracht ist (…) sodann, nach und nach, vom ganzen Feld der historischen, ökonomischen und politischen Einschreibung, auf dem der Antrieb zur Signatur (…) erzeugt wird. Keine *Theorie*, keine *Praxis*, keine *Theorie-Praxis* kann wirksam in dieses Feld eingreifen, wenn sie nicht (auf) den Rahmen abwägt [Nachdruck legt], die entscheidende Struktur des Einsatzes (…)."[10]

the title read: "Suum Cuique," meaning *to each according to his or her own merits*.[11] There was a tremendous uproar in the media in Holland when these images were presented, and eventually the whole plan was cancelled as the commissioner withdrew the commission. The designers maintained in all interviews that they "were using an iconography that is part of our history." They also claimed they were artists and that art's aim after all is to shock. These are two curious lines. Artists? Both are trained as designers. Their pieces are in a few museums and private collections, but does this mean their works are art pieces? And does it mean they are artists? Second strange line: "Art's aim is to shock." Were does that come from? Is it art's aim to shock or provoke? And don't artists have an artistic and social responsibility; can't they be kept accountable for what they communicate through their work? There's another design they made at the same time,

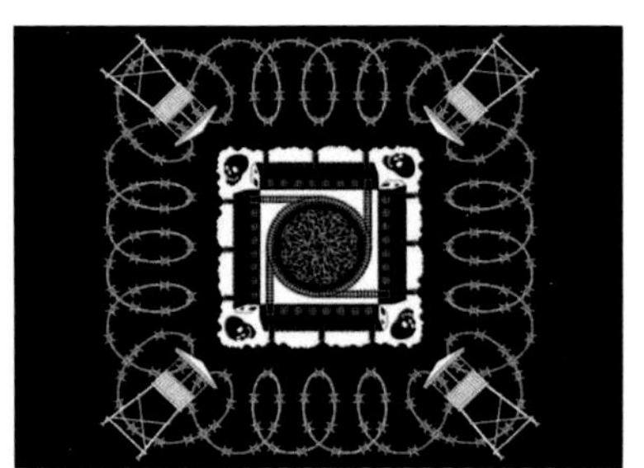

which also refers to Buchenwald: a styling of shocking symbols. If an artist or a designer intends to shock the audience, the shock should mean something, should accomplishsomething. Should offer a better understanding of a theme. What in my view is shocking here is the mere styling of offensive symbols without taking their content and the consequences of playing with them seriously.

The contexts of design, art, and craft are so different that forgetting about them turns the venture of all these professions into a mere play of visual likenesses, in which styling and preconceived assumptions seem to take the lead. In order to create Crossovers, to cross borders, one must know the borders. The word "crossover" already points to this. In order to create multidisciplinary cooperation in a sensible and effective way, one must know the essence and the historical meanings of each discipline and what can be viewed as the elements that are inevitably linked to them. The frame and the pedestal, as well as the white cube of the museum and the gallery are linked primarily to painting and sculpture.

However, designs are also presented in galleries and put on pedestals within museum spaces. This offers interesting challenges both to designers and to curators. If one decides to take a functional object, a design, out of its usual context and put it on a pedestal, this has a meaningful consequence, which adds meaning to the design, offers new perspectives on the design, revealing layers of meaning that usually escape from the attention. A curator can consciously play with these notions, but being unaware seems to be a weird option.

Ob es uns gefällt oder nicht: der Begriff des Wertes in der Kunst definiert sich nicht über irgendeine mysteriöse objektive Qualität. Die Bedeutung von Kunst hängt auch von einer Reihe externer Faktoren ab. Der Kontext eines Werkes bestimmt, wie wir es sehen, erleben und interpretieren.

DESIGN ≠ KUNST

Natürlich gilt dies nicht nur für die Kunst, sondern auch für Design. Folglich muss jeder Designer das *hors d'oeuvre* berücksichtigen, das außerhalb des Werkes Liegende, die Parerga des Designs. Seit einigen Jahrzehnten können wir beobachten, dass Kunstobjekte, handgefertigte Objekte und Designstücke oft ähnliche Merkmale haben. Sie können sogar gleich aussehen. Aufgrund dieser Gleichartigkeit scheint eine Unterscheidung zwischen Design, Kunst und Handwerk obsolet geworden zu sein. Eine Verschmelzung der Disziplinen, ein Verschwinden der Grenzen wird weithin begrüßt. Aber hilft dies dem Designer oder dem Künstler, der neue Wege im Design oder in der Kunst beschreiten möchte? Ich glaube nicht. Es ist sicherlich wenig hilfreich, die Unterschiede zu negieren, da diese Vermischung der Disziplinen zu einer Negierung der Unterschiede zwischen den Parerga der verschiedenen Felder führt. Die Parerga der Kunst unterscheiden sich von jenen des Designs, die sich wiederum von denen des Handwerks unterscheiden. Dies möchte ich anhand der nächsten Arbeit thematisieren, dem einzigen hier präsentierten Werk, das ich überaus kritisch sehe: Das Designduo Studio Job (Job Smeets und Nynke Tynagel) entwarf einen Zaun für ein privates Anwesen. Dabei ließen sie sich von dem Eingangstor des deutschen Konzentrationslagers Buchenwald inspirieren. Das von Studio Job entworfene Tor ist mit einer hängenden Glocke und zwei Schornsteinen verziert, die durch hervorquellenden Rauch verbunden sind – ein Verweis auf die Krematorien –, und der gleichen Inschrift ausgestattet, die auch das Tor des Lagers Buchenwald trug. Inschrift und Titel lauten: „Suum Cuique", „Jedem das Seine". Die Präsentation dieser Entwürfe löste einen immensen Sturm der Entrüstung in den holländischen Medien aus und schließlich wurde das Projekt aufgegeben, da der Auftraggeber seinen Auftrag zurückgezogen hatte. Die Designer beharrten in allen Interviews darauf, dass sie „eine Ikonografie benutzten, die Teil unserer Geschichte ist". Außerdem sagten sie, sie seien Künstler und das Ziel der Kunst sei schließlich, zu schockieren. Das sind zwei eigentümliche Aussagen. Künstler? Beide sind ausgebildete Designer. Ihre Stücke finden sich in einigen Museen und Privatsammlungen; aber bedeutet dies, dass ihre Arbeiten Kunstwerke sind? Und kann man daraus ableiten, dass sie deshalb

As a conclusion, I want to stress the necessity to take the parerga of design into account when creating designs and creating design exhibitions. What are the parerga of design? What is its most essential aim? What is its context? Is it functionality? Which roles do the materials and techniques, and all the historical and cultural meanings that are linked to them, play? In which context does design find its natural habitat? In the end, all of these elements define how we — the viewers and users — view, experience, and *read* a work. If one passes the borders, other meanings, other parerga have to be taken into account. Those other parerga afford a design with different meanings. A designer who proves he is well aware of this and can play with its meanings is the German designer Konstantin Grcic. In his exhibition design *Industrial Design Parade*, which he created for Museum

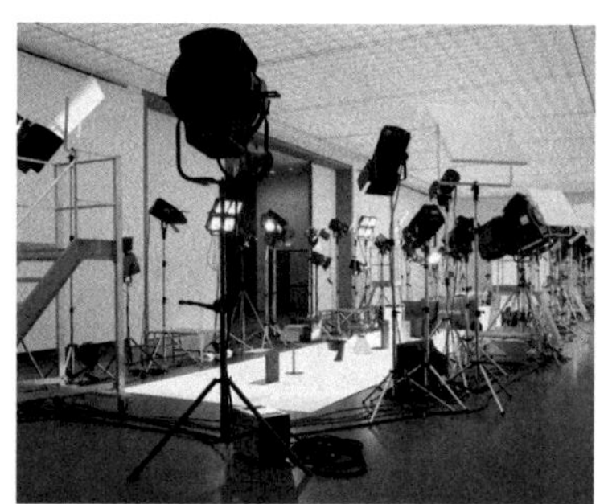

Boijmans Van Beuningen in Rotterdam in 2006, mere functional objects were exposed on a catwalk like structure in a museum of modern art. The white cube space and the elevated floor refer to a pedestal, symbolizing eternal art value. The catwalk, however, refers to the evasive nature of fashion. Its value depends on the moment, on trends and on taste. By exhibiting his functional designs in this way, Grcic says: the meaning of design is no longer about functionality, of which we might say their value is evasive and depends on trends and changing times. The meaning, and value, has stretched beyond the confines of the discipline. The discourse on contemporary design takes place within a temple of high art, which used to afford to its objects the value of eternity. What are the consequences of these changes? The object plays the leading role in Grcic's installation. The user has no significance, he can merely peep through the bundle of flashing lights that allow him a glimpse on the functional objects that he may not use within this context, thereby forcing him to consider the deeper meanings hidden within.

Künstler sind? Die zweite seltsame Aussage: Ziel der Kunst ist es, zu schockieren. Woher stammt dieses Argument? Zielt Kunst darauf ab, zu schockieren oder zu provozieren? Und haben Künstler nicht eine künstlerische und soziale Verantwortung, können sie nicht für das verantwortlich gemacht werden, was sie durch ihr Werk kommunizieren? In derselben Zeit entwickelte Studio Job noch ein weiteres mit Buchenwald im Zusammenhang stehendes Designobjekt: einen Entwurf mit schockierenden Symbolen. Wenn ein Künstler oder Designer die Betrachter schockieren möchte, sollte der Schock einen Sinn haben und zum besseren Verständnis eines bestimmten Themas beitragen. Das Schockierende besteht hier meiner Ansicht nach darin, dass provozierende Symbole als reines Stilmittel verwendet werden, ohne ihren Inhalt oder die Konsequenzen des Spiels mit derlei Symbolik ernst zu nehmen. Der Kontext von Design, Kunst und Handwerk ist jeweils so unterschiedlich, dass die Ignoranz desselben die Projekte dieser Berufsfelder zu einem reinen Spiel mit visuellen Ähnlichkeiten werden lässt, in dem das Styling und vorgefasste Ansichten die Führung zu übernehmen scheinen. Um ein Crossover zu schaffen, die Grenzen zu überschreiten, muss man die Grenzen kennen. Um auf sensible und effektive Art zu einer multidisziplinären Zusammenarbeit zu kommen, muss man die Grundlagen und die historische Bedeutung jeder Disziplin sowie die unvermeidlich mit ihnen zusammenhängenden Gegebenheiten kennen.

Der Rahmen und der Sockel, der weiße Raumwürfel des Museums und der Galerie sind in erster Linie mit Malerei und Skulptur verknüpft. Allerdings werden auch Designobjekte in Galerien ausgestellt und in Museen auf Sockeln präsentiert. Dies bedeutet sowohl für Designer als auch für Kuratoren eine interessante Herausforderung. Wenn man sich dafür entscheidet, ein funktionales Objekt, ein Designstück, aus seinem gewohnten Umfeld zu lösen und es auf einen Sockel zu stellen, dann fügt man dem Designstück eine Bedeutungsebene hinzu, eröffnet neue Perspektiven auf das Design, die normalerweise der Aufmerksamkeit entgehen. Ein Kurator kann bewusst mit diesen Ideen spielen. Unbewusst damit umzugehen, wäre eine befremdliche Alternative.

Zum Schluss möchte ich betonen, wie wichtig es bei der Gestaltung und beim Kuratieren von Designausstellungen ist, die Parerga des Designs zu beachten. Was sind die Parerga des Designs? Was ist dessen wichtigstes Ziel? Was ist der Kontext? Was ist die Funktion? Welche Rolle spielen Materialien und Techniken und all die historischen und kulturellen Konnotationen, die mit ihnen zusammenhängen? In welchem Kontext findet Design einen natürlichen Lebensraum? Schließlich definieren all diese Elemente, wie wir, die Betrachter und

Nutzer, eine Arbeit sehen, erleben und „lesen". Wenn man Grenzen überschreitet, müssen andere Bedeutungen, andere Parerga Beachtung finden. Diese anderen Parerga laden ein Designobjekt mit neuen Bedeutungen auf. Ein Designer, der zeigt, dass er sich dessen sehr bewusst ist und mit diesen Bedeutungsaspekten spielen kann, ist der deutsche Designer Konstantin Grcic. In seiner Ausstellungsgestaltung der „Industrial Design Parade" für das Museum Boijmans Van Beuningen in Rotterdam 2006 wurden rein funktionale Gegenstände auf einer Art Catwalk im Kontext eines modernen Kunstmuseums präsentiert. Der weiße Würfel des Museumsraums und die erhöhte Ebene verweisen auf einen Sockel und symbolisieren so den immerwährenden Wert der Kunst. Der Catwalk hingegen verweist auf den schwankenden Charakter der Mode. Ihr Wert wird vom Moment, dem Trend und dem Geschmack bestimmt. In dieser Form der Präsentation seiner funktionalen Designobjekte verweist Grcic auf den Umstand, dass die Bedeutung des Designs nicht mehr in dessen Funktionalität liegt, von der wir sagen können, dass ihr Wert schwankend ist und von Trends und Änderungen des Zeitgeschmacks abhängt. Die Bedeutung und der Wert haben die Begrenzungen der Disziplin überschritten. Der Diskurs über zeitgenössisches Design findet in einem Tempel der Hochkultur statt, der seit jeher den dort ausgestellten Objekten den Wert der Ewigkeit beifügt. Was sind die Konsequenzen dieser Veränderungen? Das Objekt spielt in Grcics Installation die Hauptrolle. Der Benutzer ist unwichtig, er kann lediglich durch ein Gewirr von Blitzlichtern spähen, das ihm einen Blick auf die funktionalen, in diesem Kontext nicht benutzbaren Objekte gewährt und er wird so gezwungen, die ihnen innewohnenden tieferen Bedeutungsebenen wahrzunehmen.

Figures

Notes

This essay is based on a transcription of the speech by Louise Schouwenberg held on 5.12.2012 at the symposium Art and / or Design? at ABK Stuttgart.

[1] Martin Heidegger: *Being and Time,* translated by John Macquarrie & Edward Robinson, London 1962
[2] Naturally, it would be easy to show bad examples of this phenomenon. Bad examples of very expensive pieces that are exclusively targeted to an elitist market generally don't mean anything — neither as art nor as design.
[3] Tejo Remy, *Rag Chair* (fabrics of New York based company Maharam), 2011
[4] The word *Bergmann* means coal miner.
[5] Jacques Derrida: *The Truth in Painting.* Translated by Geoffrey Bennington and Ian McLeod. Chicago 1987, p. 61
[6] This is not the usual way of thinking about the parergon.
[7] Jacques Derrida: *The Truth in Painting.* Translated by Geoffrey Bennington and Ian McLeod. Chicago 1987, p. 61
[8] Ibid., p. 9
[9] Ibid., pp. 60–1
[10] Ibid., pp. 61
[11] In German: "Jedem das Seine."

Abbildungen

Anmerkungen

Dieser Beitrag basiert auf einer Transkription des Vortrages von Louise Schouwenberg, gehalten am 5.12.2012 im Rahmen des Symposiums Kunst und/oder Design? an der ABK Stuttgart.

[1] Martin Heidegger: *Sein und Zeit,* Tübigen 1927 (11. veränderte Auflage, Tübingen 1967) Drittes Kapitel §§ 61–66, S. 301–331
[2] Es wäre natürlich leicht, schlechte Beispiele für dieses Phänomen aufzuzeigen. Schlechte Beispiele wären sehr teure, ausschließlich auf einen elitären Markt ausgerichtete Stücke, die prinzipiell weder im Hinblick auf Kunst noch auf Design von Bedeutung sind.
[3] Tejo Remy: *Rag Chair* (Stoffe des New Yorker Unternehmens Maharam), 2011
[4] Sic!
[5] Jacques Derrida: *Die Wahrheit in der Malerei,* Wien 1992, S. 24–25
[6] Dies weicht von der üblichen Auffassung des Parergon ab.
[7] Jacques Derrida: *Die Wahrheit in der Malerei,* Wien 1992, S. 82
[8] Ebda. S. 74
[9] Ebda. S. 25
[10] Ebda., S. 80f

Alex Coles

Von Designart zur Transdisziplinarität

—

Beyond DesignArt / Towards the Transdisciplinary

Eleven years ago, I wrote an article for the London-based magazine *Art Monthly* focussing on the work of a generation of artists who became visible in the mid- to late-nineteen-nineties — including, Pae White, Jorge Pardo, Tobias Rehberger, and Andrea Zittel — which expanded on a newly coined term introduced by Jo Scanlan earlier that year: that term was *designart*.[1] The following year, I began to research the deeper history of the subject of art's interface with design — I say art's interface with design rather design's interface with art advisedly because it was the impact of design on art practice that interested me at this point — by going back to the Arts and Crafts movement in the UK and the historical avant-gardes in Russia, Holland, and Germany. The trajectory I traced, in my manuscript, then ran up through Henri Matisse and Sonia Delaunay — both artists who practice what I called a tactics of simultaneity, by running many different platforms in parallel with one another (think of Delaunay with her paintings and fabrics and Matisse with his paintings and interiors) — and up through Ed Ruscha, Donald Judd and Richard Artschwager. I found the key thing that happened in the postwar period was that not only did design begin to be denigrated — with the likes of Ed Ruscha being invited to design *Artforum* in the early nineteen-sixties, which he did, but not being invited to be in its pages as an artist until much later — but art that had been impacted by design was also disparaged. Certain types of formalist painting from the period were, for example, referred to as merely "good design" — a nod to the middle-brow MoMA exhibitions of the nineteen-fifties.

I planned a publication about these investigations into the phenomenon of *designart*. After much to-and-fro, with most publishers being visibly nervous about publishing a book on something they'd never heard of (namely, *designart*), Tate finally agreed to work with me on the book, which after being researched and written in 2002–2004 was published in 2005.[2] The book met with successful sales but heavy criticism: Rick Poynor immediately published a long critique of it titled "Art's Little Brother" in *Icon;* his diatribe turning on the fact that design itself was not a considered part of the equation, and that designers had in fact been working in the gray area between art and design for decades.[3] While at the time, this was not my interest — it was, as I said before, design's impact on art that drew me — Rick was nevertheless spot-on: a whole area had been overlooked. There then followed some attempt to negotiate this dis-balance with my edited anthology *Design and Art,* released through MIT Press/Whitechapel in 2007.[4] Besides running over some of the same history that *DesignArt* had covered, my remit had broadened to include the concerns of designers

Vor elf Jahren schrieb ich für das Londoner Magazin *Art Monthly* einen Artikel über eine Künstlergeneration, die Mitte der 1990er Jahre auf den Plan getreten war – darunter waren Pae White, Jorge Pardo, Tobias Rehberger und Andrea Zittel. Darin beschäftigte ich mich mit einem von Jo Scanlan kurz zuvor neu eingeführten Begriff: *designart*.[1] Im darauffolgenden Jahr begann ich mich eingehender mit der Geschichte der Kunst an der Schnittstelle zum Design zu befassen – ich spreche hier ganz bewusst von der Kunst an der Schnittstelle zum Design und nicht etwa von Design an der Schnittstelle zur Kunst, da mich zum damaligen Zeitpunkt der Einfluss des Designs auf die künstlerische Praxis besonders interessierte – zumal ich die Arts-and-Crafts-Bewegung in England und die historische Avantgarde in Russland, Holland und Deutschland untersuchte. Das Spektrum, das ich in meinem Artikel behandelte, reichte von Henri Matisse und Sonia Delaunay – beides Künstler, die das umsetzten, was ich als Taktiken der Simultaneität bezeichnet habe, indem sie sich parallel verschiedener Medien bedienten (man denke nur an Delaunays Gemälde und Stoffentwürfe oder Matisses Gemälde und Innenausstattungen) – bis hin zu Ed Ruscha, Donald Judd und Richard Artschwager. Die wichtigste Erkenntnis daraus war, dass in der Nachkriegszeit Design wenig Wertschätzung erhielt – was sich am Beispiel von Ed Ruscha verdeutlichen lässt, der in den frühen 1960er Jahren eingeladen wurde, das *Artforum* zu gestalten, um erst sehr viel später auch als Künstler darin in Erscheinung zu treten –, und dass auch jene Kunst, die durch Design beeinflusst war, eine Abwertung erfuhr. Bestimmte Formen formalistischer Malerei wurden damals zum Beispiel lediglich als „gutes Design" bezeichnet, ein Verweis auf die für ein durchschnittliches Publikum konzipierten MoMA-Ausstellungen der 1950er Jahre.

Über diese Untersuchungen zu dem Phänomen der *designart* plante ich eine Publikation. Doch da die meisten Verlage sich offensichtlich scheuten, ein Buch über etwas zu publizieren, von dem sie noch nie gehört hatten, wie zum Beispiel *designart,* gab es ein ziemlich langes Hin und Her, bis sich der Verlag Tate Publishing schließlich bereiterklärte, mit mir zusammenzuarbeiten, sodass das Buch 2005 erscheinen konnte.[2] Die Publikation war kommerziell sehr erfolgreich, stieß jedoch auf heftige Kritik: Rick Poynor veröffentlichte unter der Überschrift „Art's Little Brother" sofort eine lange Kritik in *Icon,* wobei sein Verriss hauptsächlich darauf abhob, dass Design für sich genommen noch nie eine anerkannte Größe gewesen sei und dass Designer eigentlich schon jahrzehntelang in einer Grauzone zwischen Kunst und Design gearbeitet hätten.[3] Das interessierte mich damals eigentlich nicht, doch hatte Rick vollkommen recht: Ein ganzes

such as Dieter Rams, and his dialogue with Richard Hamilton, and Hella Jongerius, M/M Paris, Mevis & ven Deursen, and Experimental Jetset. Cheekily, Rick's critique of *DesignArt* was also included.

Between 2002 and 2007 there had been rampant commercial activity in the field of *designart,* with DesignMiami and Phillips de Pury's *designart* auctions entering the field and art galleries such as Gagosian exhibiting the work of designers like Marc Newson. As a result, sales of both of my books increased. But there was some confusion: why didn't my book include Marc Newson and Ron Arad, two of the heroes of the scene? My answer was simple: because they don't explore new creative aspects of the interface between art and design. Occasionally DesignMiami and Phillips de Pury's focus on what they also referred to as *designart* led to some interesting things, such as Martino Gamper's series of performances of works on Gio Ponti, or El Ultimo Gritto's blown glass works. But for the most part, it was ugly: there were tables and chairs with bits of twig sticking out from them. Worse still, neither promoted dialogue about design's interface with art: *designart* was obviously good for business but bad for the brain. Through the rest of 2007 and 2008, I sat and watched as the spectacle of *designart* reached new heights until things turned sour in late 2008. Then in 2009, I was invited to give a paper at a conference organized by Gareth Williams and hosted by the V&A Museum based on a new exhibition there called Telling Tales, which spotlighted the works of the likes of Tord Boonje — i.e., the aforementioned designer of the "twigged" chairs. The paper was titled "Beyond DesignArt" and was based on my brief visits to the studios of designers such as Konstantin Grcic, artists like Jorge Pardo and Olafur Eliasson, and architects like Shigeru Ban. The paper argued for the urgent necessity to move beyond *designart,* which by now had resulted in a static synthesis of aspects of art with design, and towards a more mobile notion of the interrelations between creative disciplines. This entailed a shift, I argued, from the interdisciplinary towards the transdisciplinary.

One way to begin defining transdisciplinarity, I argued, is by clearly distinguishing it from interdisciplinarity.[5] In "From Work to Text" (1971), Roland Barthes describes how interdisciplinarity begins "when the solidarity of the old disciplines breaks down … in the interests of a new object and a new language, neither of which has a place in the field of sciences, that were to be brought peacefully together."[6] For Barthes, "this unease in classification," is "precisely the point from which it is possible to diagnose a certain mutation" in a discipline.[7] What Barthes terms a "certain mutation" assumes that the disciplines will remain in place — just in an altered form — and this is precisely what has

Forschungsgebiet war außer Acht gelassen worden. Also versuchte ich in der Folge, dieses Manko auszugleichen, und gab die Anthologie *Design and Art* heraus, die 2007 bei MIT Press/Whitechapel erschien.[4] Darin wurde eine Reihe von Aspekten, die schon in *DesignArt* Thema waren, behandelt. Allerdings hatte ich mein Spektrum erweitert, um Designer wie Dieter Rams und seine Auseinandersetzung mit Richard Hamilton sowie Hella Jongerius, M/M: Paris, Mevis und van Deursen und Experimental Jetset mit aufzunehmen. Recht keck erschien auch Ricks Kritik zu *DesignArt* in diesem Band.

Von 2002 bis 2007 entwickelte sich *designart* in kommerzieller Hinsicht rasant. Die Messe DesignMiami und Phillips de Purys *designart*-Auktionen stiegen in diesen Bereich ein und Galerien wie Gagosian stellten Arbeiten von Designern wie Marc Newson aus. Die Folge war, dass sich meine Bücher besser verkauften. Allerdings war man leicht irritiert: Warum wurden darin Marc Newson und Ron Arad nicht erwähnt, zwei der Idole der Szene? Meine Antwort lautete schlicht: weil sie keine neuen kreativen Aspekte der Schnittstelle zwischen Kunst und Design erschlossen. Gelegentlich entstand bei DesignMiami und Phillips de Pury im Rahmen der Beschäftigung mit *designart* etwas Interessantes, wie etwa Martino Gampers Performancereihe zu Arbeiten von Gio Ponti oder El Ultimo Gritos Arbeiten aus mundgeblasenem Glas. Das meiste war jedoch hässlich: Tische und Stühle, aus denen Fragmente von Zweigen herausragten. Schlimmer noch war, dass bei beiden kein Dialog über die Schnittstelle von Design und Kunst entstand: *designart* war offensichtlich gut fürs Geschäft, aber schlecht für den Kopf. 2007 und 2008 lehnte ich mich zurück und beobachtete, wie das Spektakel um die *designart* neue Höhepunkte erreichte, bis die Stimmung Ende 2008 kippte. 2009 wurde ich eingeladen, bei einer von Gareth Williams und dem Victoria & Albert Museum veranstalteten Konferenz einen Vortrag zu halten. Das Ganze fand im Zusammenhang mit der Ausstellung „Telling Tales" statt, die Arbeiten von Designern wie Tord Boontje in den Mittelpunkt stellte, jene bereits genannten Designer mit den „verzweigten" Stühlen. Der Vortrag hieß „Beyond DesignArt" (dt.: „Jenseits von DesignArt") und war das Ergebnis einiger Kurzbesuche in den Studios von Designern wie Konstantin Grcic, Künstlern wie Jorge Pardo und Olafur Eliasson sowie Architekten wie Shigeru Ban. In dem Vortrag vertrat ich die Auffassung, dass es dringend nötig sei, über *designart* hinauszugehen, die mittlerweile zu einer erstarrten Synthese aus Aspekten von Kunst und Design geworden war, um einen beweglicheren Denkansatz hinsichtlich der Beziehungen zwischen den kreativen Disziplinen zu entwickeln. Dies, so führte ich aus, zöge einen Wechsel vom Interdisziplinären zum Transdisziplinären nach sich.

happened with *designart*. By contrast, a number of Felix Guattari's lesser-known, collaboratively written essays from the nineteen-sixties are devoted to developing a working definition of transdisciplinarity. In "From Pluridisciplinarity to Transdisciplinarity via the Complex Objects which Compose the Object World and its Interdependant Hypercomplexity," Guatarri explains how the transdisciplinary is a call to rethink relations between science, society, politics, ethics, and aesthetics through a new meta-methodology. For Guatarri and Vilar, it is crucial that this meta-methodology be adequate to discussing the continually expanding field of relations they perceived to be unfolding before them. They claim: "... the organization of human culture by disciplines belongs to the past," but remain a "necessary point of departure in the advance towards domains of knowledge that involve new practices and changing styles of individual and collective life."[8]

In 1970, Jean Piaget developed the following description of transdisciplinarity at the international workshop: "Finally, we hope to see succeeding to the stage of interdisciplinary relations a superior stage, which should be 'transdisciplinary', i.e., which will not be limited to recognize the interactions and or reciprocities between the specialized areas of research, but which will locate these links inside a total system without stable boundaries between the disciplines."[9] Piaget is describing a new space of knowledge that is, he says, "without stable boundaries between the disciplines" — a space that is at once between, across, and beyond all disciplines. This space can only be generated by what Guattari and Vilar refer to as "new practices," as previous forms of interdisciplinary practice are exceeded. It was precisely these *new practices* that I then turned to: spending up to three months in the studios of Konstantin Grcic Industrial Design, Studio Olafur Eliasson, Jorge Pardo Sculpture, and Åbäke, using the participant observation method developed by anthropologists to study a particular environment and community. The environment I chose was the studio and the community inhabiting it.[10]

An eight-hundred-dollar copy of Diego Velazquez's *Las Meninas* (1656), executed by local artisan Jesus Chucho, hangs in the reception room cum micro studio of Jorge Pardo's private house in Merida, the Yucatan. The painting is the very image of self-reflexivity — nothing less than a representation of the classical form of representation itself. Michel Foucault was the first to trace the perspectival line traveling from between the eyes of the individuals represented in *Las Meninas* — the King and Queen of Spain and their court — through the real picture, and projecting into the space of the beholder. The dynamic

Als Ansatz zur Definition der Transdisziplinarität schlug ich eine klare Abgrenzung von der Interdisziplinarität vor.[5] In „Vom Werk zum Text" (1971) beschreibt Roland Barthes, wie Interdisziplinarität wirksam wird, „wenn der Zusammenhang der alten Disziplinen (...) zugunsten eines neuen Objekts und einer neuen Sprache aufbricht, die beide nicht im Feld der Wissenschaften lagen, die man friedlich zu konfrontieren trachtete".[6] Weiter heißt es bei Barthes: „(...) eben anhand dieser Schwierigkeit einer Klassifizierung" einer Disziplin „läßt sich eine gewisse Wandlung feststellen".[7] Was Barthes hier eine „gewisse Wandlung" nennt, setzt voraus, dass die Disziplinen erhalten bleiben, wenn auch in veränderter Form, und das ist genau das, was mit der *designart* geschehen war. Felix Guattari hingegen hat sich in einigen seiner weniger bekannten, in Zusammenarbeit mit Sergio Vilar in den 1960er Jahren entstandenen Essays der Entwicklung einer gültigen Definition der Transdisziplinarität gewidmet. In „From Interdisciplinarity to Transdisciplinarity via the Complex Objects which Compose the Object World and its Interdependant Hypercomplexity" erklärt Guattari, dass die Transdisziplinarität ein Aufruf zum Überdenken der Beziehungen zwischen Wissenschaft, Gesellschaft, Politik, Ethik und Ästhetik durch eine neue Meta-Methodologie ist. Für Guattari und Vilar ist es entscheidend, dass diese Meta-Methodologie der Diskussion des sich permanent erweiternden Beziehungsgeflechts, das sich vor ihnen auftut, gerecht wird: „(...) die Organisation der menschlichen Kultur in Disziplinen gehört der Vergangenheit an", bleibt aber „ein notwendiger Ausgangspunkt für den Weg zu neuen Wissensbereichen, die neue Praktiken und einen veränderten Lebensstil sowohl des Individuums als auch des Kollektivs erfordern".[8]

1970 entwickelte Jean Piaget auf einem internationalen Workshop mit dem Titel „Interdisciplinarity: Teaching and Research Problems in Universities" die folgende Beschreibung der Interdisziplinarität: „Schließlich hoffen wir, dass dem Stadium der interdisziplinären Beziehungen ein höheres Stadium folgt, das als ‚Transdisziplinarität' zu bezeichnen wäre, das also nicht darauf beschränkt ist, die Beziehungen und Wechselwirkungen zwischen speziellen Forschungsgebieten zu erkennen, sondern diese Verbindungen innerhalb eines umfassenden Systems ohne feste Grenzen zwischen den Disziplinen auszumachen in der Lage ist."[9] Piaget beschreibt hier einen neuen Wissensraum, der, wie er sagt, „ohne feste Grenzen zwischen den Disziplinen" ist, einen Raum, der gleichzeitig zwischen allen Disziplinen liegt, sie durchdringt und über sie hinausgeht. Dieser Raum kann nur durch das entstehen, was Guattari und Vilar als „neue Praktiken" bezeichnet haben, da die bislang gültigen Formen der interdisziplinä-

established here between the image of the painter working in his makeshift studio, his subject, and the viewer, is then telescoped through the mirror at the back of the room in which the scene takes place. The reflection in the mirror produces what Foucault refers to as "a metathesis of visibility."[11] And it's surely the painting's capacity to produce this metathesis — an additional commentary on the mechanics of representation — that has caused Pardo to commission the copy and hang it in such a prominent position in the first place.

Velazquez gazes out at us over the course of a dinner in the humid evening air at the house in Merida, summer 2010. All I can see are Foucault's lines of convergence reaching into the room and the dynamics in the painting being played out in contemporary costume. The group sitting around the table eating consists of: the artist; his patrons Claudia and Roberto Ramirez Hernandez, who have commissioned an enormous hacienda from Pardo an hour's drive away in Tecoh; the project's architects Mecky Reuss and Anna Paula Ruiz Galindo, from Jorge Pardo Sculpture, and me. Pardo never says anything about the painting and no one ever asks.

Next morning, the painting is in shadow, and the design of the house itself comes alive. While the other houses on this nondescript backstreet in Merida typically let the outside in by leaving their doors wide open, Pardo's house (2002–2009), achieves the same effect by opening both the roof and each of the ground floor rooms to the central atrium. Dotted around each room are billowing lamps and chairs that Pardo designed and fabricated in the Yucatan. The patterns hand-painted on to the walls of the reception room reference a series of paintings Pardo began producing in Los Angeles in 2008. Even though the reception room cum micro studio is where the main action always takes place, the raw, winding concrete staircase towards the back of the house is undoubtedly its conceptual centerpiece. This tightly wound spiral orients the viewpoint of the person ascending it. During the first few steps, a blank back wall blocks any possible view making it all the more dramatic when, a few steps further, the kitchen and the swimming pool come into view. A few more steps and the bedroom comes into focus; a few more again, and the upper level is reached with its panoramic views of the city. The effect of walking up the spiral staircase is akin to the way a slide carousel works, clicking between images as it rotates. The dynamic of this mechanism generates a reflection on the composition of the house and its place within the broader composition of the city. In other words, the staircase serves the same office as the mirror in *Las Meninas* — providing a metathesis on the very object being experienced.

ren Praxis ausgeschöpft sind. Und genau diesen „neuen Praktiken"
wandte ich mich zu, indem ich annähernd drei Monate lang die Studios
von Konstantin Grcic Industrial Design, Olafur Eliasson, Jorge Pardo
Sculpture und Åbäke im Hinblick auf ihr spezielles Arbeitsumfeld und
ihre Gemeinschaft als teilnehmender Beobachter auf quasi anthropo-
logische Weise untersuchte. Das Arbeitsumfeld, das ich mir ausge-
sucht hatte, war das Studio und das Kollektiv, das darin tätig war.[10]

In Jorge Pardos Privathaus in Merida, Yukatan, hängt in dem mit einem
Ministudio verbundenen Empfangsraum eine von dem lokalen Künst-
ler Jesus Chucho für 800 Dollar gefertigte Kopie von Diego Velazquez'
Las Meninas (1656). Das Gemälde ist ein Urbild der Selbstrefle-
xion – nicht weniger als eine Repräsentation der klassischen Form der
Repräsentation selbst. Michel Foucault war der erste, der beobachtet
hat, wie die perspektivischen Linien zwischen den auf *Las Meninas*
Dargestellten – dem König und der Königin von Spanien und ihrem Hof-
staat – durch den Bildraum selbst verlaufen, um dann in den Raum des
Betrachters vorzudringen. Die Spannung, die hier zwischen dem in seinem provisorischen Atelier arbeitenden Maler, seinem Motiv und dem
Betrachter entsteht, überlagert sich durch den Spiegel im Hintergrund
des Raumes mit dem Geschehen, das darin stattfindet. Die Reflexion
im Spiegel bringt das hervor, was Foucault als „eine Metathese
der Sichtbarkeit" bezeichnet hat.[11] Ganz bestimmt war diese kraft
des Bildes entstehende Metathese – ein weiterer Kommentar zu den
Mechanismen der Repräsentation – das, was Pardo dazu veranlasst
hat, die Kopie in Auftrag zu geben und sie dann an so prominenter
Stelle aufzuhängen.

Während eines Abendessens im Sommer 2010 schaut Velazquez
uns durch die schwüle Abendluft in dem Haus in Merida an. Ich
erkenne nur Foucaults Fluchtlinien, die in den Raum hineinreichen und
die Dynamik des Bildes, die sich in barockem Kostüm präsentiert. Um
den Tisch versammelt sind: der Künstler Jorge Pardo, seine Auftraggeber Claudia und Roberto Ramirez Hernandez, die ihn mit der Gestaltung einer riesigen Hacienda im eine Stunde Fahrt entfernten Tecoh
beauftragt haben, die Architekten des Projekts, Mecky Reuss und
Anna Paula Ruiz Galindo von Jorge Pardo Sculpture und ich. Pardo verliert nie ein Wort über das Gemälde und es fragt auch niemand danach.

Am nächsten Morgen liegt das Gemälde im Schatten und der Entwurf
des Hauses selbst wird lebendig. Während die anderen Häuser in dieser
unscheinbaren Nebenstraße von Merida traditionsgemäß durch weit
geöffnete Türen einladen, entsteht dieser Effekt in Pardos Haus (2002–
09) durch die Öffnung des Daches und jedes Raums im Erdgeschoss auf

Galindo and Reuss arrive and search the house for a packet of cigarettes. Even the numerous non-American members of the studio favor the American *health* brand: American Spirit. Inspiration, it seems, is contingent upon cigarettes, and when they run out, which is often — this brand evidently being difficult to obtain in Mexico — then inspiration wanes. Fortunately, after a concerted group effort, Pardo's stash is located in one of the kitchen cabinets and the interview can begin. Galindo explains: "The studio culture is beginning to develop at the shop, where everything is fabricated. Our office is set up in one room of our house in the center of Merida. The carpenters we work with who produce the doors, the chairs, the cabinets ... constitute a different kind of studio culture."

An hour goes by and no sign of Pardo; Reuss and Galindo are deciding which of them will face the unfortunate task of waking him up. Suddenly inspiration strikes Reuss and he turns to me: "You want to participate in the culture of the studio, so you wake him. We have to do this every damn day!" So informal is the way Jorge Pardo Sculpture operates, the visitor soon becomes implicated — perhaps too much so. On this occasion, Reuss' frustration is so convincing and I am so keen to get going that eventually I accept and climb the staircase to the artist's room (acknowledging the metathesis one more time on the way). The day is beginning to warm up and moisture drips down the ornate door of Pardo's room; the air-conditioning is obviously on full blast.

The journey to Tecoh begins slowly only after lunch in Merida at Pardo's favorite fish restaurant, Muelle 8, and a quick stop at his workshop. The usual lunch routine developed over the years in LA — where studio members gather at a large table at noon everyday to enjoy Mexican-style chicken and pork dishes prepared by the studio's cook — is less ceremonious in Merida, with just a small table being shared by the three of them, and on this occasion four. After shots of tequila and espressos, it's time to go. As we drive to the workshop on the outskirts of the city, Pardo responds to my first question about the role of the studio in his practice. The window of the Toyota 4 x 4 is down, American Spirit in hand, Pardo quips, "Alex, wherever I am, the studio is." This would appear flippant if it were not for the fact that a significant proportion of Pardo's time in the Yucatan is spent in the car. Rather than having everything — home, studio, workshop, and office — under one roof like in LA, in the Yucatan, Pardo's studio is dispersed between his house in Merida, Reuss and Galindo's house nearby, the workshop and the site itself. The car is Jorge Pardo Sculpture's mobile studio, which is not uncommon for Angelinos.

das zentrale Atrium hin. Jeder Raum ist mit von Pardo entworfenen, in Yukatan hergestellten Lampen und Stühlen in sich üppig wölbenden Formen ausgestattet. Die handgemalten Muster, die die Wände des Empfangsraums schmücken, gehen auf eine Serie von Bildern zurück, die Pardo 2008 in Los Angeles begonnen hat. Obwohl sich die meisten Aktivitäten in dem Empfangsraum mit dem Ministudio abspielen, ist die rohe, gewundene Betontreppe im hinteren Teil des Hauses zweifelsohne das konzeptuelle Kernstück. Diese sich eng windende Spirale lenkt die Blicke des Emporsteigenden. Während der ersten Schritte blockiert eine leere schwarze Wand jeden Ausblick – umso dramatischer ist der Eindruck, wenn nach wenigen Schritten Küche und Swimming-pool ins Blickfeld geraten. Noch einige Stufen und man erreicht das Schlafzimmer, nach wenigen Schritten ist man in der obersten Ebene angekommen, von der aus man einen Panoramablick über die Stadt hat. Der Effekt, den das Emporsteigen auf der spiralförmigen Treppe auslöst, erinnert an einen Diaprojektor mit Karussellmagazin, bei dem durch die Rotation immer neue Bilder freigegeben werden. Diese Dynamik löst eine Reflexion über die Komposition des Hauses und seine Lage in der Stadtstruktur aus. Anders gesagt, erfüllt die Treppe denselben Zweck wie der Spiegel auf *Las Meninas*, nämlich eine Metathese zu dem Objekt zu generieren, mit dem man sich gerade befasst.

Galindo und Reuss kommen an und durchsuchen das Haus nach einem Päckchen Zigaretten. Sogar die vielen nicht-amerikanischen Mitarbeiter des Studios bevorzugen die „gesunde" amerikanische Marke American Spirit. Die Inspiration, so scheint es, hängt von Zigaretten ab und wenn diese ausgehen, was oft der Fall ist, da diese Marke in Mexiko offenbar schwer erhältlich ist, schwindet die Inspiration dahin. Nach einer konzertierten Gruppenaktion findet sich glück-licherweise Pardos Geheimversteck in einem der Küchenschränke und das Interview kann beginnen. Galindo erklärt: „Die Studiokultur hat ihren Ausgangspunkt in der Werkstatt, in der alles hergestellt wird. Unser Büro befindet sich in einem Raum unseres Hauses im Zentrum von Merida. Die Tischler, mit denen wir arbeiten und die die Türen, Stühle und Schränke herstellen (...), lassen eine ganz eigene Art der Studiokultur entstehen."

Eine Stunde vergeht und von Pardo ist nicht das Geringste zu sehen. Reuss und Galindo entscheiden, wer die unliebsame Aufgabe überneh-men soll, ihn zu wecken. Plötzlich hat Reuss eine Eingebung und wendet sich an mich: „Du möchtest doch an der Kultur des Studios teilhaben, also kannst du ihn ja wecken. Wir machen das jeden verdammten Tag!" So ungezwungen ist der Betrieb bei Jorge Pardo Sculpture, der Besucher wird sofort mit einbezogen – vielleicht mehr, als ihm lieb ist. In diesem

As we begin the hour-long drive to the hacienda in Tecoh, I press Pardo about his thoughts on the notion of the post-studio artist. With no music playing — a detail common to each of his studios — Pardo contemplates the question for a minute, flicks some ash out of the window, and clears his throat: "[John Baldessari] is representative of a particular period and that period still plays quite large today," he says. "Basically, the guys in his generation were hippies and they really believed that by changing the representation of their studio model they would change art. Their naivety has led to the total recuperation of their original project." Pardo pauses, I press that there must be more, as the *post-studio* concept has been important to a number of generations of LA artists, and he continues: "Where previously I felt that the notion of the post-studio practitioner was bullshit, now I think this concept is actually the only thing interesting about the work. At its core is an attempt to resolve the moral issue of not making something yourself. If you look at post-studio art from that generation, it's always about legitimizing being an artist who doesn't actually make things with their hands. If you are in a culture and place where you are actually surrounded by manual work, then there is much less of an issue here and there is no need for such theoretical gymnastics to legitimize your feelings about it. At root, this version of the post-studio artist, with all of its hang-ups, is very Southern Californian.

There have been countless essays devoted to the post-studio artist but no one has ever put it quite like that before. And as Pardo runs through it a second time with more depth and nuance, his reading of Baldessari's distance from the means of production gains more weight. From weeks spent with Jorge Pardo Sculpture in LA in the winter of 2008/2009, it's clear how this remoteness is at odds with Pardo's own studio setup, which seems to me more like that of his contemporary, Andrea Zittel, who is currently engaged in a long-term, large-scale project of her own in Nevada. But Pardo disagrees: "It's all about controlling the frame, and each of us has a different way of doing that. But the essential difference between our bodies of work is that Rirkrit [Tirivanija] and Andrea strive to establish a dynamic that includes presenting themselves as very much a part of the picture. As a result, their work becomes highly emotive and at times even narcissistic. Channeling the point of entry and exit in this way is a deeply problematic gesture as it prescribes where the discourse on the work begins and ends. I think of what I do as my job — a job I very much like and one I am very well remunerated for."

Fall ist Reuss' Frustration so nachvollziehbar und ich bin so wild darauf, loszulegen, dass ich mich schließlich einverstanden erkläre und die Treppe zum Zimmer des Künstlers emporsteige (wobei ich auf dem Weg einmal mehr die Metathese wahrnehme). Der Tag beginnt, wärmer zu werden und Feuchtigkeit perlt von der verzierten Tür zu Pardos Zimmer – die Klimaanlage läuft offensichtlich auf Hochtouren.

Die Fahrt nach Tecoh beginnt gemächlich nach einem Mittagessen in Merida im Muelle 8, Pardos Lieblingsfischrestaurant, und einem kurzen Zwischenstopp in seiner Werkstatt. Die im Laufe der Jahre in Los Angeles entwickelte Mittagsroutine, bei der die Mitarbeiter des Studios sich jeden Tag um einen großen Tisch versammeln und die vom Studiokoch zubereiteten mexikanischen Gerichte aus Huhn und Schwein genießen, ist in Merida weniger zeremoniell. Hier teilen sich nur drei von ihnen – heute vier – einen kleinen Tisch. Nach Tequila und Espresso wird es Zeit zum Aufbruch. Auf dem Weg zu der Werkstatt am Rande der Stadt antwortet Pardo auf meine erste Frage nach der Rolle des Studios für seine Arbeit. Das Fenster des Toyota-Geländewagens ist geöffnet und Pardo, eine American Spirit in der Hand, scherzt: „Alex, wo ich bin, da ist das Studio." Das könnte etwas flapsig wirken, wüsste man nicht, dass Pardo in Yukatan einen beträchtlichen Anteil seiner Zeit im Auto verbringt. Anders als in LA, wo alles – Wohnung, Studio, Werkstatt und Büro – unter einem Dach ist, verteilt sich Pardos Studio in Yukatan über sein Haus in Merida, das nahegelegene Haus von Reuss und Galinda, die Werkstatt und das Baugrundstück selbst. Das Auto ist das mobile Studio von Jorge Pardo Sculpture – für in Los Angeles Beheimatete kein ungewohnter Zustand.

Auf unserer einstündigen Fahrt zu der Hacienda in Tecoh befrage ich Pardo zu seiner Ansicht über das Phänomen des Post-Studio-Künstlers. Wie in allen seinen Studios läuft auch hier im Auto keine Musik. Pardo denkt einen Moment über die Frage nach, schnippt etwas Asche aus dem Fenster und räuspert sich: „[John Baldessari] ist Repräsentant eine[r] bestimmten Epoche und diese Epoche ist noch heute von ziemlicher Bedeutung", sagt er. „Die Leute in seiner Generation waren im Grunde Hippies, die wirklich glaubten, dass sie durch eine veränderte Repräsentation ihres Studiomodells die Kunst verändern könnten. Allein dank ihrer Naivität ist es ihnen gelungen, ihre ursprünglichen Ideen zurückzugewinnen." Pardo macht eine Pause, ich insistiere, dass das nicht alles sein kann, da das Post-Studio-Konzept eine ganze Reihe von Künstlergenerationen in Los Angeles bestimmt hat. Also fährt er fort: „Während ich früher dachte, die Idee der Post-Studio-Praxis wäre Quatsch, glaube ich heute, dass dieses Konzept eigentlich das einzig Interessante an dieser Arbeit ist. Genau genommen

Even though a section of Pardo's house on Sea View Lane in LA was temporarily used as a studio, and a large part of the current studio in the Alhambra region of the city has recently been turned into his apartment, Pardo's proximity to the studio does indeed remain a very practical one. The studio is where he goes to do his job; if the studio is temporarily located within his house, then this is for purely practical reasons.

Eventually, we arrive at Tecoh. Because the site can only be accessed through a bumpy overgrown path, for once an American driving a 4 x 4 seems appropriate. The hacienda is an extensive project, spanning 300 hectares of jungle and entered through a dilapidated archway. A few hundred yards down the track and the first building comes into view. Opening the door of the car, the humid air of the Yucatan rushes in and competes with the conditioned air of the Toyota and soon wins.

What was once a stone ruin has now been expanded and functions as a two-bedroom unit with an accommodating kitchen. As we enter through the front porch, Pardo stops dead, scrutinizing the sliding mechanism recently fitted onto the screen. Through an unlit cigarette fitted between his lips, he mumbles: "These look fine, Mecky. Should we put a mosquito curtain in front of them?" Reuss pauses for a moment, and then responds, "Yes, we can do that but we'll have to design something special so it doesn't look too stuck on. If the mesh was built into the screen it would have been better — it'll be difficult now to make it look integral to the structure," his words barbed with more than a little frustration. Galindo agrees. There is silence. Pardo pats the empty upper pocket in his coarse linen shirt, rapidly being dampened by humidity and sweat. "Mecky, you gotta light?" he asks, cutting the conversation short.

We walk around the back of the building, and I can't help but notice a trace of another doorway just to the right of where the door now stands. "There was … a little mistake," says Reuss, noticing the way I'm staring at the position of the old doorframe, "but the great thing about being down here is that you can move things around because of the cost of labor." From observing the three of them, it's clear that the site is treated as an extension of both their macro studio in LA and their micro studio in Merida. The hacienda is a constantly evolving model, with important structural decisions being taken at the point of construction and then being revoked, developed, or changed at any time. The skilled Mexican artisans facilitate this back-to-front process, whether they are carpenters, working on the doors and furniture, or laborers working with cement and bricks. But they can make mistakes too: during an earlier visit I witness how Reuss and Galindo's com-

ist es der Versuch der Auflösung des moralischen Konflikts darüber, dass man etwas nicht selbst herstellt. Wenn man sich die Post-Studio-Kunst dieser Generation anschaut, geht es immer um die Rechtfertigung des Künstlers, der Dinge nicht eigenhändig herstellt. Wenn du dich jedoch an einem Ort, in einer Kultur befindest, in der du von Handwerksarbeit umgeben bist, dann ist das kaum noch ein Thema und es bedarf nicht mehr dieser theoretischen Verrenkungen, um dein Verhältnis dazu zu legitimieren. Im Grunde ist dieser Typ des Post-Studio-Künstlers, mit all seinen Blockaden, sehr südkalifornisch."

Es gibt unzählige Essays über den Post-Studio-Künstler, aber so wie Pardo hat ihn noch niemand durchleuchtet. Und als Pardo sich ein zweites Mal mit mehr Tiefe und nuancierter äußert, wird seine Interpretation von Baldessaris Distanzierung von den Produktionsmitteln noch konturierter. Im Winter 2008/09 habe ich einige Wochen bei Jorge Pardo Sculpture in LA verbracht. Diese Erfahrung macht mir klar, wie sehr Pardos Studiosituation zu Baldessaris Zurückgezogenheit im Widerspruch steht. Sie erinnert eher an die seiner Zeitgenossin Andrea Zittel, die momentan an einem großen Langzeitprojekt in Nevada arbeitet. Aber Pardo widerspricht: „Es geht darum, den Rahmen zu definieren und wir beide tun das auf ganz unterschiedliche Weise. Aber der grundlegende Unterschied zwischen unseren Arbeiten ist, dass Rirkrit [Tirivanija] und Andrea eine Dynamik erzeugen möchten, in der sie selbst sich ganz deutlich als Teil des Werkes präsentieren können. Das macht ihre Arbeiten sehr emotional und manchmal sogar narzisstisch. Es ist höchst problematisch, den Punkt des sich Hinein- und Hinausbegebens auf diese Weise zu kanalisieren, da dies vorschreibt, wo der Diskurs über die Arbeit beginnt und endet. Das, was ich tue, begreife ich als einen Job – einen Job, den ich sehr mag und der sehr gut bezahlt ist."

Obwohl ein Teil von Pardos Haus an der Sea View Lane in LA zeitweise als Studio genutzt und ein großer Teil des derzeitigen Studios in Alhambra kürzlich zu seiner Wohnung umgewandelt wurde, hat Pardos Nähe zum Studio hauptsächlich pragmatische Gründe. Ins Studio geht er, um seine Arbeit zu tun. Wenn das Studio sich zeitweise in seinem Haus befindet, dann ist dies aus rein praktischen Gründen so.

Schließlich erreichen wir Tecoh. Da das Grundstück nur über einen holprigen, verwachsenen Pfad erreicht werden kann, scheint es ausnahmsweise mal sinnig, dass ein Amerikaner einen Geländewagen fährt. Die Hacienda ist ein riesiges Projekt, das sich über 300 Hektar erstreckt und durch einen baufälligen Torbogen zugänglich ist. Nach ein paar hundert Metern erblicken wir das erste Gebäude. Als wir die Wagentüren öffnen, strömt die schwüle Luft von Yukatan hinein,

puter-generated drawings for the tile laying were hung upside down on the walls of one of the buildings, while the laborers obliviously worked away. Reuss and Galindo are on-site almost every day to work with the contractor, Carlos Cuevas and his team of artisans and the laborers. This creates a loose transdisciplinary team of architects, artisans, and laborers, designing and building the structure and then detailing it. Often, the team is spread out between many different locations, but because the site is where they all meet, it becomes a creative location where new designs are generated rather than just executed.

The hacienda is framed by an archway that lies a few hundred yards down a mud track. Mushrooming from the dense jungle is the hulking central building. To the right is the main room, brightly illuminated by an enormous sliding glass door. Painted in a soft pink, the ceiling of this room consists of a series of irregularly grouped triangular shapes. The sliding glass door leads outside onto a large spiral staircase. What this staircase lacks in conceptual dynamism, it makes up for in formal lyricism. On a previous visit in late December 2009, it was just a raw, winding concrete sculpture rising out of the floor at an obtuse angle and then erratically spiraling upwards — as if a regularly shaped staircase had been violently stretched while the concrete was still wet. The staircase has a carefully welded iron balustrade, finished with a smooth wooden handrail. The ironwork is phenomenally intricate, with a once relatively simple pattern being fed through a computer program that has contorted it to an unrecognizable degree. When complete, the effect will be a continuous surface of vegetation — an infinity garden. The only visual interruptions are the reverse sides of the skylights jutting through the roof towards the sky. With the transitions between them being carefully negotiated and articulated by the studio, the central building is evidence of how sculpture, painting, architecture, and design all come together in Pardo's hacienda at Tecoh to create a total environment.

Back in the air-conditioned car, everyone soon rouses from their tropical sleepwalk through the hacienda. The conversation returns to the studio, this time focusing on its relationship to place. Pardo: "Judd is someone who had his work fabricated using post-industrial methods. At the same time, he felt the need to isolate himself in the overpowering natural landscape of the dessert. In a way, the landscape of Marfa became a kind of object in his studio. This happens with me in the Yucatan. The difference is that I'm interested in how my work has some sort of relationship to the place that can be thoroughly embedded in the studio and its output. Judd's sense of place and location was much more puritanical than mine: he left New York and established himself in

beginnt einen Zweikampf mit der klimatisierten Luft in dem Toyota und gewinnt in wenigen Augenblicken.

Was einmal eine steinerne Ruine gewesen ist, wurde ergänzt und ist jetzt eine Wohneinheit mit zwei Schlafzimmern und einer Küche. Als wir über die Veranda gehen, bleibt Pardo plötzlich stehen und untersucht den Schiebemechanismus, der kürzlich auf die Scheibe montiert worden ist. Eine unangezündete Zigarette zwischen den Lippen murmelt er: „Die sehen gut aus. Sollen wir ein Moskitonetz davorsetzen?" Reuss hält einen Moment inne und erwidert: „Ja, das können wir machen. Aber wir müssen etwas Besonderes entwerfen, damit es nicht zu aufgeklebt aussieht. Es wäre besser gewesen, das Netz in das Fenster zu integrieren – jetzt wird es schwierig, es so aussehen zu lassen, als sei es Teil der Konstruktion." Die Frustration gibt seinen Worten Schärfe. Galindo stimmt ihm zu. Es wird still. Pardo klopft auf die leere Brusttasche seines groben Leinenhemdes, das schon von Schwüle und Schweiß durchnässt ist. „Mecky, hast du Feuer?", fragt er und beendet so das Gespräch.

Wir gehen um die Rückseite des Hauses und ich kann nicht umhin, unmittelbar rechts von der jetzigen Tür die Spuren einer Türöffnung zu erkennen. „Das war … ein kleiner Fehler", sagt Reuss, nachdem er bemerkt, wie ich auf die Stelle mit dem alten Türrahmen starre, „aber das Tolle hier ist, dass man Dinge einfach ändern kann, weil die Arbeitskraft so günstig ist." Wenn man die drei beobachtet, wird klar, dass sie diesen Ort als eine Erweiterung des großen Studios in LA und des kleinen Studios in Merida betrachten. Die Hacienda ist ein Projekt in stetiger Entwicklung, bei dem während des Baus wichtige, die Konstruktion betreffende Entscheidungen getroffen oder zurückgezogen und jederzeit neu entwickelt oder verändert werden können. Die gelernten mexikanischen Handwerker ermöglichen diesen ungewöhnlichen Schaffensprozess, seien sie nun Tischler, die Türen oder Möbel bauen, oder Arbeiter, die mit Zement und Ziegeln umgehen. Aber auch sie können Fehler machen: Bei einem früheren Besuch sah ich, wie Reuss' und Galindos computergenerierte Zeichnungen für die Verlegung von Fliesen kopfüber an der Wand eines der Gebäude hingen, während die Arbeiter offensichtlich munter vor sich hin arbeiteten. Reuss und Galindo sind fast jeden Tag auf der Baustelle, um mit dem Bauunternehmer Carlos Cuevas und seinem Team aus Handwerkern und Arbeitern zusammenzuarbeiten. So entsteht ein lockeres, transdisziplinäres Team aus Architekten, Handwerkern und Arbeitern, die die Gebäude entwerfen und bauen, um sie dann noch feiner auszuarbeiten. Oft arbeitet das Team an vielen verschiedenen Punkten gleichzeitig. Die Hacienda ist jedoch der Ort, an dem sie alle

Marfa because he found the city and the art world too stifling. The Yucatan is not a place of escape for me, but more a place where I can get things done — things that couldn't happen in LA."

Keen to emphasize the dialogue between LA and Merida, at this point Pardo interjects: "Having an axis like this can be dynamic. Things produced in the studio in Mexico can serve as a portal through which to view the studio production in LA." This is further underscored by the constant movement of Pardo, Reuss and Galindo — now constituting half of Jorge Pardo Sculpture since its contraction in the autumn of 2008 — between the two cities. "[We] tend to travel back and forth between the main studio and the micro studio," Galindo affirms. Referring to the easy chairs I witnessed being fabricated in the workshop, Galindo details how it "was designed in LA, and then redesigned, prototyped, and fabricated in Mexico." No matter where the main base of Jorge Pardo Sculpture is, the method it operates by is a type of critical regionalism in overdrive. Particularly when experienced at 150 kilometers per hour in their icy mobile studio on the way back to their micro studios in Merida.

With the hacienda, Pardo is responding to the precise characteristics of the site, the available local materials and skills, his previous architectural works, and the archaeology of discourse generated by others in the region, including Robert Smithson with his *Hotel Palenque* (1969–71) and *Incidents of Mirror Travel in the Yucatan* (1969). Dispersed between Pardo's house and the micro studio in Reuss and Galindo's house in Merida, the workshop on the outskirts of the city — and with the mobile studio trafficking them in between them all — Jorge Pardo Sculpture's studio is a totally flexible, and fully reflexive, transdisciplinary operation that generates everything from paintings and sculptures, through furniture and interiors, to entire buildings. The studio could only handle the hacienda project the way they do here: as the spaces available for construction, the artisanal skills practiced, the cost of labor, the relationship to the ruins, and an amenable and flexible client are all specific to the Yucatan, and Pardo sees no need to question any of them. As Pardo says, "It's crucial to my work that all of these skills and processes are embedded in the studio model. Without them, the work would be very different: after a while, it would become static." If Pardo's practice remained purely within the gallery system, it certainly wouldn't continually develop at the pace it does. In terms of the precise way members are added to Jorge Pardo Sculpture, and the nature of the dynamics between them, Pardo comments on his tendency to collect people who can "work in the studio on the understanding that I ... direct their particular skills and biases."

zusammentreffen, wodurch sie zu einem kreativen Zentrum wird, an dem neue Entwürfe nicht nur einfach gebaut, sondern auch stetig neu entwickelt werden.

Einige hundert Meter einen morastigen Weg hinunter öffnet ein Torbogen den Weg zur Hacienda. Wie ein Pilz erhebt sich das schwere zentrale Gebäude aus dem dichten Urwald. Zur Rechten liegt der Hauptraum, der dank einer riesigen Schiebetür aus Glas großzügig beleuchtet ist. In sanftem Rosa gestrichen, besteht die Decke dieses Raums aus einer Reihe von unregelmäßig angeordneten Dreiecksformen. Die Schiebetür aus Glas führt hinaus zu einer großen Wendeltreppe. Was dieser Treppe an konzeptueller Dynamik fehlt, macht sie durch ihre formale Poetik wett. Bei einem früheren Besuch Ende Dezember 2009 war sie lediglich eine rohe gewundene Betonskulptur, die in stumpfem Winkel aus dem Boden wuchs, um sich dann in unregelmäßigen Spiralen emporzuwinden, so als wäre eine ganz normale Treppe mit Gewalt auseinandergezogen worden, während der Beton noch feucht war. Die Treppe hat ein sorgfältig ausgearbeitetes schmiedeeisernes Geländer, das von einem glatten hölzernen Handlauf abgeschlossen wird. Die Schmiedearbeit ist überaus raffiniert: Ein zunächst recht einfaches Muster wurde mittels eines Computerprogramms bis zur Unkenntlichkeit verzerrt. Einmal fertiggestellt, wird es wirken wie ein einziges Pflanzengeflecht, ein unendlicher Garten. Die einzige sichtbare Unterbrechung sind Rückseiten der Oberlichter, die durch das Dach gen Himmel ragen. Die vom Studio sorgfältig abgewogenen und ausgearbeiteten Übergänge zwischen Skulptur, Malerei, Architektur und Design zeugen davon, wie auf Pardos Hacienda in Tecoh ein Gesamtkunstwerk entsteht.

Zurück in dem klimatisierten Wagen erwachen alle bald aus ihrem tropischen Schlafwandel über die Hacienda. Das Gespräch wendet sich wieder dem Studio und seiner Beziehung zu dem Ort zu. Pardo: „Judd ist jemand, der seine Arbeiten mit postindustriellen Methoden fabrizieren ließ. Gleichzeitig hatte er das Bedürfnis, sich in der überwältigenden Naturlandschaft der Wüste zu isolieren. In gewisser Hinsicht wurde die Landschaft von Marfa eine Art Motiv in seinem Studio. Das geschieht auch mir hier in Yukatan. Der Unterschied ist nur, dass ich mich dafür interessiere, inwiefern meine Arbeit mit dem Ort in Beziehung steht und wie diese in die Arbeit und Produktion des Studios integriert werden kann. Judds Vorstellung von Ort und Lage war sehr viel puritanischer als meine: Er hatte New York verlassen und sich in Marfa niedergelassen, weil er die Stadt und die Kunstwelt zu niederdrückend fand. Für mich ist Yukatan kein Zufluchtsort, sondern eher ein Ort, an dem ich Dinge schaffen kann – Dinge, die in LA nicht möglich wären."

Though already clear from observation, this comment demonstrates how collaboration is not the basis of Pardo's transdisciplinary studio model: instead the "artist as director" model of production is. To different degrees, Pardo is involved with every stage of every project and seldom openly defers to someone else's expertise. Were the studio to shrink back to just one, the same range of projects could still be undertaken because Pardo can design and fabricate himself — the pace would just be much slower. Due to the way they test the studio, Pardo's architectural scale works are the most dynamic aspect of his practice: his gallery-based exhibitions appear static in comparison.

Meanwhile, we return to the reception room cum micro studio in the house in Merida. With his copy of *Las Meninas*, Chucho has embedded (as Pardo would say) the Yucatan into the image. Working in a makeshift studio himself, Velazquez is surrounded in the painting by the regal court of his subjects. Instead of being engaged in their activities, which are focused on the royal couple, Velazquez knowingly stares out into our space. In the three years Velazquez has been staring into this room, Pardo has surely been one of the Spaniard's most frequent admirers. As the two artists gaze at one another, they produce an endless series of metatheses.

Um dem Dialog zwischen LA und Merida Nachdruck zu verleihen, wirft Pardo noch ein, dass „eine Achse wie diese sehr dynamisch ist. Dinge, die in Mexiko im Studio entstehen, können zu einem Portal werden, durch das man die Arbeit des Studios in LA betrachten kann." Dies wird durch Pardos, Reuss' und Galindos – die seit der Schrumpfung von Jorge Pardo Sculpture im Jahr 2008 die Hälfte des Teams ausmachen – permanentes Pendeln zwischen den beiden Orten noch unterstrichen. „[Wir] reisen für gewöhnlich zwischen dem Hauptstudio und dem Ministudio hin und her", bestätigt Galindo. Zu den Sesseln, deren Anfertigung ich in der Werkstatt zugesehen hatte, führt Galindo aus, dass „der Entwurf in LA entstand, um dann in Mexiko überarbeitet zu werden, wo auch der Prototyp hergestellt und produziert wurde." Gleichgültig, wo sich die Basis von Jorge Pardo Sculpture befindet, ist die Arbeitsmethode stets eine Art kritischer Regionalismus im Turbogang. Besonders, wenn man ihr bei 150 Kilometern pro Stunde in einem eisigen fahrbaren Studio auf dem Weg zurück in die Ministudios von Merida beiwohnen kann.

Mit der Hacienda reagiert Pardo auf die speziellen Charakteristika des Ortes, die verfügbaren regionalen Materialien und handwerklichen Fähigkeiten und die Archäologie des Diskurses, den andere in dieser Region geschaffen haben, darunter Robert Smithson mit seinen Arbeiten *Hotel Palenque* (1969–71) und *Incidents of Mirror Travel in the Yucatan* (1969). Verteilt auf Pardos Haus und das Ministudio in Reuss' und Galindos Haus in Merida, die Werkstatt am Rande der Stadt und das fahrbare Studio, das sie von einem Ort zum anderen transportiert, ist Jorge Pardo Sculpture ein total flexibles Studio mit einer vollkommen reflektierten, transdisziplinären Vorgehensweise, das von Gemälden und Skulpturen über Möbel und Innenausstattungen bis zu ganzen Gebäuden alles schaffen kann. Nur hier konnte das Studio das Hacienda-Projekt umsetzen: die räumlichen Gegebenheiten für den Bau, die handwerklichen Fähigkeiten, die Arbeitskosten, die Beziehung zu den Ruinen und ein offener, flexibler Kunde – all das ist typisch für Yukatan und Pardo sieht keine Veranlassung, irgendetwas davon infrage zu stellen. Wie Pardo sagt, „ist es für meine Arbeit ausschlaggebend, dass all diese handwerklichen Fähigkeiten und Prozesse in das Studiomodell eingebettet sind. Ohne sie wäre die Arbeit ganz anders. Nach einer Weile würde sie statisch werden." Wenn Pardos Arbeit sich lediglich in der Welt der Galerien präsentieren würde, würde sie sich bestimmt nicht in dem Tempo entwickeln, das er so vorlegen kann. Auf die Frage, nach welchen Gesichtspunkten die Mitarbeiter für Jorge Pardo Sculpture ausgewählt werden und welche Dynamik zwischen ihnen herrscht, antwortet Pardo, dass er dazu neigt, Menschen um sich zu

versammeln, die „bereit sind, unter der Bedingung im Studio zu arbeiten, dass ich (…) ihre speziellen Fähigkeiten und Neigungen steuere." Obwohl dies schon durch Beobachtung festzustellen war, verdeutlicht dieser Kommentar, dass gleichberechtigte Zusammenarbeit nicht die Grundlage von Pardos transdisziplinärem Studiomodell ist. Vielmehr gilt hier das Arbeitsmodell des „Künstlers als Regisseur". Pardo hat in unterschiedlichem Maße an jeder Arbeitsstufe jedes Projekts teil und fügt sich dabei selten der Fachkenntnis eines Mitarbeiters. Würde das Studio auf einen Mitarbeiter schrumpfen, könnte dieselbe Anzahl von Projekten durchgeführt werden, da Pardo sowohl Entwurf als auch Produktion übernehmen könnte. Nur das Tempo wäre sehr viel langsamer. Die Herausforderungen, die Pardos architektonische Arbeiten an das Studio stellen, machen sie zum dynamischsten Aspekt seiner Tätigkeit. Seine Ausstellungen in Galerien wirken im Vergleich dazu statisch.

Mittlerweile sind wir wieder im Empfangsraum mit Ministudio in dem Haus in Merida angekommen. Mit seiner Kopie von *Las Meninas* hat Chucho Yukatan in das Bild eingebettet (wie Pardo sagen würde). Auf dem Bild ist Velazquez, der selbst in einem provisorischen Atelier arbeitet, umgeben von seinen königlichen Modellen. Anstatt an ihrem Tun teilzuhaben, das wiederum auf das Königspaar bezogen ist, starrt Velazquez wissend auf uns, die Betrachter. In den drei Jahren, in denen Velazquez in diesen Raum gestarrt hat, ist Pardo ganz sicherlich einer der treuesten Bewunderer des Spaniers gewesen. Während die beiden Künstler einander anschauen, produzieren sie eine unendliche Reihe von Metathesen.

Notes

[1] Alex Coles: "Art Décor: On Art's Romance with Design", in: *Art Monthly*, 253/2002

[2] Alex Coles: *DesignArt: On Art's Romance with Design*, London 2005

[3] Rick Poynor: "Art's Little Brother", in: *Icon*, 23/2005, http://www.iconeye.com/read-previous-issues/icon-023-%7C-may-2005/art-s-little-brother-%7C-icon-023-%7C-may-2005 (last access on 02.05.2013)

[4] Alex Coles (ed.): *Design and Art*, MIT/Whitechapel 2007

[5] Different interpretations of interdisciplinarity are presented in: Alex Coles and Alexia Defert (Eds.): *The Anxiety of Interdisciplinarity*, London, 1997. The volume includes interviews with Julia Kristeva and Hal Foster and articles by Rosalind Krauss and Howard Caygill.

[6] Roland Barthes: "From Work to Text", in: *Image Music Text*, London 1977, p. 155

[7] Ibid.

[8] Felix Guattari, as quoted by Gary Genosko: "Félix Guattari: Towards a Transdisciplinary Metamethodology," in *Angelaki: The Journal of the Theoretical Humanities, Vol. No. 1* (April 2003), p. 136

[9] Jean Piaget, as quoted by Basarab Nicolescu Palestra in "Transdisciplinarity: Past, Present and Future," paper given at the Congress of Transdisciplinarity (Brazil: September, 2005), 1. Article via the website of the Centre for the Study of Transdisciplinarity: www.cetrans.com.br/novo/textos/transdisciplinarity-past-present-and-future.pdf (last access on 05.05.2010)

[10] What follows is an excerpt from the book *The Transdisciplinary Studio* (Sternberg Press, 2012) on Jorge Pardo Sculpture.

[11] Michel Foucault: "Las Meninas," *The Order of Things: An Archaeology of the Human Sciences*, Routledge 2002, p. 9

155

Anmerkungen

[1] Alex Coles: *Art Décor: On Art's Romance with Design,* in: *Art Monthly,* 253/2002

[2] Alex Coles: *DesignArt: On Art's Romance with Design,* Tate Publishing 2005

[3] Rick Poynor: „Art's Little Brother", in: *Icon,* 23/2005, auf http://www.iconeye.com/read-previous-issues/icon-023-%7C-may-2005/art-s-little-brother-%7C-icon-023-%7C-may-2005 (letzter Zugriff am 02.05.2013)

[4] Alex Coles (Hg.):*Design and Art,* MIT/Whitechapel 2007

[5] Unterschiedliche Interpretationen der Interdisziplinarität finden sich in: Alex Coles und Alexia Defert (Hg.): *The Anxiety of Interdisciplinarity,* London, 1997. Der Band umfasst Interviews mit Julia Kristeva und Hal Foster sowie Beiträge von Rosalind Krauss und Howard Caygill.

[6] Roland Barthes: „Vom Werk zum Text" , in: *Das Rauschen der Sprache. Kritische Essays IV,* Suhrkamp 2005, S. 64

[7] Ebd.

[8] Félix Guattari, zitiert nach Gary Genosko: „Félix Guattari. Towards a Transdisciplinary Metamethodology", in Angelaki: *The Journal of the Theoretical Humanities,* Bd. 8, Nr. 1 (April 2003), S. 136

[9] Jean Piaget, zitiert nach Basarab Nicolescu Palestra, in: „Transdisciplinarity: Past, Present and Future", ein Vortrag, der auf dem Congress of Transdisciplinarity (Brasilien, 2005) gehalten wurde. Artikel auf der Website des Center for the Study of Transdiscplinarity: www.cetrans.com.br/novo/textos/transdisciplinarity-past-present-and-future.pdf (letzter Zugriff am 05.05.2010)

[10] Der folgende Text ist ein Auszug aus der Publikation *The Transdisciplinary Studio* (Sternberg Press, 2012) über Jorge Pardo Sculpture.

[11] Michel Foucault: „*Die Hoffräulein*", in: ders.: *Die Ordnung der Dinge;* Frankfurt a. M. 1971, S. 31–45

El Ultimo Grito

Design aus einer post-disziplinären Perspektive
—
Design from a Post-disciplinary Perspective

For designers, design is what we do in order to understand what design is. There is no practice without theory and no theory without practice. The gardener works in his garden, develops knowledge directly linked with his activity. He has not only figured out growing techniques, understanding plants and soil, he has learned to understand if the weather is going to turn and has developed an acute sense and under-standing of weather conditions which he uses to plan his actions. He has also observed how plants and animals interact to form a closely knitted ecosystem. Unavoidably, the gardener, like the theorist, also infers from his observations his own models of the world.

> Chance (the Gardener): As long as the roots are not severed, all
> is well. And all will be well in the garden.
> President Bobby: In the garden.
> Chance (the Gardener): Yes. In the garden, growth has it seasons.
> First comes spring and summer, but then we have fall and winter.
> And then we get spring and summer again.[1]

In 2008, we wrote our post-disciplinary manifesto, delivered to the world via Twitter, making it probably the first ever *Twitterfesto*, to a grand audience of thirty followers, no retweets. It synthesized some of the ideas that we have developed through our practice and have informed our way of working.

1. The Post-Disciplinary does not acknowledge the
   disciplinary divide and refuses to conform to academic-
   or market-led definitions.
2. Design is not a discipline, but the process we humans
   use to materialize thought.
3. Knowledge is gained, analyzed, and manipulated through
   design processes.
4. The Post-Disciplinary does not engage in cultural hierarchies,
   it is interested in the message regardless of the medium.
5. The Post-Disciplinary addresses the impossibility of understanding an "object" from a sole point of view at any given time.
6. The Post-Disciplinary abandons architectures.

Underwriter of Reality

"I want a third pill!" demands Žižek in his *Pervert's Guide to Cinema*,[2] after refusing to accept Morpheus's reductionism in the famous scene from *The Matrix*,[3] arguing that: "The choice between the blue and the red pill is not really the choice between illusion and reality, of course, the matrix is a machine for fictions, but these are fictions which already structure our reality, if you take away from our reality the

Wir als Designer verstehen Design als eine Tätigkeit, um zu begreifen, was Design ist. Es gibt keine Praxis ohne Theorie und keine Theorie ohne Praxis. Der Gärtner arbeitet in seinem Garten und entwickelt ein Wissen, das direkt mit seiner Tätigkeit verknüpft ist. Er muss sich nicht nur mit Anbautechniken beschäftigen, etwas von Pflanzen und Erde verstehen, sondern auch wissen, ob das Wetter umschlagen wird, also die Wetterbedingungen gut einschätzen können, um seine Tätigkeit zu planen. Er beobachtet, wie Pflanzen und Tiere interagieren und so ein eng verwobenes Ökosystem bilden. Zwangsläufig leitet der Gärtner, ebenso wie der Theoretiker, sein Weltbild von seinen Beobachtungen ab.

Chance (der Gärtner): Solange die Wurzeln nicht abgetrennt werden, ist alles in Ordnung. Und alles wird gut sein im Garten.
Präsident Bobby: Im Garten.
Chance (der Gärtner): Ja. Im Garten wächst alles den Jahreszeiten gemäß. Zuerst kommen Frühling und Sommer, aber dann kommen Herbst und Winter. Und dann kommen wieder Frühling und Sommer.[1]

2008 haben wir unser post-disziplinäres Manifest geschrieben und es über Twitter verbreitet, an ein großes Publikum von 30 Followers, keine Retweets – es ist vermutlich das erste *Twitterfesto*. Darin sind einige der Ideen zusammengefasst, die wir im Laufe unserer Tätigkeit entwickelt und die wiederum unsere Arbeitsweise beeinflusst haben.

1. Das Post-Disziplinäre erkennt die Aufteilung der Disziplinen nicht an und verweigert sich einer akademischen oder marktorientierten Definition.
2. Design ist keine Disziplin, sondern der Prozess, den wir Menschen nutzen, um Gedanken zu verwirklichen.
3. Im Designprozess wird Wissen gewonnen, analysiert und manipuliert.
4. Das Post-Disziplinäre fügt sich nicht in kulturelle Hierarchien, es interessiert sich für die Botschaft – unabhängig vom Medium.
5. Das Post-Disziplinäre thematisiert die Unmöglichkeit, ein „Objekt" nur von einem einzigen Standpunkt aus zu begreifen.
6. Das Post-Disziplinäre hebt die Strukturen auf.

Garant der Realität

„Ich will eine dritte Pille!", fordert Žižek in seinem Film *The Pervert's Guide to Cinema*[2] und argumentiert in Ablehnung von Morpheus' Reduktionismus in der berühmten Szene im Film *The Matrix*[3], dass „die Wahl zwischen der blauen und der roten Pille keine echte Wahl zwischen Illusion und Realität ist, natürlich ist die Matrix eine Maschine zur Herstellung von Fiktionen, aber es sind Fiktionen, die

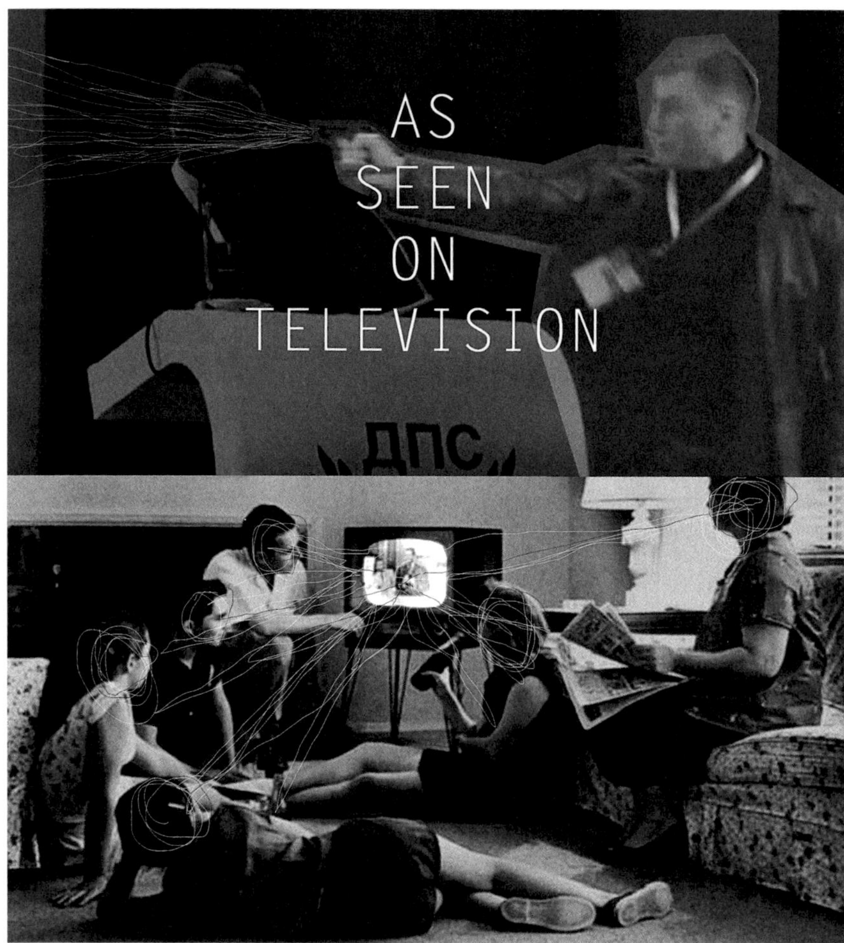

symbolic fictions that regulate it, you lose reality itself." Just before, he had shown us a clip from *Possessed*[4] where Joan Crawford, a poor girl in an industrial town, is looking through the windows of a passing train, which is making a stop in town. As the train passes by, Crawford peeks through its windows, looking into the lives of its wealthy passengers. As the train comes to a stop, Richard Skeets, playing one of these wealthy types, appears drinking champagne leisurely in the last carriage and finds himself right in front of Crawford. "Looking in?" he asks her, and as she nods he replies, "Wrong way, get in and look out." "The third pill is a pill that would enable me to perceive not the reality behind the illusion but the reality in illusion itself."

Design is this mediator. Design is found between us and everything else. It is found between us and nature, or the universe, in terms of technologies, science, philosophy, religion … between us and other people in terms of communication, history, art, politics, medicine … and between ourselves and the very things that we invent in terms of interfaces, law, binary language, applications. …Understood like this,

bereits die Struktur unserer Realität regulieren, wenn man unserer Realität die sie regulierenden symbolischen Fiktionen nimmt, dann verliert man die Realität selbst." Kurz vorher präsentiert er einen Ausschnitt aus *Possessed*[4], in dem Joan Crawford, ein mittelloses, junges Mädchen in einer Industriestadt, in die Fenster eines Zuges schaut, der in dieser Stadt Halt macht. Während der Zug vorüberfährt, schaut Crawford durch dessen Fenster auf das Leben und Treiben der wohlhabenden Passagiere. Als der Zug einfährt, sieht man Richard Skeets, der einen dieser wohlhabenden Reisenden spielt, im letzten Wagen entspannt Champagner genießen. Der Zug kommt direkt vor Crawford zum Stehen. „Sie schauen hinein?", fragt er sie, und als sie nickt, antwortet er: „Völlig falsch, steigen Sie ein und schauen Sie hinaus." „Die dritte Pille ist jene Pille, die es mir ermöglichen würde, nicht die Realität hinter der Illusion, sondern die Realität in der Illusion selbst zu erkennen."

Design ist ein solcher Mediator. Design befindet sich zwischen uns und allem, was uns umgibt. Es befindet sich zwischen uns und der Natur oder dem Universum, in Form von Technologien, Wissenschaft, Philosophie, Religion … zwischen uns und anderen Menschen in Form von Kommunikation, Geschichte, Kunst, Politik, Medizin … und zwischen uns und ebenjenen Dingen, die wir in Form von Schnittstellen, Gesetzen, Binärcode, Applikationen usw. erfinden. So gesehen steht Design im Zentrum der Kultur, Gestaltung ist Kultur und unsere Kultur ist Gestaltung. Design ist kein Medium oder eine Disziplin, es ist eben jener Prozess, durch den wir Gedanken verstofflichen.

„Die erste, natürlich am schwersten zu erfüllende Bedingung ist, dass die Menschen im Allgemeinen begreifen, in welcher Weise ihre Arbeit und ihre Erfindungen, ob sie sich dessen bewusst sind oder nicht, die Struktur unseres Lebens beständig gestalten und umgestalten."[5]

So gesehen, wäre die Geschichte der Gestaltung nicht von der Geschichte der Menschheit zu trennen und würde sich in der Evolution auf die Prozesse konzentrieren, auf die Art und Weise, wie diese Realität formen. Alles, was wir an Gestaltung kennen, ist Tradition. Wir benutzen Design, um die Realität zu beobachten, zu analysieren und zu manipulieren. Dabei schaffen wir kulturelle Modelle, die es uns ermöglichen, ebendiese Realität zu begreifen. Design fiktionalisiert die Realität und wird so zu ihrem einzigen Garanten: Wie kalt ist der Raum, wie lang ist eine Stunde oder wofür steht ein Wort etc.? Persönlich betrachtet kommen wir jedoch zu dem Schluss, dass „Design das ist, was wir machen, um Design zu verstehen."

design is at the center of culture, design is culture, and our culture is designed; it is not a medium or a discipline, but the very process by which we materialize thought.

"The first condition, of course, and the most difficult one to fulfill, is that the people in general should understand how their work and their invention — whatever they know it or not — are continually shaping and reshaping the patterns of life."[5]

The history of design, therefore, is not different from that of humanity itself, and would focus in the evolution of these processes and how these modulate reality. Everything we know in design is tradition. We use design to observe, analyze, and manipulate reality and, in doing so, we construct the cultural models that allow us to comprehend this very same reality. Design fictionalizes reality becoming its sole guarantor … how cold is the room, how long is one hour, or what does this word stands for, etc. But at a personal level, our conclusion is that, "Design is what we do to understand Design."

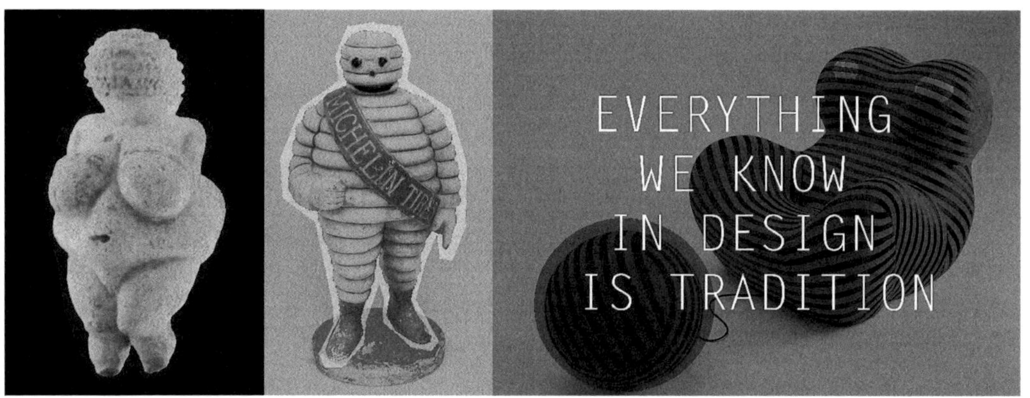

Testimonials

Prizes, trophies, medals, diplomas, honors … all designed to reassure us that what we have learned or achieved was worth knowing or doing. It sets a standard and sometimes can even substitute the very thing that they represent. Probably the best analysis of the power of awards as representational objects comes from *The Wizard of Oz* near the end of the film when Scarecrow, Tin Man, Lion, and Dorothy finally get to meet The Great and Powerful Oz. They are rewarded with brains, heart, valor, and a *return ticket* to Kansas, after the initial disappointment of finding out The Wizard's human condition. He tells them: "I am a very good man, I am just a very bad wizard." He finally makes everyone realize that they already had what they were longing for, they just didn't know it, no one had acknowledged it, so it never materialized. He gives Scarecrow a University diploma and he immediately recites the

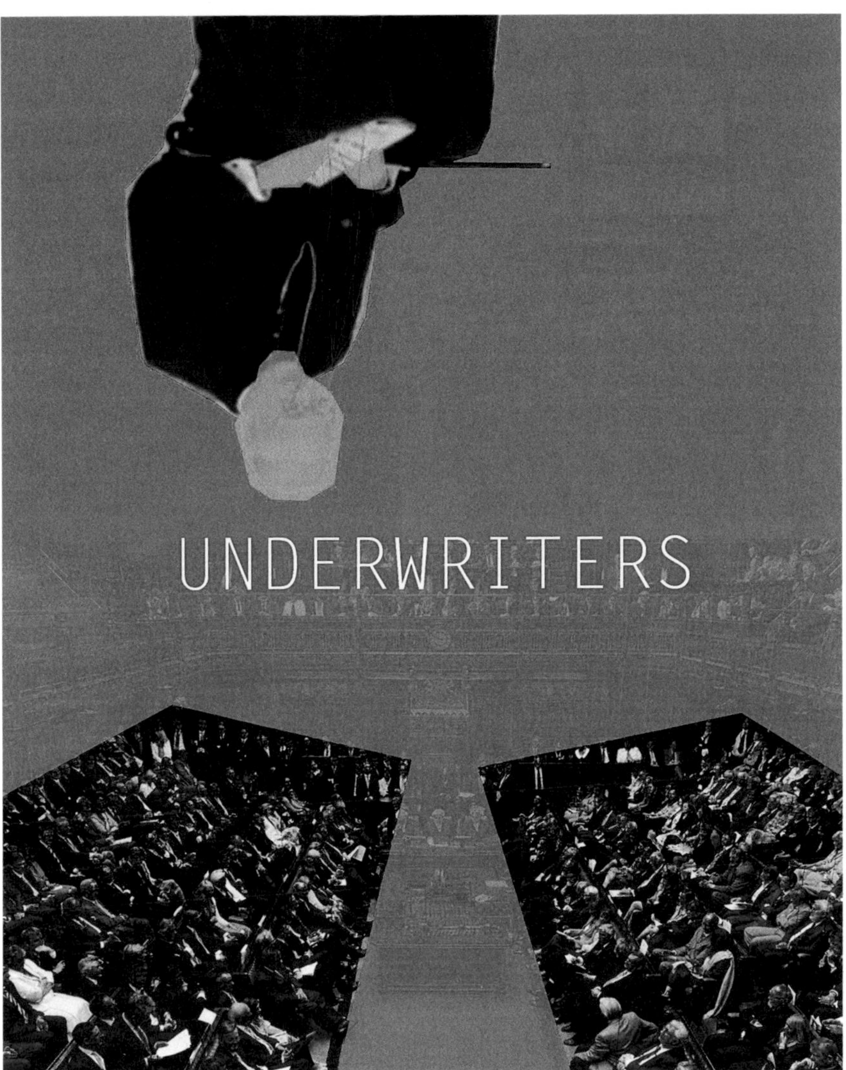

Referenzen

Preise, Trophäen, Medaillen, Diplome, Ehrenbezeugungen, etc. ... all das ist darauf angelegt, uns den Wert dessen zu bestätigen, was wir gelernt oder erreicht haben. Sie setzen einen Standard und können manchmal genau das ersetzen, was sie repräsentieren. Die wahrscheinlich beste Analyse der Macht der Auszeichnungen als repräsentative Objekte stammt aus dem Film *Der Zauberer von Oz*.[6] In der letzten Szene, in der die Vogelscheuche, der Zinnmann, der Löwe und Dorothy endlich den großen Oz treffen und nach der anfänglichen Enttäuschung der vier über Oz' menschliche Gestalt mit Hirn, Herz, Mut und einer Rückfahrkarte nach Arkansas versehen werden, sagt der Zauberer: „Ich bin ein sehr guter Mensch, ich bin nur ein sehr schlechter Zauberer." Im weiteren macht er ihnen klar, dass sie das, wonach sie sich sehnen, bereits haben, es nur nicht wissen, da niemand es ihnen

Pythagorean Theorem and realizes he, indeed, has brains. To Tin Man he offers him a clock in the shape of a heart as a token of their esteem and affection and reminds him, "A heart is not judged by how much you love, but by how much you are loved by others."

"As for you, my fine friend, you're a victim of disorganized thinking. You are under the unfortunate delusion that simply because you run away from danger, you have no courage. You're confusing courage with wisdom. Back where I come from, we have men who are called heroes. Once a year, they take their fortitude out of mothballs and parade it down the main street of the city. And they have no more courage than you have. But! They have one thing that you haven't got! A medal! Therefore, for meritorious conduct, extraordinary valor, conspicuous bravery against wicked witches, I award you the Triple Cross. You are now a member of the Legion of Courage!"[6]

We already have a diploma, and we know that, at least, our daughter loves us a lot. We were only missing a medal and we recently got one too, for our contribution to design. A great honor ... but it didn't make us better designers although, suddenly, other people thought so.

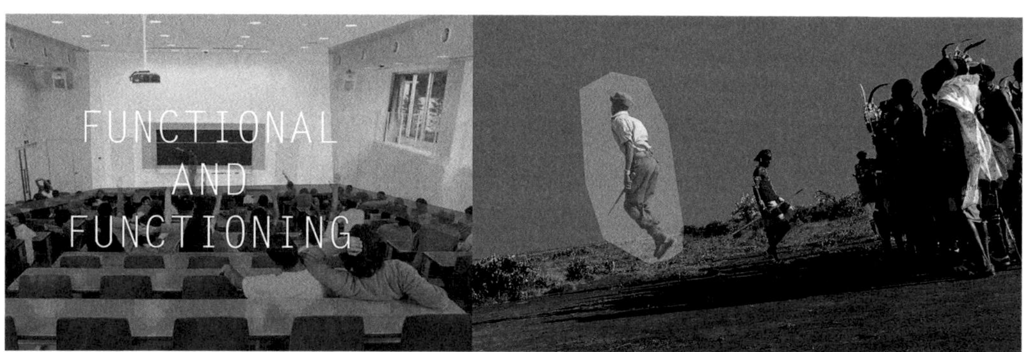

Functioning vs. Functional

In Chinese philosophy, Yin and Yang represent two seemingly opposite forces that are at the same time independent and complementary. They come together in a dynamic system, which is greater than any of the parts. When we tried to think of design as an equivalent dynamic system we came to the conclusion that design is underwritten by the idea of functionality, which, in turn, is fed by the myths of improvement and progress. This overriding principle is not compensated by any other equivalent ideal. And we find this problematic. *The Functional* is always necessarily supporting an ideology; this could be a way of living, an economic or political system, a religious practice, production system, etc. *The Functional* never questions its ideology, always working in the realm of the accepted; its meanings are understood

je bestätigt hat, sodass es für sie nicht Wirklichkeit werden konnte. Er gibt der Vogelscheuche ein Universitätsdiplom, woraufhin diese sofort den Satz des Pythagoras abrufen kann und sich bewusst wird, dass sie ein Hirn hat. Dem Zinnmann schenkt er eine Uhr in Form eines Herzens als Beweis für Wertschätzung und Zuneigung und erinnert ihn daran, „dass ein Herz nicht danach beurteilt wird, wie sehr du liebst, sondern danach, wie sehr du von anderen geliebt wirst."

„Und du, mein lieber Freund, bist Opfer eines Denkfehlers. Du leidest unter der unglückseligen Wahnvorstellung, dass du, nur weil du vor Gefahren davonläufst, keinen Mut hast. Du verwechselst Mut mit Weisheit. Dort, wo ich herkomme, gibt es Männer, die Helden genannt werden. Einmal im Jahr holen sie ihre Tapferkeit aus der Mottenkiste und stellen sie auf der Hauptstraße der Stadt in einer Parade zur Schau. Und sie haben nicht mehr Mut als du. Aber …! Sie haben etwas, das du nicht hast! Eine Medaille! Deshalb verleihe ich dir für verdienstvolles Handeln, außergewöhnlichen Mut und auffallende Tapferkeit bösen Hexen gegenüber das dreifache Ehrenkreuz. Von nun an bist du ein Mitglied der Tapferkeitslegion!"

Wir haben schon ein Diplom und wissen zumindest, dass unsere Tochter uns liebt. Nur eine Medaille fehlte uns noch, die haben wir aber kürzlich für unseren Beitrag als Designer bekommen. Eine große Ehre, die uns allerdings nicht zu besseren Designern gemacht hat, obwohl andere Leute das plötzlich so sehen.

Funktionierendes versus Funktionales

In der chinesischen Medizin repräsentieren Yin und Yang zwei scheinbar entgegengesetzte Kräfte, die sich gleichzeitig ergänzen und unabhängig voneinander sind. Gemeinsam bilden sie ein dynamisches System, das größer ist als seine Bestandteile. Bei unserem Versuch, Design als ein ähnlich dynamisches System zu begreifen, kamen wir zu dem Schluss, dass Design auf der Idee der Funktionalität basiert, die wiederum durch den Mythos von Verbesserung und Fortschritt bestimmt wird. Kein anderes Ideal macht diesem übergeordneten Prinzip hier Konkurrenz. Und das finden wir problematisch. Das *Funktionale* unterstützt immer zwangsläufig eine Ideologie, wie etwa einen Lebensstil, ein ökonomisches oder politisches System, eine religiöse Praxis, ein Produktionssystem etc. Das *Funktionale* hinterfragt diese Ideologie nie, arbeitet immer im Bereich tradierter Akzeptanz, die Bedeutungen verstehen sich immer im Rahmen des tradierten Sprachgebrauches. Das *Funktionale* kennt keine Alternativen, nur Verbesserungen oder effizientere Systeme. Sein Untergang sind Nutzlosigkeit, Ineffizienz und Überalterung; aber das sind Konzepte,

165

within the framework of the language that uses. For *The Functional*, there are no alternatives, just improvements or more efficient systems. Its nemeses are uselessness, inefficiency, and obsolescence, but these are charged concepts aimed at perpetuating this longing for improvement. This potential for improvement is its own functional fiction — this belief in the system's infinite capability to improve engages us in a shared idea of purpose and destiny. What it discards is automatically forgotten.

It seems clear to us, that to have a truly dynamic design system, we need to adopt a valid Yang to its functional Yin. We propose the idea of *The Functioning*, which deviates from the ideological framework of *The Functional*, offering a vision of other possible functionalities, alternative industries, economies, technologies, politics, narratives, fictions. *The Functioning* is necessarily experimental, it has to work in a point of poetic tension, transcending the design language and demanding our attention to the alternatives that might lay ahead (or behind) and to reconsider if where we are is really where we were meant to be. *The Functional*, like any living organism, will keep fighting for survival until it dies or transforms into a new form; and we will continue to justify the system, it will continue to defend its status quo, because it's the only thing it knows and believes in ... until this is no more.

The Poetic Moment

These moments of insight into a different fiction are achieved by overriding our designed languages.[7] These are poetic moments, moments where we manage to experience meanings outside the prosaic meanings of the very language we are using. Experimentation is therefore at the center of any practice that aims at creating these triggers that question the language of the object itself, whether it is an object, a movie, an event, a performance, etc. The poetic only remains poetic while it remains out of the mainstream, because it offers us an insight into reality that goes beyond language; that goes beyond what we are capable of processing culturally. It then lends itself to become a new, possible, a functioning alternative. The poetic moment can only be rationalized and built into a functioning narrative *a posteriori*. Design lives across these two paradigms: *The Functional* and *The Functioning*. On one hand, we can easily recognize the need for *The Functioning*, for possible futures other than the one we seem to be heading to; on the other, *The Functional*, the meta-narrative, tries to build these innovations into a continuity of the system. Only the poetic moments that remain poetic offer us a glimpse into what could have been. The system is always able to offer us a sense of belonging to the historical moment we were *destined to live in*.

die letztlich auch nur darauf abzielen, das Verlangen nach Verbesserungen aufrechtzuerhalten. Dieses Potenzial zur Verbesserung ist die funktionale Fiktion des *Funktionalen*. Der Glaube an die unerschöpfliche Fähigkeit des Systems zu permanenter Verbesserung fesselt uns in einer gemeinsamen Vorstellung von Bestimmung und Schicksal aneinander. Was verworfen wird, wird sofort vergessen.

Uns ist klar, dass wir, wenn wir ein wirklich dynamisches Designsystem wünschen, ein wirkungsmächtiges Yang zu dem funktionalen Yin schaffen müssen. Wir schlagen den Begriff des *Funktionierenden* vor. Das *Funktionierende* weicht von dem ideologischen Bezugssystem des *Funktionalen* ab, indem es andere mögliche Funktionalitäten, also alternative Industrien, Ökonomien, Technologien, Politik, Erzählungen, Fiktionen usw. zulässt. Das *Funktionierende* ist zwangsläufig experimentell, es muss sich an einem Punkt poetischer Spannung entwickeln, an dem die Designsprache transzendiert und unsere Aufmerksamkeit auf die Alternativen gelenkt wird, die vor (oder hinter) uns liegen könnten. Ein Punkt, an dem wir überdenken können, ob wir uns wirklich an jener Stelle befinden, an der wir sein wollten. Das *Funktionale* wird, wie jeder lebendige Organismus, ums Überleben kämpfen, bis es ausgestorben oder in eine neue Form übergegangen ist, und wir werden fortfahren, das System zu rechtfertigen, es wird fortfahren, seinen Status quo zu verteidigen, weil er das Einzige ist, was es kennt und woran es glaubt, bis es nicht mehr ist.

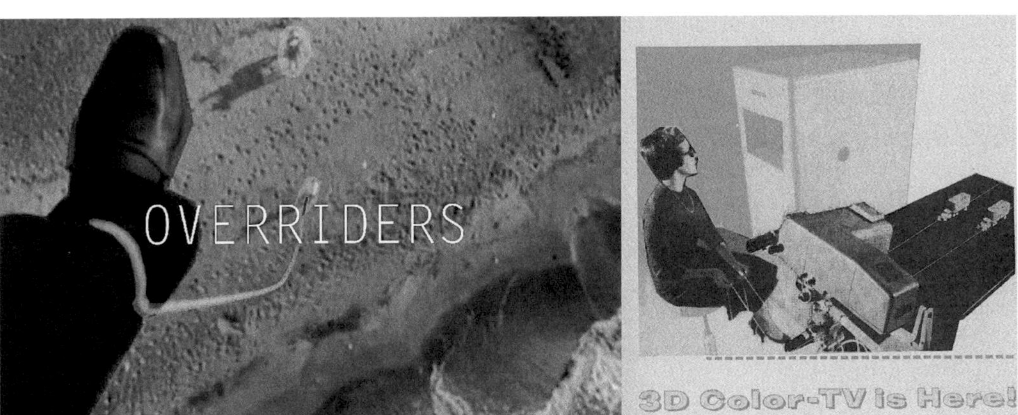

Der poetische Moment

Derlei Momente von Einsicht in eine andere Annahme gelingen durch das Aufbrechen unserer festgelegten Sprachen (Sprachen begreifen wir hier im weitesten Sinne und beziehen uns auf die Konventionen, die alle menschlichen Tätigkeiten bestimmen, das können geschriebene und gesprochene Sprachen sein, mathematische, wissenschaftliche,

One day we saw our daughter struggling to get into a small model car. She was holding it with two hands, front door open, and violently pushing her toes in. Astonished, and containing our laughter, we asked her what was she trying to do. "I want to get in the car! I want to get in the car!!" Frustration turned rapidly into anger and then frustration again … tears. "It's too small for you, can't you see?" we told her, trying to be rational. She looked at us in disbelief and looked back at the car, took a breath of air, and with regained determination, tried pushing herself in again. What was most incredible was to think that for her, not being able to get inside the car was just some sort of physical anomaly that could be overcome by perseverance. She was being poetically denied. This is a moment that will always remain poetic, as it will not find a way of incorporating itself to her own sense of reality. And for us, outsiders, it also remains poetic because it represents a moment when she was able to feel that space of the car in the same terms as that which surrounded her, and we long for those moments that our brain lost long ago.

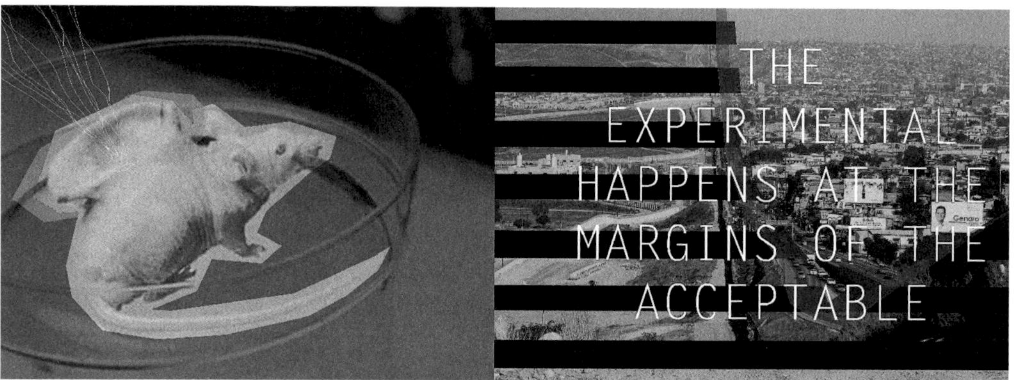

Design Does not Understand Metaphors

Design is like a genie that can materialize all your wishes, but will show no other consideration than what conforms to the materiality of the wish itself; its only goal is that of making the wish real (prompting all those "Three Wishes" jokes). But let's take the story of King Midas as an example: as a reward for bringing back Silenus, Dionysus offers Midas whatever he wishes. Midas asks that whatever he might touch would turn into gold. And so it happened. What was subconsciously just a metaphor for wealth — as it is nowadays when we use it to refer to successful businessmen — taken literally, it was clearly inconvenient. But the wish was granted and Midas was happy, everything he touched turned to gold and very quickly he had amassed a huge fortune, until the moment he realized that he could not bring food or water

ästhetische, künstlerische etc.).[7] Es sind poetische Momente, Momente, in denen es uns gelingt, Bedeutungen außerhalb der prosaischen Bedeutungen der von uns verwendeten Sprache zu erfassen. Deshalb steht das Experimentieren im Zentrum jeder Praxis, die auf die Erschaffung jener Impulse abzielt, die die Sprache des Objekts selbst hinterfragen, sei es nun ein Ding, ein Film, ein Ereignis, eine Performance etc. Das Poetische bleibt nur so lange poetisch, wie es sich aus dem Mainstream heraushält, da es uns Einsicht in eine Wirklichkeit gibt, die über die Sprache hinausgeht, die über das hinausgeht, was wir kulturell verarbeiten können. Erst dann wird es zu einer neuen Möglichkeit, einer funktionierenden Alternative. Der poetische Moment kann in einem funktionierenden Narrativ nur *a posteriori* rationalisiert und eingebaut werden. Design lebt zwischen diesen beiden Paradigmen: dem *Funktionalen* und dem *Funktionierenden*. Einerseits ist die Notwendigkeit des *Funktionierenden* für eine mögliche, von der momentan anvisierten *abweichenden* Zukunft leicht zu erkennen, andererseits versucht das *Funktionale*, das Meta-Narrativ, diese Neuerungen in die Kontinuität des Systems einzugliedern. Nur die poetischen Momente, die poetisch bleiben, erlauben uns einen Blick auf das, was hätte sein können. Das System ist stets in der Lage, uns das Gefühl der Zugehörigkeit zu jenem historischen Moment zu vermitteln, in dem wir *zu leben bestimmt* sind.

Eines Tages beobachteten wir, wie unsere Tochter versuchte, in ein kleines Spielzeugauto einzusteigen. Sie hielt es in beiden Händen, hatte die Vordertür geöffnet und presste gewaltsam ihre Zehen hinein. Erstaunt und unser Lachen unterdrückend fragten wir sie, was sie da tun wolle. „Ich will in das Auto einsteigen! Ich will einsteigen!!" Frustration schlug unmittelbar in Wut um, um dann wieder zu Frustration zu werden – Tränen – „Es ist zu klein für dich, siehst du das denn nicht?", fragten wir sie und versuchten Vernunft walten zu lassen. Sie schaute uns ungläubig an, um sich dann wieder dem Auto zuzuwenden, tief durchzuatmen und mit neuerlicher Entschlossenheit zu versuchen, sich hineinzupressen. Das Erstaunlichste daran war, dass für sie die Tatsache, dass sie nicht in das Auto einsteigen konnte, nur eine Art körperlicher Ausnahmezustand war, der durch Beharrlichkeit überwunden werden könnte. Die Realisierung ihrer Poesie wurde ihr vorenthalten. Dies ist ein Moment, der immer poetisch bleiben wird, da er sich nicht in ihre Vorstellung von Realität integrieren lassen wird. Und auch für uns Außenstehende wird er als der Moment, in dem sie den Maßstab des Autos genauso empfand wie jenen ihrer Umgebung, poetisch bleiben. Wir sehnen uns nach diesen Momenten, die unserem Denken und Fühlen schon so lange verloren gegangen sind.

to his mouth as this solidified into the precious metal ... And as with design, we have to realize that design does not understand metaphors. You get what you ask for ... the metaphor remains in the mind of whoever expresses the desire, not in the mind of whoever acts as the Google Translate and feeds this information into the design machine ... "This is the only story of mine whose moral I know. I don't think it's a marvelous moral, I simply happen to know what it is: We are what we pretend to be, so we must be careful about what we pretend to be."[8] Like the Genie, design materializes the wishes we express. Design sees that

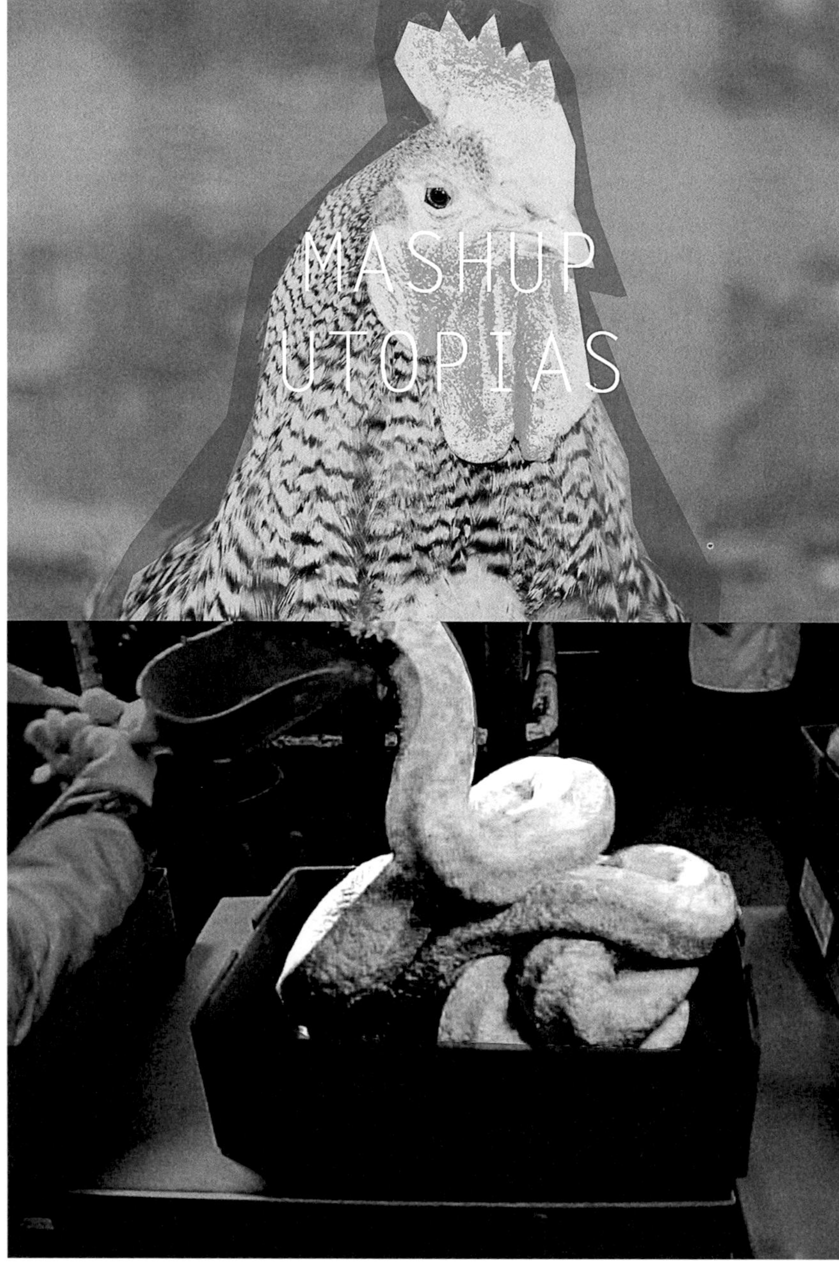

Design versteht keine Metaphern

Design ist wie ein Dschinn, der all unsere Wünsche verwirklichen kann, aber nur berücksichtigt, was der reinen Verwirklichung des Wunsches entspricht. Das einzige Ziel ist es, den Wunsch real werden zu lassen (Grundlage für all die Witze mit drei Wünschen). Nehmen wir doch die Geschichte von König Midas als Beispiel: Dionysos bot Midas als Belohnung dafür, dass er Silen zurückgebracht hatte, alles, was er sich wünschte. Midas bat, dass alles, was er berührte, zu Gold werden sollte. Und so geschah es. Was hier unbewusst nur eine Metapher für Reichtum war, so wie wir sie auch heute noch bei erfolgreichen Geschäftsleuten verwenden, erwiese sich wörtlich genommen als sehr unangenehm. Aber der Wunsch wurde gewährt und Midas war glücklich, da sich alles, was er berührte, in Gold verwandelte und er im Handumdrehen ein riesiges Vermögen anhäufen konnte. Dies änderte sich just in dem Moment, als er realisierte, dass er weder Nahrung noch Wasser zum Mund führen konnte, ohne dass diese sich in das wertvolle Metall verwandelte.

Was nun das Design betrifft, müssen wir uns darüber im Klaren sein, dass Gestaltung keine Metaphern versteht. Du bekommst, wonach du fragst, denn die Metapher verbleibt im Kopf desjenigen, der den Wunsch geäußert hat, und nicht im Kopf desjenigen, der wie Google Translate fungiert und diese Information dann in die Designmaschine eingibt. „This is the only story of mine whose moral I know. I don't think it's a marvellous moral, I simply happen to know what it is: We are what we pretend to be, so we must be careful about what we pretend to be."[8] Wie der Dschinn verwirklicht Design die von uns geäußerten Wünsche. Design ist bestrebt, diese Umsetzung auf möglichst effiziente, effektive und schnelle Weise voranzutreiben. Zu diesem Zweck sucht das Design funktionale Lösungen, keine vernünftigen, humanen, sozialen etc. Diese waren nicht Teil der Forderung.

Die Verwirklichung der Utopie

Vielleicht ist es etwas vermessen, die Allgemeine Erklärung der Menschenrechte als erste globalisierte utopische Vision zu bezeichnen, aber warum eigentlich nicht? Utopisch deshalb, weil die reine Tatsache, dass sie *erklärt* werden mussten, genau genommen bedeutete, dass sie eben keine allgemein gültigen Rechte waren und somit ein Ziel, das es erst zu verfolgen galt. Und globalisiert deshalb, weil sie eindeutig eine westliche Idee von Fortschritt und Freiheit als erstrebenswerten Standard formulierten. Es überrascht nicht (oder überrascht gerade), dass der Ostblock sich der Stimme enthielt (vielleicht war dies jener Moment, in dem sie den Kalten Krieg verloren?). Aber lassen wir die Vergangenheit ruhen. Artikel 25 besagt,

this implementation is done in the most efficient, effective, and fastest way possible. Design seeks functional solutions to this purpose, not sensible, humanitarian, social, etc. These were not part of the request.

The Implementation of Utopia

Maybe it is a bit much to say that the Universal Declaration of Human Rights was the first *globalized* utopian vision, but why not? Utopian, because the fact that it needed to be *declared* meant precisely that they were not universally extended rights and that these constituted the goal to pursue. And globalized because it clearly typifies a Western idea of progress and freedom as the standard to be aspired to. Not surprisingly (or surprisingly) the Eastern block abstained (maybe this was the moment when they lost the Cold War?). Let bygones, be bygones. Article 25 states that everybody has the right to a "standard of living" including all basic necessities food, housing, clothing, medical care, etc.

Let's take the idea of food as an example. The first question would be what constitutes the standard and what does adequate really mean. Is *adequate* the USA standard? The British one? The German? Or that of Bangladesh? But nevertheless, the design machine can already start working on its implementation; it is not going to get into further considerations just yet. It is clear that a growing population will be the result of a "better world" and that food production was already and would become more important every day. It is difficult not to digress into political commentary because this is intended just as an example of what it is required to implement an ideology. We will go directly to basic number crunching to try to understand the scale, looking at chicken production as a widely accepted source of protein and consequently one of the more industrialized, and therefore dehumanized, food industries. Today 140.000.000 chickens will be slaughtered for human consumption. This means that today, there are already 840.000.000 ready to be slaughtered by the end of the week. By the end of the month 3.920.000.000 chickens would have been consumed, and another 3.900.000.000 that hatched today will be ready for consumption by the end of the month. Large as it is, in a global context, this would only represent an average of half a chicken per person per month. Obviously, chicken is not distributed equally among all the inhabitants of the planet. Malnutrition still affects one to three people in the world. If, for example, we would take the USA standard — where as an average, each person consumes 1.8 chickens per month — and extrapolate it to worldwide population, it would mean that the actual production of chicken would have to rise to 12.600.000.000 per month, almost four times as much.

dass jeder das Recht auf einen adäquaten *Lebensstandard* hat, der alle Grundbedürfnisse wie Nahrung, Wohnung, Kleidung, medizinische Versorgung etc. gewährleistet.

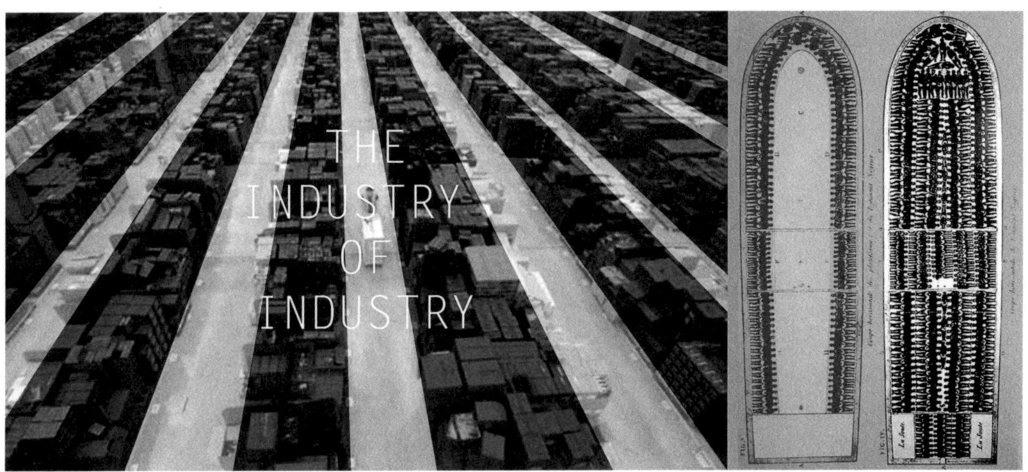

Nehmen wir uns das Beispiel der Nahrung vor. Die erste Frage wäre, was bestimmt den Standard und was bedeutet *adäquat* wirklich. Ist der amerikanische Standard adäquat? Der britische? Der deutsche? Oder jener von Bangladesch? Ungeachtet dessen kann die Designmaschine schon beginnen, an der Umsetzung zu arbeiten, sie muss keine weiteren Überlegungen anstellen. Es ist klar, dass eine „bessere Welt" zu einer wachsenden Population führen wird und dass die Nahrungsmittelproduktion noch wichtiger werden wird, als sie es bislang schon war. Es ist schwer, an dieser Stelle nicht in einen politischen Kommentar abzudriften, aber hier soll nur ein Beispiel dafür gegeben werden, was erforderlich ist, um eine Ideologie zu verwirklichen. Wir werden uns direkt mit Zahlenbeispielen beschäftigen, um den Maßstab des hier Verhandelten verständlich zu machen. Dazu betrachten wir die Produktion von Hühnerfleisch. Es ist eine weltweit nachgefragte Proteinquelle, die von einer stark industrialisierten und daher inhumanen Nahrungsmittelindustrie produziert wird: 140.000.000 Hühner werden am heutigen Tag für den menschlichen Konsum geschlachtet. Das bedeutet, dass heute schon 840.000.000 Hühner bereitgestellt werden, die bis zum Ende der Woche geschlachtet werden. Am Ende des Monats werden 3.920.000.000 Hühner konsumiert worden sein und weitere 3.900.000.000 Küken, die heute schlüpfen, werden Ende des Monats zum Verbrauch bereit sein. Auch wenn dies im globalen Kontext viel erscheinen mag, würde dies doch nur den durchschnittlichen Konsum von 0,5 Hühnern pro Kopf im Monat bedeuten. Offensichtlich wird Hühnerfleisch nicht gerecht an alle Bewohner dieses Planeten

Is easier to believe, when we are talking about this kind of consumption and production, the level of mechanization and extreme functionalism that is required to achieve them. There is no room in this machine for considerations of animal welfare, public health, etc. You could not deliver 980.000.000 chickens a week if there were. And the machinery of design continuously seeks to improve these numbers (still many mouths to feed at a profit) with new medications, new feeds, genetic modification, etc. — and it will. Functionality feeds the implementation of the dominant ideology, which supplies its own utopian narratives. These dominant utopias are no longer so; they are reality itself, materialized and underwritten by design.

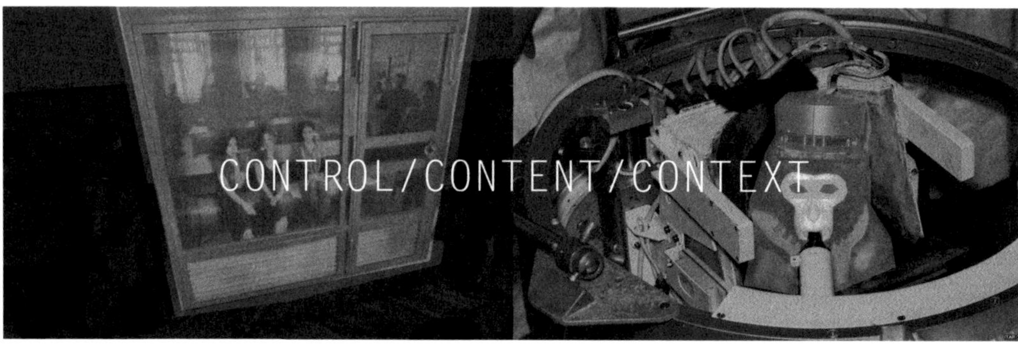

verteilt. Mangelernährung betrifft immer noch einen von drei Menschen auf der Welt. Wenn wir zum Beispiel den Standard der USA nehmen, wo jede Person durchschnittlich 1,8 Hühner pro Monat verzehrt, und diesen auf die Weltbevölkerung umrechnen, würde das bedeuten, dass die Produktion von Hühnern auf 12.600.000.000 pro Monat steigen, also fast viermal so hoch sein müsste.

Wenn wir über ein solches Ausmaß von Konsum und Produktion sprechen, ist es einfacher, das Ausmaß der Mechanisierung und des extremen Funktionalismus zu begreifen, die dafür nötig sind. In dieser Maschinerie gibt es keinen Raum für die Berücksichtigung von Tierschutz, Volksgesundheit etc., denn diese würde die Lieferung von 980.000.000 Hühnern pro Woche unmöglich machen. Und die Designmaschinerie versucht permanent, diese Zahlen durch neue Medikamente, neue Futtermittel, genetische Veränderungen etc. zu optimieren (immer noch viele Mäuler, die profitabel gestopft werden können) und das wird auch geschehen. Die Funktionalität ermöglicht die Verwirklichung der dominierenden Ideologie, die die eigenen utopischen Narrative bereitstellt. Diese dominanten Utopien sind keine Utopien mehr, sie sind zur Realität geworden, verwirklicht und garantiert durch Design.

Figures

Notes

[1] From the movie *Being There*. Directed by Hal Ashby . USA 1971. Adapted from the 1970 novel written by Jerzy Kosinski, screenplay coauthored by Jerzy Kosinski and Robert C. Jones.
[2] *The Pervert's Guide to Cinema*. Directed by Sophie Fiennes, Cast: Slavoj Žižek. AT/GB/NL 2006.
[3] *The Matrix*. Directed by Andrew Wachowski, Lana Wachowski. USA 1999.
[4] *Possessed*. Directed by Clarence Brown. USA 1931.
[5] Siegfried Giedion: *Mechanization Takes Command,* Oxford 1948, p. vi (foreword).
[6] *Der Zauberer von Oz*. R.: Victor Fleming. USA 1939
[7] When we talk about languages we do so in a general sense, referring to the set of conventions that regulate any human activity, these can be written and spoken languages, mathematical, scientific, aesthetic, art, etc.
[8] Kurt Vonnegut: *Mother Night,* New York 1961, p. v (introduction page)

177

Abbildungen

S.160–175   Collagen von El Ultimo Grito, 2013

Anmerkungen

[1] Aus dem Film *Willkommen Mr Chance*. R.: Hal Ashby USA 1979, nach dem 1970
   erschienen Roman von Jerzy Kosinski, Drehbuch von Jerzy Kosinski und Robert C. Jones
[2] *The Pervert's Guide to Cinema*. R.: Sophie Fiennes, Cast: Slavoj Žižek, AT/GB/NL 2006
[3] *The Matrix*. R.: Andrew Wachowski, Lana Wachowski, USA 1999
[4] *Possessed*. R.: Clarence Brown, USA 1931
[5] Siegfried Giedion: *Mechanization Takes Command,* Oxford 1948, dt. *Die Herrschaft der
   Mechanisierung. Ein Beitrag zur anonymen Geschichte,* Frankfurt a.M.: 1987 S. 14
[6] *Der Zauberer von Oz*. R.: Victor Fleming. USA 1939
[7] Wenn wir über Sprachen sprechen, tun wir das im allgemeinen Sinne und beziehen uns
   auf den Kanon von Konventionen, der jegliche menschliche Aktivität steuert, es können
   dies geschriebene oder gesprochene Sprachen sein, mathematische, wissenschaftliche,
   ästhetische, künstlerische, etc.
[8] Kurt Vonnegut: *Mother Night,* New York 1961, S. V (Einleitung), dt. Übersetzung: „Dies ist
   die einzige meiner Geschichten, deren Moral ich kenne. Ich denke nicht, dass es eine
   tolle Moral ist, ich weiß nur zufällig, wie sie lautet: Wir sind das, was wir vorgeben zu sein,
   also müssen wir vorsichtig sein mit dem, was wir vorgeben."

This publication is based on the Weißenhof–symposium *Art and / or Design?* held on 5th December 2012 at the State Academy of Arts and Design in Stuttgart. As a director of the Weissenhof–Institute from 2009-13 I would like to take this opportunity to thank the academy for its long-term financing.

In only a few months, we have succeeded in making the event's lectures available to a wider audience in this present anthology. I would like to extend my personal gratitude to all the authors, who have transformed their lecture scripts into printable texts within only a few weeks, as well as to Lucinda Rennison and Stephanie Rupp for their fast, professional translations. Special thanks go to Regina Fasshauer for her stalwart effort organizing the event, the picture editing, and for the assistance with the project's coordination, and to Christine Nasz for her continous engaged support, a documentation of the event and the implementation of the blog. I also owe a debt of gratitude to Moritz Hahn and Sven Tillack for their graphic design, composition, and keen commitment to the volume's preparation for printing, and to my colleague Prof. Uli Cluss for the cooperation and the financial support for this publication.

This is the fourth volume in the series *weißenhof edition* that I established together with jovis Verlag Berlin in 2009. I express my warmest appreciation here to Jochen Visscher and all his colleagues at jovis Verlag Berlin, in particular to Philipp Sperrle, Susanne Rösler, and Jutta Bornholdt-Cassetti for many years of collegial collaboration. This double publication represents the end of a cycle of events that I initiated and planned within the framework of my activities as director of the weissenhof–institut. However, this does not mean that the interdisciplinary discourse is over: it is to be hoped that it will be continued on the blog www.art-and-or-design.blogspot.de and elsewhere, for interdisciplinary questions are essential when it comes to the design of our future.

Annett Zinsmeister, Berlin 2013

Danksagung

Diese Publikation basiert auf dem gleichnamigen Weißenhof-Symposium *Kunst und / oder Design?*, das am 5.12.2012 an der Staatlichen Akademie der Bildenden Künste in Stuttgart stattfand und der an dieser Stelle zu danken ist für die langjährige Finanzierung des Weißenhof-Institutes, das ich von 2009–13 geleitet habe.

In nur wenigen Monaten ist es uns gelungen, die Vorträge der Veranstaltung in dem vorliegenden Sammelband nun einer breiteren Öffentlichkeit zugänglich zu machen. Mein persönlicher Dank gilt allen Autoren, die in nur wenigen Wochen ihr Vortragsmanuskript in einen druckfertigen Text verwandelten, sowie Lucinda Rennison und Stephanie Rupp für die schnelle und professionelle Übersetzung. Ein besonderer Dank geht an Regina Fasshauer für ihr Engagement in der Veranstaltungsorganisation, der Bildredaktion und der Mitarbeit in der Projektkoordination, sowie an Christine Nasz für ihre engagierte Unterstützung, die Veranstaltungsdokumentation und der Einrichtung des Blogs. Moritz Hahn und Sven Tillack sei für die grafische Gestaltung, den Satz und die engagierte Bearbeitung des Bandes bis zur Drucklegung gedankt sowie meinem Kollegen Prof. Uli Cluss für die Zusammenarbeit und die finanzielle Unterstützung dieses Bandes.

Dies ist die vierte Ausgabe in der Reihe *weißenhof edition,* die ich 2009 mit dem jovis Verlag Berlin gegründet habe. Jochen Visscher und allen Mitarbeitern des jovis Verlag Berlin, insbesondere Philipp Sperrle, Susanne Rösler und Jutta Bornholdt-Cassetti, sei an dieser Stelle herzlich gedankt für die langjährige kollegiale Zusammenarbeit. Mit diesem Doppelband schliesst sich thematisch der Kreis der interdisziplinären Veranstaltungs- und Publikationsreihe, die ich als Leiterin des Weißenhof-Instituts initiiert, konzipiert und organisiert habe. Damit ist der interdisziplinäre Diskurs jedoch nicht abgeschlossen, sondern findet hoffentlich in dem blog www.art-and-or-design.blogspot.de und anderenorts eine Fortsetzung, zumal interdisziplinäre Fragestellungen im Hinblick auf die Gestaltung unserer Zukunft schlicht unerlässlich sind.

Annett Zinsmeister, Berlin 2013

Katia Baudin is an art historian, curator and Deputy Director of the Museum Ludwig, Cologne since 2008. Head of the Fonds régional d'art contemporain in Dünkirchen 1997–2004 and the École Supérieure des Arts Décoratifs in Strassburg 2004–2007. Curatorial focus: dialectic of art and design. Exhibitions include: "Cosima von Bonin" (2011), "Franz West" (2009), "Trafic d'influences: Art & Design" (2004), "Split Identities: Objects at the Interstice of Art and Design" (2010).

Alex Coles is an art historian and Professor of *Transdisciplinary Studies*, School of Art, Design and Architecture, University of Huddersfield. His scientific focus is on transdisciplinary practice, interfaces, and boundaries between art and design. Publications include: *DesignArt* (2005), *The Transdisciplinary Studio* (2012), *Design and Art* (Ed., 2007) and EP Vol. 1, *The Italian Avant-Garde: 1968–1976* (Ed., 2013).

Christine Hill is an artist based in Berlin. She is the proprietor of the project *Volksboutique* and professor and Chair of *Media, Trend & Public Appearance* within the media faculty at the Bauhaus-University Weimar. Exhibitions include: "Hotel Volksboutique: A Project by Christine Hill" (GFZK Leipzig, 2012), "Do-It-Yourself Bauhaus" (Martin Gropius Bau, Berlin, 2009), "Volksboutique Collected Templates 1998–2007" (IfA Gallery Berlin, 2007) Publications include: *Inventory* (2003), *Minutes. The Volksboutique Weekly Diary 2006–2007* (2007).

Rosario Hurtado and **Roberto Feo** are London–based designers and founded the post-disciplinary design studio **El Ultimo Grito** (EUG) in 1997. EUG are self-proclaimed *post-disciplinarians*, whose work aims to question and research the nature of human relationships with objects and culture. Currently they lead the MA- Program *Space and Communication* at the University of Art and Design Geneva. Their work is in the permanent collections of MoMA in New York, Stedelijk in Amsterdam and the V&A in London. Publications include: *Designs for all* (2008), *NOWHERE/NOW/HERE Exploring New Lines of Investigation in Design* (2008), *abandon architectures* (2010).

Autoren

Katia Baudin ist Kunsthistorikerin, Kuratorin und seit 2008 stellvertretende Direktorin des Museum Ludwig, Köln. Leitung des Fonds régional d'art contemporain in Dünkirchen 1997–2004 und der École Supérieure des Arts Décoratifs in Straßburg 2004–2007. Kuratorischer Schwerpunkt: Dialektik von Kunst und Design. Ausstellungen u.a.: „Cosima von Bonin" (2011), „Franz West" (2009), „Trafic d'influences: Art & Design" (2004), „Split Identities: Objects at the Interstice of Art and Design" (2010).

Alex Coles ist Kunstwissenschaftler und Professor für *Transdisciplinary Studies* an der School of Art, Design and Architecture an der University of Huddersfield. Forschungsschwerpunkte: Transdisziplinäre Praxis, Grenzen zwischen Kunst und Design. Publikationen u.a.: *DesignArt* (2005), *The Transdisciplinary Studio* (2012), *Design and Art* (Hg., 2007), EP Vol. 1, *The Italian Avant-Garde: 1968–1976* (Hg., 2013).

Christine Hill ist Künstlerin und lebt in Berlin. Sie ist Geschäftsinhaberin des Projekts *Volksboutique* und Professorin für *Moden und öffentliche Erscheinungsbilder* an der Bauhaus Universität Weimar. Ausstellungen, u.a.: „Hotel Volksboutique: A Project by Christine Hill" (GFZK Leipzig, 2012), „Do-It-Yourself Bauhaus" (Martin-Gropius-Bau Berlin, 2009), „Volksboutique Collected Templates" 1998-2007 (IfA Galerie Berlin, 2007). Veröffentlichungen u.a.: *Inventory* (2003), *Minutes. The Volksboutique Weekly Diary 2006–2007* (2007).

Rosario Hurtado und **Roberto Feo** sind Designer und gründeten 1997 das post-disziplinäre Design Studio **El Ultimo Grito** (EUG) mit Sitz in London. EUG bezeichnen ihre Tätigkeit als *post-disziplinär*, da sie Beziehungen des Menschen zu Objekten und Kulturen hinterfragten. Derzeit leiten sie das MA-Programm *Space and Communication* an der Hochschule für Kunst und Design in Genf. Ihre Werke sind in Sammlungen vertreten u.a. im: MoMA, New York, Stedelijk Museum, Amsterdam, V&A Museum, London. Publikationen u.a: *Designs for all* (2008), *NOWHERE / NOW / HERE Exploring New Lines of Investigation in Design* (2008), *abandon architectures* (2010).

Louise Schouwenberg is an artist, author, and curator. She studied sculpture and philosophy; since 2000, her focus has been on theory. Currently she leads the master programme *Contextual Design* at Design Academy Eindhoven, and the master program *Material Utopias* at the Sandberg Instituut in Amsterdam. Curated exhibitions at a.o.: Galerie Fons Welters Amsterdam (2012), Museum Boijmans Van Beuningen Rotterdam (2010). Publications in international art and design magazines and contributions to a range of books, including: *Robert Zandvliet* (2012), *Hella Jongerius* (2010).

Wolfgang Ullrich is an art historian and Professor of Art History and Media Theory at the Karlsruhe University of Arts and Design. Publications on the history and critique of the art term, modern imagery, and image social questions and phenomenons of prosperity. Publications include: *Tiefer hängen* (2003), *Habenwollen. Wie funktioniert die Konsumkultur?* (2006), *An die Kunst glauben* (2011), *Alles nur Konsum. Kritik der warenästhetischen Erziehung* (2013).

Annett Zinsmeister is an artist, designer and author; interdisciplinary teaching since 2000. Since 2003 she is Professor at Kunsthochschule Berlin Weissensee and the State Academy of Arts and Design Stuttgart, where she was the director of the Weißenhof Institute from 2009–2013. Exhibitions and publications include: "Rasterfahndung" (Kunstmuseum Stuttgart 2012), Annett Zinsmeister – *Searching for Identity* (2012), *Ethics in Aesthetics* (Ed., 2012), *Figure of Motion* (Ed., 2011), *Update! 90 years of bauhaus. what now?* (Ed., 2010), *City + War. A trip to Sarajevo* (2008), *welt[stadt]raum. Mediale Inszenierungen* (Ed., 2007), *Constructing Utopia* (Ed., 2005).

Louise Schouwenberg ist Künstlerin, Autorin und Kuratorin. Sie hat Bildhauerei und Philosophie studiert, seit 2000 liegt ihr Arbeitsschwerpunkt in der Theorie. Sie leitet das MA-Programm *Contextual Design* an der Design Academy Eindhoven und *Material Utopias* am Sandberg Instituut in Amsterdam. Kuratierte Ausstellungen u.a. in: Galerie Fons Welters Amsterdam (2012), Museum Boijmans Van Beuningen Rotterdam (2010). Publikationen in internationalen Kunst- und Design-Magazinen sowie Beiträge in Monographien, u.a.: *Robert Zandvliet* (2012), *Hella Jongerius* (2010).

Wolfgang Ullrich ist Kunsthistoriker und Professor für Kunstwissenschaft und Medientheorie an der Staatlichen Hochschule für Gestaltung Karlsruhe. Publikationen zur Geschichte und Kritik des Kunstbegriffs, bildsoziologischen Fragestellungen und Wohlstandsphänomenen. Publikationen u.a.: *Tiefer hängen. Über den Umgang mit der Kunst* (2003), *Habenwollen. Wie funktioniert die Konsumkultur?* (2006), *an die Kunst glauben* (2011), *Alles nur Konsum. Kritik der warenästhetischen Erziehung* (2013).

Annett Zinsmeister ist Künstlerin, Gestalterin und Autorin. Interdisziplinäre Lehre seit 2000. Seit 2003 ist sie Professorin u.a. an der Kunsthochschule Berlin Weißensee und der Staatlichen Akademie der Bildenden Künste Stuttgart, wo sie von 2009–13 das Weißenhof-Institut leitete. Ausstellungen und Publikationen u.a.: „Rasterfahndung" (Kunstmuseum Stuttgart 2012), Annett Zinsmeister – *Searching for Identity* (2012), *Ethics in Aesthetics* (Hg., 2012) *Gestalt der Bewegung* (Hg., 2011), *Update! 90 Jahre Bauhaus - was nun?* (Hg., 2009), *City + War. A trip to Sarajevo* (2008), *welt[stadt]raum. Mediale Inszenierungen* (Hg., 2007), *Constructing Utopia* (Hg., 2005).

Impressum Imprint

© 2013 by jovis Verlag GmbH, Annett Zinsmeister
Das Copyright für die Texte liegt bei den Autoren.
Das Copyright für die Abbildungen liegt bei den Fotografen/Inhabern der Bildrechte.
Texts by kind permission of the authors.
Pictures by kind permission of the photographers/holders of the picture rights.

Alle Rechte vorbehalten.
All rights reserved.

Konzept und Redaktion Concept and editing Annett Zinsmeister
Übersetzung Translation Lucinda Rennison, Stephanie Rupp
Gestaltung und Satz Design and setting Moritz Hahn (www.moha-grafik.de), Sven Tillack (www.sventillack.de)
Lithografie Lithography Bild1Druck, Berlin
Herstellung Production jovis Verlag: Susanne Rösler
Druck und Bindung Printing and binding Graspo cz A. S., Zlín

Bibliografische Information der Deutschen Nationalbibliothek
Die Deutsche Nationalbibliothek verzeichnet diese Publikation in der Deutschen Nationalbibliografie;
detaillierte bibliografische Daten sind im Internet über http://dnb.d-nb.de abrufbar.
Bibliographic information published by the Deutsche Nationalbibliothek
The Deutsche Nationalbibliothek lists this publication in the Deutsche Nationalbibliografie;
detailed bibliographic data are available on the Internet at http://dnb.d-nb.de

Weissenhof-Institut
Staatliche Akademie der Bildenden Künste Stuttgart
Am Weißenhof 1
D-70191 Stuttgart
www.weissenhof-institut.abk-stuttgart.de

jovis Verlag GmbH
Kurfürstenstraße 15/16
D-10785 Berlin
www.jovis.de

ISBN 978-3-86859-255-9

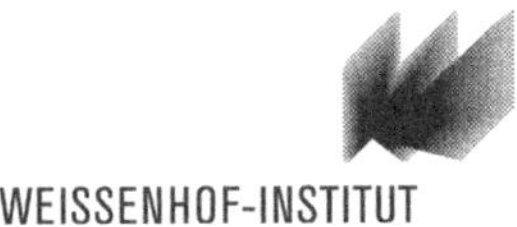